7308

D1583254

WE LIVE IN SINGAPORE

By the same author :

FAR EASTERN AGENT

WE LIVE
IN
SINGAPORE

by

DONALD MOORE

LONDON
HODDER & STOUGHTON

First Printed . . . 1955

ACKNOWLEDGMENT

For permission to quote from A BAR OF
SHADOW by Laurens van der Post we are
indebted to the author and publishers,
Messrs. Hogarth Press Ltd.

MADE AND PRINTED IN GREAT BRITAIN FOR
HODDER AND STOUGHTON LTD., LONDON, BY
HAZELL WATSON AND VINEY LTD., AYLESBURY AND LONDON

LIST OF ILLUSTRATIONS

All the photographs are
by the Author.

August 1st, 1954

The war in Indo-China ended yesterday, and, to many of us who have grown accustomed to living on the fringe of Communism, it was ended by an Eastern Munich. It seems to us that peace was bought at a price no less than that which Chamberlain, in his day, was obliged to pay to Hitler, and with no greater honour.

There was a war and men were being killed, and if the war went on more men were going to be killed. The men of Geneva, concerned not so much with the killing as with what their electors would say if it continued, decided to lose the war that had drained France to the brink of disaster for almost a decade, and agreed that what the French had fought for for so long, and for which so many had died, was not really worth fighting for after all. They had died, as others had died before them, in vain. Their names will be inscribed on pious rolls of honour, and statues will no doubt rise to commemorate their leaders. But apart from that, they have returned to the dust where all things are forgotten. And all this would be acceptable if the war were over. But it is not. It is only just beginning. At least, that is what a good many Malayans believe.

When you have read in your newspaper each day for years that men and women have been killed and injured by Communists within the bounds of your own country, you are no longer disposed to grant to Communists any of the more common virtues of humanity. When they have tied a few dozen defenceless men to trees and slowly hacked them to pieces with knives; when they have flung women, screaming, into blazing smokehouses; when they have shot children, apparently without caring; then it is difficult to resist the conclusion that you are no longer dealing with men, but with a species of wild animal. These murderers of Malaya are not misguided youths; nor are they ill-advised and foolish adults. They are loathsome, degenerate killers waging a horrible war that knows no quarter. At the same time, they are heroes and objects of praise and admiration in Communist countries.

When our politicians sit down at Geneva and parley with the representatives of Russia and China and their miscellany of satellites, when they undertake to lunch with them, to dine with them and to drink with them, they are dealing with men who believe that the Malayan Communists are acting rightly, who believe that eventually Malaya should be governed by them, and who see very little that is inconsistent in this view, since they themselves, almost without exception, came to power by an identical process of merciless inhumanity.

The war in Indo-China has ended. The war in Korea has ended. But the war in Malaya goes on; and it is easy to forget that our war is the same war as that which the politicians say they have now ended. In fact, all that has happened is that one of the theatres of operations is about to be shifted.

All else, it now seems to some of us here, should now be subservient to the containing of Communism. All the old problems are irrelevant. Why a man is a Communist, how he became a Communist, when he became a Communist, all are equally unimportant now. Whether the present government of a country is good or bad, or whether the people of a country would be better off under Communism: these things, as separate problems, scarcely matter any more. The inflexible aim must be to stop Communism at its present boundaries and to root out the pockets of Communism that exist beyond its boundaries, by whatever means we have, and at whatever cost. We in Malaya, who are sickened beyond all possibility of charity by Communism and all its works, say this, not because we are afraid of losing what we have here, not because we do not like the idea of being reduced to the level of the common denominator, nor even because we simply dislike Communist economic theory, but because we have seen the dead, watched the maimed, and looked upon men who have had acid flung into their defenceless faces. We know from our own experience in our own country that the Communist is a man whose trade is butchery, who, if he is not killed first, will certainly in the end kill us.

That is why Malaya did not rejoice, unreservedly, yesterday.

August 4th, 1954

We have been having cook trouble. Our last cook, who stayed with us for several years, was a kindly old Chinese with a shaven head and horn-rimmed spectacles. He reigned in the kitchen with a serene benevolence, and only became upset when it was suggested that he should hurry. Foo was constitutionally incapable of hurrying, and therefore quite unable to deal with any situation that approached within nodding distance of an emergency. The sight of the swiftly rising bubbles in a saucepan of boiling milk would, it is true, send him into a paroxysm of activity, none of which was of any use, however, since it was never directed towards the immediate problem of removing the saucepan from the stove. He would search frantically for a cloth, fling open cupboard doors, almost split his polished cranium in collision with the sink or some similar obstacle, gaze up to heaven and beat his breast, only to find the cloth where he had left it —over his shoulder. But for all his faults, he was a nice old chap and we were sorry to see him go.

We think he felt an urge once more to sleep with his wife. As far as we knew, he had only seen her during the last few years while he himself was in motion on his bicycle. Every week he had a day off, and we think he invariably spent it bicycling doggedly up and down Holland Road. This habit worried us, not because we thought he would wear himself out or that his wife would not be seeing enough of him, but because there was every possibility of his being killed. He would affect, on these solitary outings, an enormous topee of the kind Europeans used to wear and which only American tourists wear today, which enveloped not only his head but also the greater part of his face. It was, in fact, the greatest wonder that he was able even to breathe, although it was clear that he drew sufficient breath to enable him to converse with his wife as he sailed past her, from time to time, in the main street of Holland Village.

In all the time we knew him he never spent a night away from his solitary couch in his room by the kitchen. He was always back about half-past nine or ten o'clock, and fast asleep and snoring, with all available lights switched on by ten-thirty. He was a frugal man, was Foo, except in his one extravagance for electric light.

He had four children, which was why he did not bring his family to live with him. We think that even he quailed at the prospect of himself, his wife and four wailing children, all on two single beds in one small room, with the door bolted and all the shutters tightly closed, as, so often, is the Chinese wont. We think perhaps his wife quailed too. So, as I have explained, she stayed in Holland Village with three of the children and sent one to live with his father. But this arrangement, seemingly so satisfactory to all concerned, evidently palled, and a few weeks ago we received a letter, neatly typed on foolscap paper. It read something like this:

Dear Madam,

Due to the domestic situation I am reluctantly compelled to ask that my employment with you be terminated at the end of the present month. I am desirous of obtaining a post where the accommodation provided can contain both my wife and children, and in such a household as can employ my wife simultaneously.

Your respectful servant,

Foo.

God knows who had composed this document and, presumably, typed it for him. He could speak little English, and could read and write it not at all. But there it was, laboriously signed, neatly folded in an envelope addressed to Madam, lying on the breakfast table. We saw his point at once and only wondered that it had not been made before. And so, with much flashing of gold teeth and a great bobbing of polished skull, he went.

Now, almost every day, either in the morning early, or on my way home from the office in the evening, I see a rotund, white shape surmounted by the enormous helmet, bent determinedly over the rusty frame of a familiar bicycle. Usually he is half-way up a most exhausting hill, the varicose veins standing out like ropes on his straining calves, wobbling drunkenly from side to side in a furious endeavour not to dismount. We think that perhaps he has taken to bicycling as a career and would not be surprised to find him entered for next year's Round-the-Island bicycle race.

But the fellow we have now! Oh my goodness! We are trying to be charitable, but we think he will drive us, eventually, to an interest in bicycles, a subconscious longing for the absent Foo. He came for an interview armed with the most convincing references. He was a good cook, willing, conscientious, trustworthy, clean, tidy and slightly oiled. In none of them was there the faintest suggestion of a note of dissatisfaction with his excellent service. Among the string of school report clichés there was not even a "could-do-better." The man was a paragon, a genius, one who could do no wrong. Or so we thought.

He arrived in an American shirt of the type that is worn outside the trousers. We have since discovered that he has another shirt, a T-shirt of the kind usually associated with Mr. Montgomery Clift. Then there is his brilliantine—Rocky Mountain Bouquet I believe it is called—and the entire house now reeks and swoons with the smell of it. Even the food tastes remotely of *edelweiss*.

We think perhaps he worked in an iron foundry before, or a motor-car repair shop. Wherever it was, it was clearly of no consequence if he dropped anything. Fortunately, our crockery is not priceless.

But things are seldom as bad as they seem, and we think he will improve. Meanwhile, there is never a dull moment. One never knows what one is going to be given next. It is a humdrum life, after all, when a request for a whisky-and-soda produces just such a beverage. This evening, in response to this request, I received a tumbler of almost neat brandy, and I am still recovering from the first, too hasty, gulp. Later, after dinner, we were brought two tiny coffee-cups and a gigantic water-jug full to the brim with steaming coffee—ready mixed with milk and sugar. But at least it was coffee.

Later this week we are having some people to dinner and we are praying that the calamity that overtook our friends the H.'s will not, too, be our misfortune. They are in government service and, with due solemnity and with a respect proper to the occasion, they invited the august head of their department to dinner. He arrived with his wife and, after the usual preliminaries, they sat down to what Mrs. H. fondly thought was going to be a meal worthy of her guests. The soup undoubtedly was good, and H. felt encouraged to ask if anyone would take sherry with it. The response was unanimously in favour, and he called to Aminah, their new Malay *amah,* to serve it. Aminah complied immediately, but it was only after the guests had been served that H. discovered that it was being dispensed from a teapot. After that, I believe, they became so drunk that the incident mercifully was forgotten.

August 5th, 1954

S. has at last taken me to meet his adopted grandmother, as he called her. She lives on the top of a hill not far from the centre of Singapore in an enormous house built decades ago by her father. Later, a second house was built adjacent to the first, and a connecting passage placed between them. Today the second house lies empty and derelict, while the daughter lives in the half she knew as a child. That was a very long time ago; so long ago, in fact, that to talk to S.'s adopted grandmother is rather like reading one of the old books on Singapore, which tell of a city where once existed calm, graciousness and peace.

She is now an old lady with an erect, dowager's figure. She has straight grey hair and fine Jewish eyes, and when she speaks she speaks softly and with a quiet authority. About her hangs the aura of days that are gone, and although she faces the very different present and the unpredictable future with the calm assurance with which she will always meet every eventuality, she is a part of the past that can never return.

Her father was a very rich man, and one can imagine his household: orderly, autocratic, yet hospitable and generous, a household engaged single-mindedly in the business of good living, a bustling busy organisation of individuals towards a common aim of happiness.

"I remember," she said, as we ate our Gentleman's Relish sandwiches and delicious cheesepuffs, and sipped our China tea poured out by the companion who spoke only when addressed, "I remember at one time helping with the census in this area, and when I came to count the souls who lived in our servants' compound they amounted in all to seventy-three."

As I sat there, cool on the marble floor and surrounded by the pale, cold, distempered walls, looking out over the decaying roofs towards the Cathay Building, I could hear for a moment the voices of that vast household rising to another day. Here the sun rises dramatically, and the grey, shot light of the dawn dies quickly before the great, red ball that soars out from below the horizon. The earth is fresh with dew, and the cold of the night lingers, before the sun, rising to the open blueness of the sky, makes all things hot again. By then the house would have been a hive of activity. Coachmen would be washing down carriages, and Malay grooms would be noisy with buckets and brushes and food. The immaculate garden, which still reaches out from all four sides of the house, would be receiving its usual daily attention from its several gardeners, Tamil or Malay. The Sikh watchman at the gate would be moving his bed into a remoter, more shaded spot. In the house itself Chinese boys and *amahs* would be dusting and scrubbing and polishing, and in the kitchens and servants' quarters the cooking of the first meal of the day would be well under way. In and out of everywhere, except the main rooms of the house, would be the cheeky, half-naked children of the servants—Malay, Indian and Chinese—all dependent, as their parents and possibly their grandparents, on the owner of the house. I have no doubt that he took due cognisance of his responsibilities and looked after them in their troubles. It was, indeed, a benevolent autocracy; a little kingdom which, for a while, was happy, because its inhabitants had not then bothered to consider the rights and wrongs of it all.

"Do you see that house just there? That, too, has been empty for a long time, but I believe someone has taken it just recently. When I was a little girl it was occupied by a Russian who, I think, must have been a little mad. He built baths in practically every room of the house and was for ever using them himself. I remember him so clearly. He used to wear a great number of bangles and bracelets. But he went away, I do not know where to.

"Slowly we are getting the house back into order—but it takes time and things are very expensive." I could see her running her methodical accounts, obtaining full value for every dollar. "You know, it was empty for years, and before that it was used by the army. During the war the Japanese billeted their soldiers here, and when they were defeated it was used by Indian soldiers. It was in a dreadful state when we finally returned. Now I want to make it as my father knew it."

I was shown over the house, and I walked through the great empty rooms, full of chairs which had never been sat in, carpets which had scarcely been walked on, guest-rooms which had seen no guests, and verandahs from which no visitors ever admired the view. Only the ghosts of the past were there, and even the living were partly ghosts. There were no more meetings of the Jewish Community, no more house parties, no more ceremonial dinners in the great dining-room, no more soirées in the stately music-room. There were not even any books, beyond an illustrated guide to Israel and a complete set of the *Encyclopædia Britannica.*

She walked to the porch with me, followed by her impassive companion and her sister. She thanked me for coming and I said I was grateful for her kindness. I walked out on to the unkempt drive, where grass and weeds forced a way through the worn stones. She watched me drive away, and I think perhaps she did not see a motor-car but a smart turn-out with a pair of horses in jingling harness, making their way at a spanking pace down to the Esplanade. Sixty years ago the band would have been playing there, and most of the residents would have congregated on the green padang, not only to listen to the music but to take the air and meet their friends. It was a regular institution.

"We used to go in the evenings to the Botanic gardens, where the band would play. The bandstand is still there, but I do not know when a band last used it. We would all drive there in our carriages, right up to the stand, and there we would spend perhaps an hour or so. Hundreds of our friends would be there too, and we would get out and talk to them. We would go and sit in each other's carriages and talk and gossip—oh! it was such fun! Then we would all drive home, and the air would be filled with the clip-clip-clop of horses' hooves."

Now the house that has known so much life, that has heard so many girlish voices raised in laughter and happiness, has grown old, and those who have returned to it have grown old also. When they die, their memories will die, and when their memories die the house will die with them.

August 7th, 1954

Malaya is divided in many ways; in particular, it is divided between those who think self-government a good thing and those who believe that it can never possibly be made to work. R. has something to do with the hospital, and she shudders at the thought of Asians in control.

"They simply have no idea of organisation. When the Europeans are no longer at the top, the standards will fall. Of course, the hospital will go on, people will still come to it when they are ill, and no doubt most of them who are curable will be cured, but standards will inevitably fall. There will be confusion and lack of positive direction. There will be slackness, and all the drive will disappear. No one any more will accept responsibility, and we shall all have a glorious time passing the buck. Fine, flowing reports will be issued, continual and unnecessary meetings will be held, and meaningless resolutions will be adopted. But not very much of practical value will be achieved."

It is not an uncommon view, this theory of Asian ineptitude, and it has solid backing in every-day experience. That so many Asians are inept in the things they tackle is undeniable. This is most noticeable of all, perhaps, in the politicians who go on record in the daily newspapers with the quaintest ideas. Yet John Summerfield, who occasionally comes to waste my time in the office, has an explanation for it all.

"What do you expect?" he thunders. "A Colonial govern-

Chinese dialects, which in themselves are almost different languages, and Malay and English. If you want your efficiency, you are the chap who should be speaking these languages to him. After all, you're supposed to be the bright boy in the outfit.

"You will find that the European Company is gradually on the way out in this country, through sheer force of circumstances. Business in this country lies in the hands of the Chinese and no one else. The essential thing to remember is that that is the only way you will get efficiency—to let the country Orientalise itself. Let it run itself its own way, as the people want it. And you? What will happen to you? You will probably become a big executive, with more power than you have ever known before, responsible to Chinese directors. Have you not noticed this trend? When a local company gets big enough, it employs Europeans to execute the policy of the board. They become General Managers, Sales Managers, Production Managers and so on. That's what I call sense. Then you get the natural abilities of the West and the East working together for once. But that won't last for ever. Sooner or later their business will be conducted in Chinese. If I were you, old boy, I'd buy myself a Cantonese primer. They say it's an easy language after the first five years."

The other day I met Dick Fennings. He asked: "What are you going to do when self-government arrives?" I said that I didn't know; that for so long I had been so preoccupied with the present that I had had no time to worry about the future. But I asked him what he was going to do. "I'm off to New Zealand," he said.

August 15th, 1954

To a press conference for Mrs. Pandit. It is held in the Public Relations Office in the new Assembly House where also meets Singapore's semi-elected government.

There are perhaps a hundred journalists present and I do not know of which I am more ashamed—their questions, or their readers who demand the answers to them. Surely it is possible to ask this most brilliant woman a more pertinent question than whether she has any message for the women of Malaya? Or whether she has any message for the Indians of Malaya? One almost expected to see her draw a little packet of prepared messages from the elegant folds of her white sari. It would scarcely have been surprising if one of our more enterprising reporters had asked her whether she cared for the new flat-chested look!

But those who asked questions at least said something. The remainder—Indians, Chinese and Europeans—simply sat in a glazed, unreceptive silence and scribbled occasionally.

Mrs. Pandit reiterated two points in her answers, which she had already made several times in her tour through Malaya: that one must, instead of deploring Communism, concentrate on praising and promoting the benefits of democracy; and that war and the instruments of war, even though they were not used, never solved any problem—they simply created bigger and more dangerous ones.

These are easy arguments, easy to hold and easy to convey. They are even right; unquestionably right, as far as they go. But I cannot persuade myself that they contain the real answer to our danger, since neither of them takes cognisance of the equally unquestionable fact that the Communists lose no opportunity both to run down democracy and to attack us with guns.

It is in this that the essential weakness of the Indian position lies. It is all very well to turn the other cheek, but in this world of deadly realism someone then hits it so hard that you never recover. What, for example, would Mrs. Pandit have us do in Malaya? We believe it wrong to go to war. We believe it wrong to shoot and kill and hound men through wet and inhospitable jungle until they die. We believe war—and it is a war that we have in Malaya—to be a mode of conduct repugnant to civilised man. But what would Mrs. Pandit have us do? No one thought to ask her that question. Presumably, according to the press, the people of Malaya are not interested in the answers to such questions.

Then again, she said that it was a matter of pride to her that the Indian Army had been used only, so far, as a truce-administering force in Korea. Quite apart from the exceptionally doubtful veracity of such a statement, what does Mrs. Pandit suggest *ought* to have happened in Korea once South Korea was attacked? But no one thought to ask her that question either.

There can be no doubt that Mrs. Pandit would have shot her questioners down in flames, leaving them to slink into their corners to think up their belated answers. It would have been fascinating to watch her clear and incisive brain demolishing them one by one.

But there are more important considerations than this, and perhaps the most important of all is to try to put a finger on the flaw in the Indian argument. It is, I think, largely connected with the degree to which a country has been exposed to Communist methods. We in Malaya have been exposed in a way that no other country has been exposed and yet survived. We believe—or many of us believe—that the standard of living of all Asian countries must be raised, and raised quickly. If it remains low, as it is abysmally low today, then it remains low at our immediate peril. If one would destroy Communism, one must destroy poverty, want, hunger and all forms of gross inequality. We believe—or many of us believe—in this doctrine just as much as India believes in it. But I think the essential difference lies in the fact that we no longer believe that this is more important than military defence; I think we no longer believe that the two aspects of protection are even of equal importance; I think we believe that unless we are strong enough to defeat the enemies at our gates, then we can never hope to defeat the less warlike machinations of the enemies within our gates. India, militarily, is impotent. Would Mrs. Pandit please tell me what would have happened had Malaya been equally impotent? I fancy, among other things, that Mrs. Pandit would not have been speaking her mind in Singapore this sunny Sunday morning.

August 21st, 1954

We have been having a conference in Singapore—the Second Assembly of the World Assembly of Youth. A great number of youths of ages ranging, curiously enough, from eighteen to forty have descended upon Singapore, at a quite phenomenal expense, from all over the world. They have come here to talk, to talk endlessly and, it seems to me, to remarkably little effect. I cannot help feeling that they would be far better occupied climbing Snowdon or playing baseball. But that is beside the point. They came here, and Singapore decided to make the best of the matter.

Tonight we had a concert on the Padang. The steps of the classical City Hall, facing across the green padang to where Raffles once landed, were turned into a stage with a highly theatrical backcloth of waving palms and a tropical moon. Seats were arranged for the delegates in front of the stage, and the whole was then roped off so that there would be no danger of the delegates mixing with the common herd.

Behind the ropes there assembled a great concourse of people. It was impossible to count them, but they must have numbered from thirty to forty thousand. The City Hall was floodlit, and the stage itself was picked out in spotlights. The Padang, packed to suffocation, was in darkness.

The concert was one that only Singapore could give : an exhibition of the Malay art of self-defence, Balinese dancing, European singing, the Chinese sword dance, Indian dancing and so on for what seemed like hours, turn after turn. The vast audience was equally mixed—racially, nationally, culturally. There is perhaps nowhere else on earth where this can happen to this degree. And if Singapore is ever to become great it will be because eventually she must epitomise and synthesise all of the East and all of the peoples of the East. As I stood among that dark crowd I thought I sensed the greatness of a city that is yet young. It was possible, as one watched the subtlety of the Malay dancing or the dash of the Chinese sword dance to dream dreams and see visions. It was possible, fleetingly, to see Singapore as the hub and the centre of the East because only she had assimilated all that lay about her.

August 22nd, 1954

It is still dark when Cho calls for me. As we drive to the airport the day comes quickly, and by the time we reach Kallang night is as though it had never been. In spite of the early hour there is a delegation of Indians standing aimlessly at the entrance to see off a visiting dignitary. I know one of them slightly : he comes from Kuala Lumpur, and there is no doubt that he has travelled 250 miles just to see his countryman leave for his homeland—national and racial solidarity!

The day passes slowly; a day of dull roaring and white flecks of cloud miles below. The only land we see are the isolated Paracel Islands and the gigantic elliptical reef that stands to the west of them. I wonder if anyone lives there?

It is hot in Hongkong, and Henry Foo is there to meet me. He has not changed—except that he has bought a bigger American car, a swish, utterly silent job that appears to have no engine. We drive to the Peninsula, where we have tea and then get down to a couple of hours' work. He invites me to a party at his house in the evening. We reach there at eight o'clock and the guests are just arriving.

The party is in honour of one of Henry's relations, a South African Chinese, who is returning the following day to South Africa. His father went there years and years ago, a land-hungry Chinese from over-populated Kwantung, a penniless migrant from the rigours of survival in China. He made good there and built up a flourishing grocery business which now employs his son. And his son has been on a six months' holiday, nearly, but not quite, to the land of his fathers.

Bob, he is called. It is strange to be calling a Chinese Bob. But then a lifetime's residence abroad seems to have modified even his appearance. He has no trace of accent, except perhaps South African, and in a crowd of Europeans would scarcely be noticed as being different. Apparently the Chinese communities in South Africa are quite self-contained or, at least, they look after one another. In official eyes they are not white and therefore they go to their own schools. This seems to me to be so utterly incredible, coming, as I do, from Singapore, where such overt discrimination is an impossibility, that I question him closely on his reactions to such a practice. I find him strangely unhostile, and I find, or I think that I find, that the reason for this is possibly because he is just as afraid of the blacks as the whites are. He fears their overwhelming numbers and their brutal, superstitious ignorance. *Apartheid*, to him, is understandable—at least it is realistic from a non-black point of view.

I meet two Malayans from Singapore—a young Chinese doctor and his wife—and I talk to him as we eat our way through a tremendous spread, a completely European meal except for the gigantic prawns flown frozen from Tientsin. We talk, naturally enough, of Malaya and of what will happen when British power is removed. The conclusion we come to is that there is no future for the Malay in Malaya, and neither of us can understand why the Malay is so vociferous in shouting his pathetic *merdeka*. Once he has freed himself from the British, to whom is he to turn for protection from the far more powerful enemy, the Chinese? The Malay today will look towards Indonesia, but I cannot see what Indonesia can do for anyone in the next fifty years. It is little enough, goodness knows, that Indonesia can do for itself, let alone for its helpless brothers over the narrow seas. And so my Chinese friend agrees that his two and a half million countrymen in Malaya must inevitably subjugate an approximately equal number of pleasing, easy-going Malays for precisely the same reason that a pair of scales tips to the side with the greater weight upon it. The Chinese in Malaya cannot possibly prevent the scales tipping their way, even if they wanted to. But the puzzle remains: why, apparently, cannot the Malays sense the inevitability of their approaching disaster? Or is it simply that they are led by fools?

Henry drives me back to the Peninsula in his silent car. The prostitutes still parade in droves in Nathan Road and the back-cloth of lights on the Peak of Hongkong still staggers one with its beauty.

The Chinese liftman takes me up to the sixth floor and remembers me. He has been operating the same lift for twenty-six years. Jobs are not easy to find any more.

August 23rd, 1954

Lily works in Hongkong and lives in a tenement in Kowloon. She commutes each day on the ferry. For 420 Hongkong dollars a month she writes out bills in a tailor's shop. Her expenses total approximately $1,000 a month. She supports her mother and her young sister, who goes to a convent school in Kowloon. Her mother is old, so she also has to employ a servant to do the washing and manual work. Then there is the rent, food, her own clothes, her sister's school fees and the midday meal. Regularly every month it works out at something like $1,000—and she earns $420 precisely, with no possibility whatever of earning any more—at least not by regular means.

Lily was born in Peking where her father had a good job in a bank. It must have been reasonably well paid for he was able to support two wives—Lily's mother was the number one wife. Lily hates her father—although she does not now know where he is. He was missing during the revolution and has not been heard of since. As far as Lily is concerned, it is best that he stays lost, for she has known the heart-break of a house that attempts to contain two women who, ostensibly, are the wives of the same man. She has known the arrogance of the predominant male, and she has come to the conclusion that, although, in his time, a man may have many women, it is better that he have them one by one.

Somehow, her mother and sister got away to Formosa and then, with the last that remained of their money, they came to Hongkong. All through they had one idea: to go back, eventually, to Peking. Now they have been in Hongkong for two and a half years, and they think they will never see Peking again, not because of the Communists, nor because they are not allowed to enter China again, but simply because there is no prospect of their ever saving enough money to buy the railway ticket. Lily and her family have simply added three more souls to Hongkong's population problem.

It was Lily who kept the family together; it was she who paid the room rent in the ramshackle hotel they lived in at first, she who got a job as a waitress in a cheap café to bring in enough money to buy some food. Then she found work on the Hongkong side writing out bills in a tailor's shop at $420 a month. It kept them alive, but only just.

Then Lily discovered something. She discovered that if she dressed well, she was not unattractive to men, to the thousands of men who used the ferry, as she did, every day. She discovered that it was not necessary actively to solicit, but that a look and a slow walk were often sufficient. Conversation would follow, an appointment at a hotel, and she would earn as much in a couple of hours as she would in a week in the tailor's shop. She found that, without undue exertion, she could just make up the extra $580 she needed to run the home. Her mother thinks she has a post of considerable responsibility at the tailor's shop; her sister scarcely gives a thought to where the money comes from. Some people would call her a prostitute, but then, sometimes, you haven't much option, especially if you want to go back to Peking.

August 24th, 1954

Once more I see the unearthly sight of Tokyo from the air by night. In two years the lights have increased, and now they are blue, red, white, green and yellow, shimmering like water in the sunlight. As we circle, white streaks of lightning shoot through the air illuminating the clouds that stand like mountains before us. It is not so very long ago that aeroplanes flew in successive fleets over this city dropping their high explosive into the velvet darkness.

Sukitomo is waiting for me, dear old Sukitomo, considerate, indomitably polite Sukitomo. I have a tremendous admiration for this unassuming man, who will never make a material success of life simply because he is too honest and has not enough push. But he is not worried about this because that is not the way he wants his life to be.

We drive into Tokyo in the pouring rain to the Marunouchi Hotel, a box-like structure full of tiny, doll-like rooms. We eat together an enormous underdone steak in the smartly decorated dining-room. Then Sukitomo goes home into the darkness to his unpretentious home, to which he will never take me, and I go off to my cripplingly undersized bed. The night is made hideous with the clatter of suburban trains as they rush over the iron bridge just below my window.

In what way has Tokyo changed in the two years I have been

away—if it has changed at all? Can the addition of more neon on the old worn buildings be called a significant change? Or the filling in of just a few potholes in the shabby roads? There are fewer Americans, and the people are better dressed. There is more traffic in the streets, and the streets themselves are cleaner.

But all these things are superficial, and I think that perhaps the greatest change has taken place within myself. This time, for the first time, I have become properly aware of the essential soul-rotting tawdriness of Tokyo. The novelty and the glamour have to some extent gone, leaving behind a consciousness of acres of drabness, an almost illimitable drabness of mean little buildings in mean little streets. Perhaps before it was bombed and before fifteen years of neglect brought about the present extreme of shabbiness, perhaps then Tokyo had a pleasanter face. But even then it could never have been attractive. Tokyo is like a worn old whore whose looks have become so ravaged that not even paint can restore them.

You can go now and stand by the great gate of the Imperial Japanese grounds. By the gate towers the dark, grey gatehouse with its curved Japanese roof. All around stand the graceful pines and, below, the water of the moat lies placid in the pale sunlight. Here for a moment you can glimpse in the centre of Tokyo the true, ancient Japan, where the things that man made had to fill an essential requirement by being in tune with nature. As you look at these gentle buildings set among the trees, you may almost wonder which of them God created. Then turn round and see what man made later—the concrete cubes and stuccoed walls, the sightless windows and the mountains of worthless merchandise—and you will wonder how any man ever came to reject the former in favour of the latter.

Yet I cannot wholly condemn it, for I myself am a part of this century. If the buildings hurt the eyes and the product of the work of the people for the most part displeases, there still remain the people and the spirit of the people. They are as ugly or as beautiful as ever they were, in this century or ten centuries back in time. Because of the people, I think I could live with this raddled old whore.

August 26th, 1954

Watanabe is a fat and genial Japanese. He is not rich; in fact he is almost poor and, although I do not think he is an extravagant man, I have no doubt that he would not be averse to being able to live rather less economically than he does today. His interests lie chiefly in art and literature, and he is able to revel in the mysteries of Japanese and Chinese poetry. More than anything else he would like to see Japan as a strong, well-ordered country, taking a respected place among the nations of the world.

"Tokyo," he says, "is a fool's paradise. Here people go on in the same old sweet way, taking no thought for tomorrow. We waste our money on television and automatic washing machines, and our exports are so dear they will not sell overseas. And yet no one worries, least of all the Government. I suppose we must all believe in an act of God that is going to arrive at the last moment and save us all from our inevitable doom. That, certainly, can be the only explanation of the Government's behaviour.

"Why do the people vote for Yoshida and his party or for any other party that manœuvres itself into power? What can they do for the people? Nothing. What, for example, does Yoshida know about the people? Nothing. He rides about in a foreign car and puts his fingers into innumerable and lucrative pies, but he has no thought whatever for the people, whom he has never even met. And yet, you may be quite certain that when we have another election, Yoshida, or people like Yoshida, will be voted for. Why? I can't answer, except to repeat that Japan is a fool's paradise.

"And even if the Japanese people became so tired of their poverty, so worn out with the drudgery of their lives, that they rebelled against the present order and actually voted for a socialist government, that government would in no way be better than the present one: being Japanese, it would consist largely of incompetent fools, sycophants and corrupt hangers-on. Japanese Governments are like that; there seems to be no escaping them or the consequences they bring upon us. Does it not seem to you to be a terrible thing that we should be plagued in this way?

"It is to this aspect of Japanese life that I refer when I speak of our living the life of slaves. We are the slaves of our own shortcomings. It is precisely because the people still have so remarkably little conception of democracy that we get the paralysed governments we are blessed with today. We act like sheep. Now take ear-rings, for instance. Not long ago a number of Japanese women began to wear ear-rings. Now *all* Japanese women wear ear-rings. It has become a craze which everyone must follow. Our people behave in politics in the same way. We follow the herd. And what do we get? Yoshida.

"But, nevertheless, there must come a time when the Japanese people will become tired of the inefficiency, the bungling, the corruption, the gross inequalities and the poverty. Then no one can know what will happen. But it may be something terrible."

August 28th, 1954

M. entertained me royally this evening to dinner. Dinner in Japan means assembling no later than six p.m. and dispersing from the table no earlier than ten p.m. It can be a ceremony of marathon proportions.

We went to a house by the river where we were shown to a room at the water's edge. It was an exquisite Japanese house, almost wholly of wood—plain, polished wood—of many kinds and grains. Some of the walls were papered with light-coloured wallpaper of Japanese design, and other walls slid away to open one side of the room to the river. We sat on our cushions on the floor, at the one-foot-high lacquered table, and awaited the arrival of the girls of the house, seemingly so indispensable to the Japanese banquet.

Then they came—laughing, tripping girls whose purpose in life is to make men forget whatever it is they have been worrying about. They were Yoshiko, Sunsuke, Suzaya, Kayo, Masaya, Hanko and Yaeko. Looking back, I cannot remember which was which, except that they were all, in varying degrees, beautiful. They all wore kimonos and obis, colourful and supremely decorative. These are the real geishas of Japan—witty, intelligent, graceful creatures, who scarcely ever stop talking. Only one was made up in the traditional geisha style, with her hair standing in a great circle over her head. Her face was an almost dead-white mask, and it was just possible to detect that the painted lips of the mask did not correspond to the real ones below the layers of powder. The white powder covered her neck, too, except for a deep V of natural flesh at the nape, which the kimono is pulled away to reveal. I am told that this mask-like make-up originated in the idea that the model Japanese girl of old should never betray her emotions. They were delicate flowers to be admired, and such things as anger, sadness or jealousy might well have marred the illusion of the flower. Today many Japanese men prefer their geishas to look more natural.

Japanese food has æsthetic as well as calorific values. A dish that does not look right, however well it may taste, is but a poor thing, and the person who prepared it to be pitied. And so the delicate mounds of raw fish, served on dishes of a great variety of shapes, are balanced on the porcelain among little hillocks of horseradish and graceful trees of parsley. The dish of hors d'œuvres containing fish, pickles and a whole roast chestnut, complete with the prickly skin, is arranged to form a perfect design. Here is no mess of gravy, no ungainly heaps of potatoes or untidy mounds of vegetable; here is a lesson in the artistry of composition, as well as a gastronomic experience of consider-able magnitude.

Yoshiko is perhaps the most talkative of them all. She tells an incredibly long and seemingly hilarious story, which Suki-tomo tries hard to translate for me, of a Japanese female musician who went to America and found herself locked in her dressing-room. I did not get to the bottom of the story at all, but such was the vivacity of the teller, and the good humour induced in all present, that I found myself laughing at each successive but incomprehensible sally.

And that, of course, is the function of the geisha; to make men laugh, to make them feel good and to persuade them that they are better, more clever, kinder and wiser than they are.

After a number of dishes and startling quantities of *saki*, the meal came to a temporary halt while the geishas sang. On the river, small motor-boats hung with coloured lanterns chugged up and down with guests of the same house and their tinkling geisha companions. Yoshiko sang, another played the *shamisen* (a plucked string instrument resembling a lute), and the traditionally dressed girl danced the ancient classical dances of Japan. First she was a fisherman and then the rain. Her movements were simple, studied, always restrained and always graceful. As she slowly pirouetted, her fan moved through geometrical arcs and planes, and her head, moving laterally from side to side, peeped from behind it. The song, like so many Japanese songs, was mournful and plaintive, and Yoshiko, kneeling on the floor, looked straight before her as she intoned her words to the softly strident *shamisen*.

Then a newcomer appeared on the scene. He came from the river. He wore a black kimono and was accompanied by his wife, who wore a white one. They both carried *shamisens*, and they stood before the open room. He was an intense, very thin man, with a narrow, hatchet face, large, sunken eyes and gold-filled teeth. His wife, who stood beside and a little behind him, was much sturdier, with a determined expression on her round, young face. She looked at her husband, and her look expressed clearly her confidence in his greatness.

He was a *kabuki* singer, a master of his art. A note was struck on their instruments and instantly a silence fell in the room, which a moment before had resounded with talk. His song was of unrequited love, and the sorrow of Japanese songs seemed to reach a peak in the anguish that poured from this frail man. He seemed able to hold sound deep within his throat and to control it from his throat; he sang with the whole of his being, so that his mouth was simply the channel through which the music reached us. He was able to slide his voice to incredibly high levels, and great waves of a desperate sadness floated from him into the night. As he sang he played, and so did his wife, who seemed as transported as her husband. They achieved a oneness in the dark world around them, plaintive, crying aloud to a harsh, uncontrollable reality, a poetic outpouring of humbleness and sorrow.

In the room there was rapt and silent attention. There was no movement. Not an eyelid fluttered. All was concentration. One was drawn into this sadness as a moth is drawn into an enveloping flame. Then the pæan subsided, fell and died, and returned to the silence that first bore it. We applauded madly; he smiled, bowed low and returned to his boat, a thin shadow of a man followed by his sturdy little wife.

Then the aura of the East deserted us and we played riotous party games—"American Baseball Game" and "Japanese Drinking Game," the latter a form of musical chairs played on cushions.

But, stranger than all else, we finally went to another softly lit room in another part of the house. Here was a small dance-floor with a tiny bar in the corner. In another corner was a shiny radiogram, and we danced to the music of modern America. Here, if anywhere, was that astonishing mixture of the old and the new that is Japan. During this evening we travelled through endless centuries of time and found ourselves, finally, in Dixieland.

August 29th, 1954

A visit to the Florida is inevitable. It is the only place in Tokyo, according to my friend K., where the girls cannot be bought. They can, I believe, be persuaded; but it takes time.

Many of the girls are those who were here two years ago, still milling incessantly round the polished floor. The band is the same, still perhaps the best in the whole of the East. The same tawdry strip show is still held at nine-thirty p.m. Very little has changed except that the customers are far less numerous than they used to be. Times are not so good in Japan now there is no war in Korea.

I dance with a girl who knows no English except "me no English," "very sorry" and "thank you very much." She is almost beautiful in the half-light, and her name is Issimaru. Her knowledge of the world is gained from American films. She is able to tell me that she has seen "The Glen Miller Story." She clearly enjoyed it far more than she can possibly say. Dear old Glen Miller. What would life have been like if America had gone to war without him?

August 30th, 1954

A letter to a Japanese newspaper:

LIVING ON THE BRINK OF HELL

To the Editor.

I read with much pain the letter from "A Sick and Scared E-Serviceman" translated from the "Mainichi" entitled "Living on the Brink of Hell" in your Column (The Japanese Viewpoint) yesterday.

I lost my only son in the war, but I feel very deeply that those remaining maimed, and suffering in no less measure, have given their lives for their country. The war destroyed my property, took my son and my husband, so I do not have much to give but what I earn myself now, but even in a small measure I should like to contribute something to this hero, made helpless through no fault of his own. I am sure he was glad, like every true Japanese, to suffer for his country, and I hope with all my heart your powerful paper will take the matter up, not for him personally, but for all those like him who are now neglected by the very land they hoped to save. Do not let the matter rest until each one of them has been assured a livelihood at least, with the dignity and gratitude they deserve from us all. I have never written a letter to an Editor before in my life and I feel diffident doing it now, but I am greatly moved by the plight of the wounded and neglected soldiers of Japan.

May I also add that I and my students never fail to read the letters in your paper each day, and I wish to congratulate whoever it is on your staff who does such distinguished translating.

To the writer of the letter I, of course, prefer to remain anonymous, but will appreciate your letting me know how and where to send my "widow's mite."

MRS. SABURO KURUSU.

August 31st, 1954

Hara is worried about the irresponsibility of the Japanese. He sees in the present and the future only a terrible necessity for economy, planning and work. He sees a future for Japan that

From the top of the Asia Building, Singapore.

A Honkong Street.

can only be met by the same spirit evinced in Britain when Churchill offered the people blood, toil, tears and sweat. Without these things he fears a desperate future.

Hara is a mild-enough little man, educated, tolerant, and conscientious. He is the sort of Japanese who would like to believe in democracy, the sort of Japanese who will go along with democracy if it appears to be governing his country effectively. But Mr. Hara has come to the conclusion that democracy is making a terrible mess of his country, and because he is a patriot he must search for an alternative form of government. I do not think that he himself has found it, but he is quite certain that the Japanese people will find it when it finally becomes necessary to do so. He thinks that the sort of government that will solve Japanese problems will differ but little from the military dictatorship which brought about the last war. It will be either that, he believes, or Communism. In this way Mr. Hara, in common with a great many other thinking Japanese, is caught between his great desire to see a Japanese government able to raise his country to its former stature and his fear and utter distrust of another war. There is the Japanese dilemma: the government that is needed is almost certainly not a democratic one, and if it is not democratic then the danger of a future war is greatly increased. This very failure of democratic institutions must inevitably lead to dictatorship.

Mr. Hara, searching desperately for the right words, deplores the conduct of the people as much as that of the government.

"Western people like to think that we have changed, that we believe and understand democracy. But it is only our own irresponsibility that allows them to think these things. To some extent we are reluctant to hurt your feelings; we would not like you to see Japanese democracy as a kind of jolly charade, which is what in fact it is. For the time being we are willing for you to believe almost anything about us—as long as it keeps you happy. And this is just one aspect of our irresponsibility.

"Look about you wherever you go in Tokyo. We are supposed to be poor. We *are* poor. And yet we seem to be able to find plenty of money for our innumerable pin-ball halls, our television, our streets of night clubs, dance-halls, cafés, bars and brothels. How can one reconcile this flourishing life of expensive pleasure with our national and individual poverty? Look at our undirected building, our almost totally unplanned economy, the failure of our manufacturers—a fact hitherto unknown in history—to compete in world markets. It is incredible that our goods should be outpriced by Britain and Germany—but it is so.

"Then look at the Unions, for ever demanding more pay, shorter hours and increased benefits. They show no sense of responsibility towards either themselves or their country.

"Then, when our people vote, they have not the remotest conception of their responsibility towards the country. They will vote for the man they are told to vote for, without any realisation that in voting they are making themselves ultimately responsible for the government of the country. It has been this way since the war and is likely to continue so until the condition of the people becomes so bad that they will take things into their own hands. This may seem like a paradox to you. On the one hand I blame the people for irresponsibility, and say on the other that they themselves will end it. But this is not a paradox; it is, as you say, the heart of the matter. I say that the Japanese for years have been living in a dream world where everything, in the end, was going to be all right. But the time is swiftly coming when conditions will become intolerable. Our goods will not sell overseas. As a nation we are unable to pay our way. The time must come when we shall be bankrupt. The situation will then only be retrieved by a ruthless, powerful government which the Japanese people themselves will put into power—not, perhaps, by voting for it, but by the same processes of irresponsibility which operate today.

"It is sometimes very difficult to understand Japan. Sometimes I, myself a Japanese, am unable to understand it. But Japan is an old, proud country with a long and great tradition. No one really knows where my people came from, but they came to these beautiful islands many centuries ago. Here they lived their own lives, subjects of great Emperors, developed their art and their culture, built their cities and their palaces. In this land, whose name means 'origin of the sun,' they created something that is indestructible, a corporate, national life under their

Emperor. The Emperor represented their country; they were united in him even as they were united in the snowy pinnacle of Fuji-san, that dazzling emblem of our land. Japan cannot live without that point of unity provided by the Emperor. That he should be superseded by a gang of brawling fools in the Diet is unthinkable. The Emperor, or some other figure-head, or, if you like, some other Son of Heaven, must come back and save Japan. I know that he will come. It cannot be otherwise.

"The more I think about it the more I see that whereas the purpose of Western art is often the assertion of man among his surroundings, here in Japan it is to identify and integrate him with his surroundings. Our singing, our art, our poetry and our music all tend to strive towards this identification with nature. You can see this most strongly, perhaps, in our buildings; in our villages, which are almost invisible until you step inside them. Always we try to be a part of nature, a part of our country, a part of a gigantic family. When our country dies, then we die; when our country is sick, then we are sick; when our country is strong, then we are strong. And although we ourselves are not afraid of dying, we can never allow our country to die. We will die for our country, for our home, for our Emperor, for the shining idea you can see in Fuji-san. The 'I' in us is not afraid to die, for our being is contained in a greater conception of life which cannot die.

"You must think me an old man who talks too much. Perhaps I am, but so few of us understand. So few of us, in the West or in the East, are conscious of these inflexible motives driving us on to an unavoidable future. And I think that with more understanding some of the horror might be removed from the future.

"I am an old man who has seen much trouble. I know that there was never a greater folly than Japan's entry into the war with England and America. But I say that I am afraid that the killing will have been in vain if Japan is not allowed to achieve the destiny that lies within all of her sons.

"I do not know what this destiny is, but I know that it is a great one. I would ask you to do two things; I would ask you, one day, to go to the most crowded part of Tokyo, watch the people, and listen to the beat of life that can plainly be heard. It is not a hysterical rhythm, nor is it the rhythm of a tired people. It conveys a sense of power and of solidarity, a dogged, plodding, simple, all-embracing, all-containing beat of power. We Japanese are perhaps waiting for someone to harness, control and direct that power.

"And the following morning I would ask you to go early to the outskirts of Tokyo and watch for the first sunlight to glint from the white summit of Fuji-san. There you will see the wondrous focus of Japan, which also, like the people, waits in the knowledge that it will not wait for ever."

When Hara left me I sat for a long time, knowing the truth of what he had said. As I sat I remembered an illustrated article that appeared in, I believe, *Picture Post*. It purported to be a discussion between a Lancashire textile manufacturer and a Japanese. As I recalled the gentle but determined arguments of the Japanese and the uncouth effrontery of the Englishman, I felt the cold hand of the future and saw more clearly than ever that what Hara had told would indeed come to pass.

September 1st, 1954

A whole day and night in the plane, distinguished only by my meeting, over two a.m. coffee at Okinawa, a perfect stranger who had read my book *Far Eastern Agent*. He had so agreed with what I said about the uniform of the British army abroad, that he had showed the passage to his General. But from what I see around me still, I can only assume that the General did not agree.

September 2nd, 1954

She cared not how she came by the name, nor did she ever perceive its beauty: she knew it only as a constant reminder of her Eurasian ancestry and therefore disliked it. Somewhere in time, in the last three or four centuries, a swarthy, bright-toothed, swaggering adventurer from Europe came to the East and set in motion a series of reproductive events which resulted ultimately in Lynn—Lynn Marianne de Vegas. Lynn, however, had scant regard for the possibly romantic story of this early de Vegas; the fascination which her family tree might have held for the less prejudiced aroused in her only a cynical regret. The virile streams of life which had joined together in perfect synthesis would have been better, in Lynn's view, had they never flowed at all.

When I first met Lynn, she had few friends and practically no interests; the appalling emptiness of her life was frightening in one so young. The circumstances of her life had been such that she could no longer be induced to enthuse over anything if by any means she could avoid doing so, and she found her refuge in a permanent and obdurate state of indifference. Her life became circumscribed by an inarticulate and impotent revolt against her lot. This is the story of Lynn, very much as she told it to me, without, in the beginning, my even asking for it. She told it to me, when the first bloom of her youth had died and when she was faced with the interminable prospect of an empty maturity.

Lynn was born in Kuching in Sarawak, where her father had a respectable job as a minor overseer in a sawmill. He was black —as black, as some would have it, as your hat—and hailed from Southern India, a part of the world he first left as a child. To all appearances he was a pure Tamil, the blood that had given him his name in the distant past having, by the time it reached him, become diluted to the point of extinction. Her mother was the product of a drunken Dutch sailor, who loved lasciviously in many ports and what must have been a very beautiful Siamese woman.

They, Lynn's father and mother, had met in Singapore, where she had drifted to work in a cabaret and where he had come to look for work. If his visit did not find for him employment, at least it provided him with a fertile and prolific wife. De Vegas in those days was a handsome enough fellow. Tall, well-developed and always fashionably dressed, he experienced no difficulty in sweeping Marianne Haas right off her shapely little feet. But perhaps Marianne's circumstances at the time had something to do with her easy capitulation to his undoubted charms, since she had little to look forward to then but a nightly succession of fat Chinese paunches.

Marianne, like her mother, was beautiful. Her face was a perfect oval, with that purity of outline and feature to be found only among Orientals. Its Siamese flatness had been gently erased by her Dutch father, and her skin was fairer than that of most Siamese; otherwise she was not noticeably un-Asian. Her eyes were the true eyes of the East, set quite obliquely in the smooth, flawless, almond skin, and her pert, perfectly-shaped lips were able to evoke the most immediate response in almost any man. She had been born, mercifully, with black hair and not, as might well have been the case, with hair drearily mouse or dirtily red, and it had grown into a rich and glossy crown.

All that I have said about Lynn's parents was gleaned from Lynn herself. I myself never met them and so I have no verification, except to look at Lynn: then I know that she speaks the truth. She loved her mother and came to hate her father—partly because of his colour, partly because of the way he treated his wife, and partly because of the way, towards the end, he treated Lynn herself. He had, in the first place, no conception of birth control, or, if he had, his religion forbade him even to think about it. He was, of course, a Roman Catholic, and therefore a willing believer in the idea that God would provide in spite of numerous, manifest, and persistent indications to the contrary. His wife, too, was a Catholic, and was therefore also unversed in the methods of planning the arrival of her babies. But, although they shared their prejudices and their ignorance, there was a marked divergence of opinion between them on the subject of offspring. Louis de Vegas was prepared to go on making his wife pregnant just so long as she was fertile and he was potent. That his wife began to look thirty years old when she was twenty, and forty-five years old when she was thirty, until at forty, or thereabouts, she might be expected to die, was not important. That was simply the way things went. Marianne, on the other hand, tried to think that that was not the way that life was intended to be lived. She preferred not to die. But she found that, short of running away, she might as well try to resist the advances of an elephant. And so, year by year, she bore her husband children. She gave birth, usually, not long after Christmas, until, when she had been married for thirteen years, she had produced thirteen children, three of whom, fortunately or unfortunately, had died before they had learned to go hungry. It was during the birth of the fourteenth child that Marianne de Vegas died, a shapeless, middle-aged drudge of thirty-two. Perhaps she would not have died had she received competent medical attention, had the disreputable Malay midwife groped and prodded less. Either way it was a miracle that the baby lived, to be duly baptised into the Roman Catholic Church.

Lynn was the second child and so, when her mother died, she was old enough to know what was happening. It was from this point that she began to loathe her father. Picture the dark, stifling bedroom, lit by a single oil lamp. Outside the air is still, the only sound the dry, shrill scream of cicadas. The grubby mosquito net, patched in a dozen places, has been thrown aside and the midwife crouches by the side of the bed, fearing her own ignorance, yet knowing that she will not be blamed. The shiny linoleum on the floor is littered with the debris of the gigantic household that has tried unsuccessfully to contain itself within three small rooms. The two eldest children are there and their father, he sitting uncomfortably on the only chair, they squatting on the floor. No one speaks; there is no sound except the incessant noise of cicadas and the slow, unsteady panting of Lynn's mother. All know now that she is dying, and also that there is nothing that they can do about it. They are content in their helplessness, but they have asked the priest to come since it would not be right to die without the priest. And so he comes, a fat, sweating man with an Irish accent, pushing his way through the patterned curtain that divides the bedroom from the living-room. He has a smiling face, as though any moment he is going to make a joke. Then he does not, because he sees the woman and even he knows that she is dying, and he thinks for a moment that it might be better in some ways if the father instead were lying there, breathing his last.

"Hello, Marianne," he says in his soft Irish voice. He takes her brown hand and holds it in his, and slowly, like a terribly wounded animal, she turns her head and looks at him, but she does not smile. The father stands uncomfortably in the shadows, feeling but not recognising the guilt of all men. The children sit still, wide-eyed and fearful. Outside, beyond the curtain, sits Lynn, knowing nothing except that her mother is dying, and for a moment she wishes that she, too, were going to die. And there is no sound except the thin scream of cicadas and the distant noise of a yelping bitch. Then there is the gabbled low murmur of prayer and the cockroach sound of the midwife, scuttling before the magic she does not understand.

Lynn's mother died that night and they buried her in the Catholic cemetery the following afternoon. Lynn went to the service with all the other children and her father. They all wore black bands on their arms, and carried flowers that they placed afterwards on the little heap of soil which was all that remained to remind them of their mother. After the funeral they all trooped home again, and their father went down to the sawmill. Lynn watched him go and felt the surge of an impotent rage that was never entirely to leave her. He had lost his wife. It was a pity, but it was the will of God. There were other wives. It would not be long before he found another. After all, a man was a man, and someone had to look after the children. But Lynn had lost her mother and there were no other mothers like the one she had known. Her mother had died and she knew that it was her father who had killed her. She knew that, quite certainly. She snatched up the snivelling child at her side and strode home, dry-eyed, and hurt beyond remedy. Then she went to the bedroom and lay on her mother's bed and cried until she could cry no more.

Next day life started all over again. It was much the same as it had been before, except that a good deal of the love had gone out of the house. The system was that the elder children looked after the younger, and Louis de Vegas, out of his slender pay, engaged a Malay servant to look after the baby which, considering the circumstances of its birth, turned out to be remarkably healthy. A year passed, and then Lynn joined her sister at school. Whatever else might be said against Louis de Vegas he did, to his everlasting credit, place an astonishingly proper value, for one so ignorant, upon education. All his children went to Catho-

lic schools for a few years and learnt to speak English with a
modicum of accomplishment. On leaving school they qualified
for jobs that did not require manual labour, which was, of
course, the object of their education. There was no doubt about
the pride Louis de Vegas took in the number and the quality
of his children. It was simply a pity that he had never taken a
proper pride in his wife.

Lynn went to school for the first time during the week that
saw the arrival in the house of the new Mrs. de Vegas. Her name
was Lily Chen, a widow, who, as her name implies, was Chinese.
She was a fat, raucous, blowsy Chinese woman whose husband
had committed suicide after losing such money as he possessed
in gambling. Chen Ah Lim had gambled all his life with everything he had. His very nature was to gamble. He preferred to
put his shirt on a horse than wear it himself, and a dollar in his
pocket represented only an opportunity to turn it into two or
several without actually working to produce the increase. More
often than not he would lose it. He would bet on anything containing the slightest element of chance, and it was because of
this propensity that his unstable little business came to an end.
One day Lim woke up and found himself bankrupt beyond re-
call, so he cheerfully walked out and shot himself with a revolver no one ever dreamt he possessed.

His wife Lily was a slut—a dirty, idle but, unfortunately, fertile slut. She had been having children so long she scarcely
needed to go to bed to give birth. The last infant she gave to her
husband was born five minutes after she had got into bed, and
she was up and about the next morning. In the process she had
grown fat and shapeless, and her thin, pendulous breasts hung
down inside her *samfoo* jacket like malignant deformities. She
was thirty-six, and for twenty years had slept each night with a
man. So much a habit had this become that she believed she
could no longer do without one, and that was why she married
Louis de Vegas, who by then shared her sentiments.

Lily Chen had never let her children occupy her time. She
produced them very much as a by-product of her enjoyment and
recognised in them their nuisance value only. From the very
beginning they were left almost entirely to their own devices and

to their elder brothers and sisters, who, being Asian, developed very early in their lives a marked sense of responsibility towards the younger members of their family, a most useful trait, usually absent in European children. Feeding never presented a problem to Lily: if the baby cried, wherever she might be or whatever she might be doing, she would simply pull up her jacket and thrust the great brown teat into the child's mouth, not so much to feed it as to silence it. The effect, without exception, was magical.

And so this slatternly child of semi-civilisation came to live in Lynn's house and to share her father's bed. And Lynn shuddered, and resolved to leave her father's house as soon as she was able. She had to wait for four years, by which time she had three half-brothers. She was then seventeen, and already a beautiful woman—beautiful in the way that her mother had been.

She had the same perfect features, the same flawless skin and the same pert mouth. Already, wherever she went she attracted the attention of men, and already she was fully sensible of the effect she had and derived great pleasure from it. But if she had eyes for men, she had them only for Europeans. It may be that this attitude was the beginning of the end for Lynn. She would perhaps never find the acceptance among Europeans that she hoped for and desired, and would succeed only in alienating whatever affection her own people might have for her. But it was not Lynn's fault that this happened: it was the fault, largely, of her father, and, if one wished to trace the blame beyond him, it became necessary to go back to his father and to his father before him, until one arrived in a sun-drowsy port somewhere in Portugal, which, in the several hundred intervening years, would be found to have changed scarcely at all. Between the two, between Lynn de Vegas and Portugal, not a great deal of affinity remained, except, perhaps, a common faith in the Catholic Church. When the Portuguese had travelled to the East and established the first European settlements beyond India, they had come with fire and sword and the Bible. They were conquest-hungry men who sought to enlarge the boundaries of their tiny country to include the very girdle of the earth. But they differed from the Dutch and English who came after them in that they required, above all else, that the defeated should accept their faith. It was as though the converted could atone for the cruelty, the torture, and pillage that preceded their change of heart. Given a thousand new Catholics, the killing had been worth while. Given a spread of the word of God, then those who had died foully had not died in vain. A new shrine was worth the heads of a thousand unbelievers. But some will say that all the converts in the world could not atone for the Lynn de Vegas' of this world, who happened several centuries later.

There was in Kuching, at the time that Lynn left school, a European, by the name of Frank Carvell, who was engaged in an export business of a somewhat dubious nature. He dealt in timber and sundry other produce of the country, and it was well known to most local people that his own personal standards were no less dubious than those of the business he had created. He had several weaknesses, one of which was drinking and another women. He was not a particular man in either of these excesses, and usually indulged in the one in conjunction with the other. He had a very old Morris Oxford, and one day, returning from the quay on the river, he pulled into the side of the road to offer Lynn de Vegas a lift. He did not undertake this kind action from any consideration for Lynn, nor from any concern for the state of his own conscience, but simply because he had seen a pretty girl and it was his habit to offer to pretty girls anything within reach which would, in his view, lead to a closer relationship. In this case it was a lift in his broken-down vehicle. Lynn hesitated for a moment, then smiled and availed herself of the heaven-sent opportunity to save her feet. They drove off in a great cloud of exhaust smoke, accompanied by a terrible mechanical vibration that shook the old Morris to the point of disintegration. Somehow it never did disintegrate and, for all I know, it still ploughs slowly along the sparse roads of Kuching, perhaps with yet another *affaire* sprouting on its dilapidated seats and stained, frayed carpets.

Frank Carvell stood six foot three in his stockings—when wearing any, which was seldom—and his enormous chest bulged through the open neck of his habitual cricket shirt in much the same way as the bodily contours of a wrestler press outwards through the confines of his tights. The effect, at one time, had no doubt been impressive, but a good deal of the glamour was lost when fat was added to the bone and muscle in almost equal proportions. This later development consisted in particular of a paunch, sizeable in one still comparatively young. In a colder climate men similarly afflicted may hide their protuberances beneath well-cut suits, but in the tropics no such deception is possible without extreme discomfort. Carvell wore a pair of khaki shorts which, because of the disappearance of his hips beneath rolls of fat, tended continually to slip down and drape themselves in untidy folds about the lower reaches of his stomach and thighs. At this time he was thirty-five, and traces of his earlier good looks still survived. He was fair and, strangely enough, his features, with the possible exception of the lips, which were too large, were not weak. His clear, blue eyes invariably looked one straight in the face, and his chin was square and forceful. His skin was burnt a golden brown by the constant sun, and he had none of the sallow pallor of the alcoholic. Perhaps alcoholic is too strong a term to use: he simply drank heavily, a not unusual habit for a man to form in the East if he lives too long alone.

Lynn was dressed in a cool linen dress which she had made herself from a remnant. It fitted sufficiently tightly around her young body to outline clearly, and yet not too obviously, the gentle curves of her hips and breasts. It made a deep and permanent impression on Frank Carvell. Above the roar of the Morris he asked her if she would like to come to his bungalow for a drink.

"Now?"

"Yes, why not?"

"But I don't know you."

"Yes, you do. Don't you remember? We met two minutes ago."

"But I must go home first."

"Now why on earth should you want to do that? I can run you home later."

"Not today, please."

"Why?"

And so it went on, the same old conversation that Carvell had held a thousand times. But to Lynn it was something fascinating and exciting. Her sense of anticipation was excruciating. She found herself strangely short of breath and slightly trembling. But of one thing she remained quite certain: if she went to his house without permission there would be a fearful row at home, and if she allowed him to drive her home, either now or afterwards, there would be an equally fearful row. Either way there would be trouble, and she was sensible enough to avoid trouble while she could.

"Drop me here, will you, please?"

But Mr. Carvell showed no sign of bringing his shuddering mass of machinery to a halt.

"You must stop. Please stop here."

Again Carvell paid no heed, but he was about to learn that Lynn possessed a strong mind of her own, coupled with a keen business sense.

"Unless you stop," she shouted, "I shall never come to your house. Never."

Carvell considered this for a moment, looked at her, saw that she meant what she said, and obeyed.

Lynn got out and thanked him, showing no sign of her previous annoyance. He leaned over and looked at her.

"What's your name?"

"Lynn."

"Lynn what?"

"Lynn de Vegas."

Carvell had a feeling for words, and said tritely, "That's a very beautiful name."

Lynn smiled at him but said nothing. She simply waited for him to continue.

"How old are you?" he asked.

"Nineteen," she lied.

"When shall I see you again?"

"When do you want to?"

"Tomorrow?"

"All right."

"I'll pick you up at the same time."

"All right."

"Good-bye, for now."

"Good-bye."

As he let in the clutch the whole car was at once thrown into a lunatic convulsion, but gradually it gathered way and proceeded slowly and uncertainly along the road, to disappear round the bend beyond. Lynn stood and watched it go, shielding her face from the setting sun with her cheap white handbag. Then she walked home, possessed of a strange, previously unknown sense of exhilaration. When she reached the dilapidated, attap-roofed bungalow in which fourteen people attempted without success to pursue a separate existence, she felt the impulse that had come to her many times before to turn away and never again look back. But this time the impulse was stronger, and she stood for a moment on the threshold of the compound of baked mud, topped with a film of fine dust, and a vague picture of Carvell took shape in her mind. Then she crossed the dusty no-man's-land between the lane and the front steps, and went inside.

Lynn was the brightest of the entire family (none of whom could be said to be over-intelligent), and with intuition rather than logic was able to foresee the inevitable situations which would develop from given lines of action. She knew as she entered the house that there was going to be a row. There was an unnatural silence about the place that spelt the early breaking of a domestic storm, an atmosphere she had come to recognise clearly and to avoid when she could. This time, however, there was no escape, for her father bounded out of the bedroom, followed by his slatternly wife, who remained propped in the doorway, methodically picking her teeth with a spent match, as she waited for the fun to commence.

"I saw you getting into a car, a European's car, this afternoon."

"Yes."

"What were you doing? How do you know him?"

"I don't know him."

"Then why did I see you in his car?"

"Because he asked me."

Her father was enraged by the matter-of-fact innocence of her replies, and yet she could not restrain herself from making them. She knew that his temper was uncontrollable, and yet she went on.

"Anyway," she flung at him, "what is it to you?"

The shapeless bundle of human life steadily picked its teeth in the doorway, the dull, unintelligent eyes watching the defiant Lynn. One or two of the children sat in the dark corners of the room, fearing to move lest they should attract attention and bring down a storm of paternal anger upon their own heads. The Eurasian father, fully committed to an Asian life, faced his daughter, who already aspired to the life of a European. There was hatred on both sides, hatred not only of each other but between the races which, for the moment, they represented.

Louis de Vegas glared with bloodshot eyes at his daughter, and advanced a step towards her. Lynn, fearing the violence of which she knew him to be capable, backed against the wall.

"What is he going to do for you, you slut?" he bellowed. "What do you think he cares once you've given him what he wants? These white bastards will take everything you like to give them, but you'll get nothing in return but a kick in the arse. Do you hear me? And another thing—Carvell's a drunk. A no-good, dirty drunk. Do you know what they say about him? They say he will never marry except to a native. That's what you are, a native. A native whore. All right. Get yourself a native. Go and sleep with a native. But if I catch you with that bastard again, I'll kill you." He dropped his voice at the end of this, the longest speech he had ever made to his daughter. "That's what I'll do, I'll kill you."

Lynn scarcely understood what he was talking about. There were tears standing in her dark eyes, and when she could bear the sound of his obscene words no longer, she flung herself forward crying, "Stop! stop! for God's sake, stop!"

He caught her wrists and laughed in her face, as her body shook with sobs of furious humiliation. She struggled, but he held her, unable to move, until she had no strength left to struggle. He looked at her savagely.

"You think it was my fault that your mother died, don't you? Looking at me, always looking at me. You think I killed her,

don't you? Don't you?" he screamed. "Well"—his voice dropped
again—"be careful I don't kill you, you cheap little European's
whore."

Then he let go of her left wrist, raised his hand and brought
it down, knuckles forward, in a savage blow on her face. She
yelped like a rabbit, spun round and collapsed on the floor.
There she lay, holding her hand to the cut on her face, the blood
trickling between her fingers and falling in big red drops on to
the dusty floor. Louis de Vegas stared at her, his chest rising and
falling beneath his sweat-soaked shirt. Then, without a word, he
left the house.

She waited until he had gone before pulling herself to her
feet. Her stepmother made no move to help her, nor showed,
indeed, any reaction at all, and the children, as soon as their
father was out of sight, scuttled out of the house to await de-
velopments from a safer point of vantage. Her dress was torn in
a great rent where it had caught against the table, revealing her
cheap cotton briefs, the only other garment she was wearing.
She had an excruciating pain in her knee where it had clouted
the hard boards of the floor and, as she sat up, the blood that
flowed from her cut cheek dripped on to the front of her dress.

Somehow she got herself to the washbowl which was kept at
the back of the house, washed herself and, by dabbing repeatedly
at the cut on her cheek, caused the bleeding to stop. Then she
found her other dress and put it on. As she went through these
familiar motions, the rage and the humiliation left her. Her
body seemed to have purged itself of all emotion, all feeling—
even all hope. All she felt was a dull, implacable opposition towards everything represented by her father, and a similarly dull,
cold acceptance of whatever else life should bring her. In that
hour her character underwent a change which was to last for the
rest of her life. She had been wounded beyond all prospect of
recovery. There was ever afterwards a scar upon her heart, a scar
as permanent as the one she was to carry upon her cheek. She
was young no longer, but as old as her race.

When, many years later, I was to meet her, I came to know a
woman who was almost beautiful. But she did not believe in her
beauty as did others similarly fortunate. She laid no store by it.

Shopping on a small income, Hongkong.

Tokyo Miss.

Old Japanese Gateway, Tokyo.

Modern Tokyo.

She made no advances to others, but always waited for them to make overtures to her, and if they did she would accept them with an air which suggested that it would not have mattered very much to her if they had not. Lynn no longer ran any risk of being let down, since she no longer allowed herself to be up-lifted in the first place. She led a negative, passive life which gave nothing, and expected nothing. She stayed closed within herself, tight like a clam, fearing that if she ceased to protect herself in this way she would be hurt again. I was able to change her, a little, a very little, but only towards myself. Somehow she came to believe to a tiny extent in me, perhaps because I ap-proached her through the only person in the world she loved. But I am getting ahead of my story.

It was natural, I suppose, that Lynn, after the incident with her father, should gravitate to Carvell. She did not immediately leave home, for the simple reason that she had nowhere else to go except the street. She had no friends who could help her, and so she stayed in her father's house, and slept on the front veran-dah. By day she stayed away from the house, and it was only a matter of time before Carvell spotted her again. He again offered to take her to his house, and this time she agreed at once, though without enthusiasm, since she was already cultivating her new personality.

Carvell's bungalow was a nondescript wooden building with a thatch of attap. The garden was totally uncared for, and the interior of the house itself was scarcely less wild. Carvell, it appeared, was a man whose happiness was not affected by his environment or, if it was, the effect was quickly nullified by means of alcohol. There was an assortment of rattan chairs on the verandah, and one or two of the rooms seemed to be equipped with a primitive type of bed. But apart from these indications, the purpose of one room was quite indistinguishable from that of another. There was an almost complete absence of furniture, except for the essentials required by a single man living quite alone. He appeared to employ no servants and, as a result, al-most everything he possessed was kept on the floor in old packing-cases which were not even disguised with any sort of covering. In addition, the place was filthy. His water he obtained from a small spring which, quite fortuitously, welled up in his garden. But, apart from the occasional request of a guest for a glass of water, he had small use for the commodity. The washing of his clothes, and of his own person, he accomplished *in situ* at the spring.

The interior walls of the bungalow were, for the most part, bare boards, except where areas of colour-wash displayed the care of previous owners. He had no pictures, no books, and only a selection of tattered, dated magazines. Each dingy room was lit by an oil lamp.

Perhaps the most arresting feature of the house was the remarkable number of empty bottles to be found in it. They were littered in profusion in every room and, had they all been removed in one operation, a lorry of considerable size would have been needed. It is true that they had taken several years to accumulate, but even given the unquenchable thirst of a Carvell, they still seemed to represent an unconscionable amount of drinking.

The house, then, that Lynn entered less than a week after the incident with her father could be said to be furnished with old rattan chairs, old packing-cases and bottles, and little else. And this was the house which she was not to leave for a full two years.

I do not think that Lynn ever forgot that first night with Carvell. It began, as might be expected, by his offering her a drink. He drove the car up to the front verandah steps, leaving Lynn to climb out in her own time as he marched ahead, flinging over his shoulder as he went, the words:

"What can I get you to drink?"

Lynn panted after him. "Can I have a squash, please?" She walked up the front steps and examined for the first time a house which even to her was remarkable for its untidiness. As Carvell rummaged about in another room, she walked along the verandah and back again, examining the broken chairs and the stained old table. She leant on the verandah rail and looked down the hill, and when she moved away she found her hands were covered in dust. She walked back to the table and sat down. Dusk was just falling: in a few moments it would be quite dark.

Carvell reappeared from the dim recesses of the bungalow carrying a gin bottle and a couple of glasses, one of which appeared to contain orange squash. He offered her the squash. He then poured a generous helping of gin into the other glass, which already contained an inch or two of water.

"Cheers," he said.

Lynn smiled. "Cheers," she answered. She drank deeply, and a second afterwards appeared to have convulsions.

"What's the matter?"

She fought for breath, tears streaming down her face.

"What is it?" she was at length able to ask.

"Squash."

"But there's something in it."

"A little bit of gin," he said, and smiled. "It will do you good." He looked at her and saw that she was beautiful. "But don't drink it so fast," he added.

Lynn could feel the alcohol like fire in her veins. It was a sensation entirely new to her, and she had no conception of its effects.

"Don't be afraid of it," he said. "It won't do you any harm."

She sipped, and found that in small doses it did not burn her throat. She also discovered that it was not so distasteful as she had at first thought. She sipped again. Gradually she found the vague uneasiness she had felt as she entered the house slip away, and in its place she experienced a new confidence and a strange, bubbling happiness. She listened as Carvell prattled away, and found herself laughing at his sallies although, goodness knows, they were not very funny. He was telling her how he needed someone to look after his house, how he had no time for cleaning and cooking, how the servant he had at one time employed had stolen practically everything he possessed. He painted a vivid picture of his attempts to cook a meal on a charcoal stove which he could never get started, and of how very much easier it was to open a bottle or a tin. She laughed loudly at his description of his washing a shirt and then trying to iron it by sleeping on it. And as he spoke he added some gin to her squash almost without her noticing it. She was easy, very easy, meat.

Lynn decided that she quite liked Frank Carvell, whatever her father may have said about him. And, of course, it is not possible to blame her particularly for this decision, for Carvell was, when you first met him at any rate, a likeable sort of fellow. There was nothing vicious about Carvell: he was simply weak to a criminal degree. With the aid of drink his principles—those that he possessed—could be modified to the point of non-existence. I think perhaps there were occasions when he regretted the harm he had done in the world, but I am certain such moments of introspection occurred only during his rare periods of complete sobriety. At this particular moment all his wits were centred on getting Lynn into bed with him as quickly and as easily as possible. His method, perhaps, was odious, but at the time he had no thoughts of propriety. It was simply, he thought, a matter of time. And Carvell had lots of time.

"I feel so sleepy," said Lynn.

"Then why don't you go to sleep?" It was all so terribly easy. She rested her head on the hard back of the chair. "So tired . . ." she said.

"Go to sleep . . ." He picked her limp body up in his great arms, carried her into his bedroom and laid her down on the hard, unmade bed. Then he pulled down the grubby mosquito net, which hung from lengths of string stretched across the room, and tucked the ends beneath the mattress. Slowly he undressed, turned out the lamp and climbed in beside her.

Lynn, on the very ultimate fringe of the drunken sleep, still retained a dim awareness of what was happening, but when she felt his hands fumbling at the catches of her dress and her clothes being gently but resolutely drawn from her body she found herself too tired, too tired and too sleepy, to resist.

When she awoke, or came to, whichever it was, she was icily cold. Judging from the temperature, there was not much time left before dawn. She freed herself from the clinging folds of the net and, staggering as though she were still drunk, made her way to the rear of the house. After a while, with the aid of the moon, she found that she could just see her way about and discern the various obstacles that lay in her path. After an eternity of time she found what she was looking for, and poured the cold water over her naked body and bathed herself gently. Then, feeling that she was going to faint, she made her way back to the bedroom. She found a blanket at the foot of the bed which she pulled round her shivering, aching body, and collapsed once more into a deep sleep.

When she awoke it had been day for some time and Carvell had left the house.

There is no need to dwell on the next two years which she spent with Carvell. She stayed in the beginning because she was too afraid to go back home, and if she could not go to her father, then there was no one else to whom she could go. Strange as it may seem, those two years were not entirely unhappy, although they were often tinged with sorrow. Carvell came home that night full of contrition. At first she cowered in a corner, like a whipped animal, and snarled if he approached. Then she found she could come out of her corner without there at once ensuing a repetition of their first night together. They recognised the fact that they must continue to live together in the same house for some little time at least, and gradually there grew up between them a mutual appreciation of the other's predicament. Old injuries to a certain extent healed, and since they found themselves together they almost unconsciously began to make the best of it. Carvell behaved better, at least, than he might have done. He desperately wanted Lynn to stay with him and she, for her part, perhaps because she had been loved so little in her life, found that she stayed, not only because she had nowhere else to go, but later because she wanted to stay, or, at least, was content to stay.

For six months Carvell drank less—although he still drank too much—and did everything within his meagre power to make Lynn happy. The transformation in the man was astonishing. The house, too, underwent a fundamental change, and Lynn, with the aid of a broom, some paint and some cheap materials, made it almost habitable. Carvell, although chronically short of money, managed to give her small sums from time to time to spend on things which, to his way of thinking, could not be considered vitally necessary to the business of living. These she spent on little decorations for the house, and on one or two extra dresses for herself.

During this time they lived a totally isolated life. They had no friends, not even any acquaintances who thought enough of them to visit them occasionally. But this did not matter to Lynn. She had to some extent found a home and a rickety sort of security. For the moment she almost felt safe. She was fed, clothed, housed and, it seemed, in a peculiar, oafish way, loved. Many girls had less. And while her life was in this way made bearable, she was able, if not to forget, at least to push back into the farther recesses of her mind, the memory of how it had all started. It is true that the memory of her first night in the house often returned to her, but she found that with a little effort and ingenuity she could prevent herself from thinking about it. She was not concerned with shame or humiliation, for she did not feel either: she simply wished to be as happy as her circumstances would allow, and the farther she could get away from hate, and the closer she could get to love of Carvell, the happier she knew she would find herself to be.

Then she discovered she was pregnant. She did not recognise the earlier symptoms, but only knew with certainty when she saw her swelling belly. She was then just eighteen and the knowledge at first terrified her. She found herself sweating with fear. She did not tell Carvell, but went instead to see the aged Malay midwife who had helped to deliver her mother before she died. The Malay midwife was also an abortionist and, although Lynn did not know this and would not have understood the meaning of the word, she had a vague idea that the old woman was able to get rid of babies as well as to deliver them.

She searched among the riverside hovels and at last found her, filthy and almost blind. They spoke in Malay, quickly, and without any wasted words. Lynn said:

"I am pregnant."

The ancient harridan smiled, revealing her toothless gums, and answered that what she said was undoubtedly correct.

Lynn then said that she wished to be rid of the baby since she was not married to its father. She added that, this being the case, she would not know what to do with it. Again the old woman smiled, and asked what her much-vaunted religion would have to say about such a sentiment. Lynn answered that she no longer went to Mass, and that when she saw the priest coming up the hill she would lock the door and refuse to let him in. Yet because of her religion, she was afraid: she was afraid both of having the child and of not having it. Either way, it seemed to her, her religion would find her sin intolerable. The midwife then asked if Lynn had ten dollars and added that if she had no money there was little point in their continuing the conversation.

Lynn returned in three days with ten dollars which Carvell had given her to buy clothes, and the midwife gave her a little brown earthenware bottle and told her to drink the contents as soon as the moon was full. Lynn walked home through the hot sun with fear in her heart and hid the bottle in the rafters above the verandah.

She drank the stinking, sluggish, red liquid exactly a week later, and within half an hour was writhing on her bed in an extremity of pain. Carvell was lying beside her, almost asleep, and her moaning woke him, and between gritted teeth she tried to tell him what she had done. She was astonished to find that he wanted the child, and equally astonished to find, at the same time, that she herself, in that case, wanted it too.

Carvell had been long enough in the country to know something of Malay charms and potions, but he was powerless to ease the terrible pain. He wanted to fetch a doctor but she would not let him. She did not really know why she would not have a doctor, except that it was partly shame and partly fear and partly a determination to put things right herself if only she might live. As the great, griping pains swept through her body, she found herself praying for the first time since she had come to the house. During the clutching, contracting spasms she deliriously chanted a meaningless jumble of lines from almost forgotten prayers, which crystallised into "Holy Mary, Mother of God," "Holy Mary, Mother of God," repeated over and over again. "Holy Mary, Mother of God, Save me, Holy Mary, Mother of God."

Carvell watched over her all night, and brought her towels when the blood began to flow. All night it seeped slowly into the

towel stretched under her legs, until, in the morning, it ceased
to flow if she lay quite still. She lay like death, utterly spent, and
stayed thus, scarcely moving, for three weeks. After that she
could move again without starting the bleeding afresh. After a
month she was better and knew that she was still pregnant.
Perhaps there was something to be said for her religion after all.

Now she was glad, and happy, and strangely self-confident. In
the proper course of time the child was born, a boy, and from
the first it was the living image of Carvell. It was fair and had
blue eyes, and Lynn loved it far more than she had ever thought
herself capable of loving. The child, which they called Robert,
was more important to her than anything else in the world could
ever be, and for the first time in her life she was completely
happy.

Perhaps it was her adoration of the child, which inevitably
meant a lessening of the attention she paid to Carvell, that began
his gradual reversion to the old habits; or it may have been
simply that he grew tired of the unfamiliar role of respectability
which he had so recently and so suddenly embraced. Perhaps it
was a little of both, but, with Lynn happily occupied with her
baby, he began to spend riotous evenings in town, returning
home fit for nothing but a drunken slumber. Perhaps it was that
he suddenly came face to face with the added responsibilities he
had so gaily assumed and discovered he did not like them. Certainly he began to miss his freedom.

There was nothing that Lynn could do to prevent this back-
sliding. She pleaded, implored, cajoled and shouted, but nothing
could alter the fact that he was growing away from her. She
should have known, of course: she should have known that men
like Carvell are incapable of sustaining any affection beyond a
certain limited time, and that after that period nothing again
will quicken their interest. It is possible that when she went to
the midwife for the poisonous rubbish she had drunk she already had a dim premonition of Carvell's ultimate reaction. But
all along Lynn had been dogged with the knowledge that
nothing better lay waiting for her elsewhere. There was not, in
fact, much option.

One night Carvell brought home with him a Malay prostitute.

He was almost too drunk to know what he was doing, and he staggered into the bedroom and pushed her on to the bed where Lynn was lying asleep. She was awakened by the uproar to find herself faced with the spectacle of Carvell trying to rip the sarong from the now very startled woman. For a moment Lynn was too dazed to take in the full significance of the extraordinary situation that confronted her. She could see the thick, coarse face of the Malay woman clearly, and she could see that she was struggling with Carvell's insistent hands, but this picture seemed to lose its impact on its way to Lynn's brain. She simply sat there in bed, utterly stunned and utterly confused. Then it was as if a sudden electric shock surged through her, and she flew like a lithe animal at the bovine, giggling prostitute, clasping her thin hands round the loose brown neck. They went down on to the floor, taking Carvell with them. For a full five minutes the battle raged, such furniture as there was in the room was overturned and shattered, bottles and glasses rolled and crashed into the walls. Carvell stood and watched drunkenly, outside the fight and not properly understanding it, as the two women fought over his worthless hulk. They screamed and panted and bit and scratched. Then Lynn, by now quite naked, got herself on top and, seizing the Malay's head between her hands, banged it with all the strength she had left against the floor. There was a sharp crack, and the body beneath her sagged and made no further resistance. Still possessed by an uncontrollable anger, Lynn dragged it to the steps of the verandah and, panting as though her chest would burst, toppled it over the top step and listened to it go thump, thump, thump to the bottom, where it lay inert in the moonlight.

She went back into the house to Carvell, who was sitting on the bed simply staring in front of him.

"Get out," she shrieked. "Get out, you filthy swine."

He got to his feet and turned to her. He seemed suddenly and strangely sobered. He began to speak. "But——" he began.

His voice only roused Lynn to a new level of fury. "Get out. Get out—or I shall kill you."

He shambled over to the door. Lynn stood her ground as he passed. She was not afraid. Nor, I think, was she afraid of killing him. She knew where the axe was kept at the back of the house, and it was uppermost in her mind as a weapon both of defence and attack as he passed her. He stood for a moment at the top of the verandah steps, and then walked slowly down them. He staggered a little at the bottom. He went over to the old car, and backed it towards the Malay woman. He stopped the engine, got out, and walked back to the body. He looked at it for a moment, then dragged it to the side of the car and bundled it into the back. Then he climbed into the car and drove away in the moonlight, the dry dust swirling behind him. He did not return for three days.

Lynn, for one day, had had as much as she could take. She went back to her bed and collapsed upon it, hysterical with tears.

Gradually the three days passed. During that time Lynn lived the most dreadful ten minutes of her life over and over again. She felt again the rage and the terrible, consuming passion of hatred; she also experienced again the shame, the horrible injustice of it all, and the misery. And yet, and it sounds incredible, she wanted Carvell back. She missed him in the house and she missed him in bed, and the knowledge of the longing only increased the pain because she was not sure that he would come back. She discovered for the first time that she really loved him, so that his misfortunes were hers, his pain was hers, his weaknesses were hers. She did not understand this love, nor perhaps did Carvell, nor perhaps did anyone. But it was a form of love that is not perhaps unusual where the weak loves the strong, the servant the master, the oppressed—for all the oppression—the oppressor. It was in some such way that Lynn loved Carvell. And it was for this reason that she accepted him when he came back, full of humble excuses.

For a time it seemed as though life at Carvell's bungalow had returned to normal. The drinking tailed off a little. They even had some money to spare. Lynn had a few more new clothes, and they bought a battery radio set to which they would listen in the evenings. They would sit on their verandah in the soft tropical night, and fleetingly an atmosphere of domestic peace would settle over the house. They did not talk very much, for neither of them had a great deal to communicate either to the world or to each other. But they seemed to find some peace in each other's company which they could not easily find elsewhere. One night Carvell said:

"Are you happy, Lynn?"

"Mm."

"Why are you happy, Lynn?"

"Because you are here."

"But that is no reason to be happy," he said.

"I know. But I am."

Carvell had a very pleasant speaking voice. It was low, and in its gruff way possessed a kindly quality. He smiled often as he spoke, and gave the impression that at times he wanted to be good, and kind, to be of some use and to stop hurting people. From time to time an unfamiliar conscience moved within him. It did not cause him to suffer pangs of remorse, nor did it bring him to the verge of good resolutions. It simply, for the time being, made him a better person and one whom no one could wholly dislike. Lynn's love for him stemmed in large measure from these intervals of contentment, and all the hopelessness that inevitably followed could not kill the flame that they ignited.

"Lynn?"

"Yes."

"Why don't you leave me?"

"I don't want to—not when you're nice to me."

"You're old enough now, you know. You could go to Singapore. You could make your own living there. Lynn, why don't you go? Why don't you leave before it is too late?"

"But I don't want to leave you. I don't want to go to Singapore. I would rather stay here."

"It would be better if you went, Lynn. You can't always stay as the under-age mistress of an outcast European. Maybe now you are happy, Lynn, but you can't go on being happy, not this way. This way you can only go on being happy for a little while, because of me and because of this house and because of the way we live. I'm no one to give advice, but go; go, Lynn, before it is too late. Go with Robert now."

Lynn sat, still and lovely, in the cold moon's glare.
"I will never go," she said.

That was her declaration. It was not reasoned. It was not even
emotional. She simply said it. We shall perhaps never know
what amalgam of inherited and environmental influences
brought her to this decision. It is possible to read into it the pride
of the old Portuguese, the stubbornness of the Dutch or the
fatalism of the Orient. It is also possible to say that she wanted
to stay because she saw no other alternative, because she had
been ill-treated at home, or because she distrusted an outside
world in which she could only be a stranger. It is possible to
produce a welter of theories and postulations to account for her
irrational behaviour. But if you ask Lynn today why she stayed
she will say, quite simply, "Because I loved him."

There is no point in searching beyond this undoubted fact.
She loved him and that, as far as Lynn was concerned, was the
end of the matter.

Suddenly one day Carvell announced that he was going to
Singapore. He had some business to do there which could not
wait.

"How long will you be away?"

"Oh! a couple of weeks. But, you know, I've made one or two
good deals lately, and you and Robert could come too."

"Now? With you?"

"No. I'm going tomorrow. But I've got your ticket to leave in
a week's time. I'll meet you in Singapore and we'll have a week's
holiday."

A journey to Singapore was, to Lynn, a journey to the utter-
most ends of the earth. She had heard people talk of Singapore,
the great city, and she had longed to go there in much the same
way as a child in England will long to go to London. She could
scarcely believe it. Then there was the prospect of going out into
a new, strange world as Carvell's wife. Her mind flew to dresses,
and of how she would feel. A great happiness rose within her
and she flung her arms round him and pressed her face to his.
She whispered very quietly into his ear, "Is there time to get
married before we go?"

This left Carvell with nothing to say for a moment, except, "Get married?"

"We ought to get married, you know. We live together. We are man and wife. We sleep together. We have a child. I could be Mrs. Carvell, and you could be the man who is married to that attractive girl. Could we?"

"Do you really want to?"

"Yes, more than anything else, I want to be married to you."

"There isn't time here, at all. Perhaps we could in Singapore."

"Will you? Will you promise?"

"Well . . ."

"Promise! Please promise me."

"All right, I promise."

It seemed to Lynn, who dared pursue the question no farther, that he was not altogether happy at the prospect. But there was too much to be done to bother about what, after all, might only be imagined doubts. She had to have a new dress. There were tickets to buy, packing to be done and immigration people to see. There was so little time, with the future so near that it bubbled into the present.

The following day she saw Carvell off on the tiny passenger-cum-cargo boat that would be in Singapore in not much more than a day. She waved to him until she could see him no more, and even after that she watched with her heart in her mouth until the ship itself disappeared from sight. It was Monday, and she was to follow on Friday. At the moment she did not know how she could possibly live until then, but somehow she did, and almost a week later she arrived, with Robert, in Singapore.

She landed at Clifford Pier, which juts out into the seething inner roads of the great Eastern port. She was quite radiant and unbelievably lovely. She was tall, straight-limbed and exquisitely proportioned. Her face then was at its loveliest—gentle, a perfect oval, the smooth, soft skin stretched over the high cheekbones. In her arms she held her baby, Carvell's baby, the baby of the man she was going to marry. At her feet stood a cheap suitcase.

Around her the life of Clifford Pier went on oblivious of her. The porters went to and fro. People catching ferries, hiring sam-

pans and motor-boats, passed her by unheeding. The little boats
chugged round the pier in the brown water, and the sun glinted
hotly from the smooth waves they left behind them. The traffic
on Collyer Quay clattered its impersonal way up and down the
broad roadway.

She picked up her suitcase and walked to the barrier. Carvell
was not there, and a tiny, sickening fear began to gripe in her
intestines. In spite of the heat she shivered. After a while she
wanted to panic, to run wild and beg people who passed her to
find him. Her eyes darted among the men who came to the pier,
but none of them was Carvell, yet still she expected him to come
running up with some trivial excuse for being late. And all the
time the ice-cold, sweaty fear moved in her bowels. In the end
it grew dark and she sat on one of the benches with her child.
A chill wind blew from the sea and an attendant asked her if
she was waiting for anyone. That night the first Lynn de Vegas
died and a new Lynn de Vegas took her place.

I am glad, I think, that I did not know her in the early months
of her desertion by the human race. I do not think that I could
have dealt with the situation. Even now it is difficult enough :
the refusal to believe in kindness, to accept help, to believe in sin-
cerity, to grant anyone any good intentions. Even now it is possible to incite in her a rapid, implacable resentment, sometimes
followed by a sudden, unheralded reversal to an almost reluctant
gratitude. In this paradoxical behaviour lies the core of Lynn's
dilemma—a refusal to accept the world as she finds it and an
inability to do without it.

That is Lynn's story. I have tried, in telling it, to transmit a
little of the savour of her own words. I have tried, since I have
known her, to help her. But the task is difficult, for most of the
time she will not allow herself to be helped. She lives now for
her son, who goes to a free boarding-school run by a religious
mission. Every Sunday, and whenever she is free, she takes him
for an outing, perhaps to the beach, perhaps for a ride on a bus,
perhaps for a cheap ride in a boat in the harbour. They always
go alone. They share, perhaps, some secret which others cannot
share. There is one secret, though, which no one can know,
except Carvell. Did he go away for his own selfish reasons, or did

he go from some terribly misguided urge to set Lynn free? One thing is certain: whatever his motive, knowledge of it cannot make Lynn any less unhappy than she is today.

September 5th, 1954

Climbed to the top of the half-completed eighteen stories of the Asia Building this afternoon. When it is finished, it will be our highest and most imposing edifice.

Slowly Singapore is developing some of the equipment of a capital city, and gradually its miserable skyline is being altered to conform to more modern ideas. But it is a snail-slow process, and one which is not helped by the prevalent outlook of: "We're all right for a few years yet, but after that—another Indonesia? Another Burma? Another Indo-China?" Each country conjures up a different vision of hopelessness and futility. I meet many people who would like to believe in the future, but very few who unreservedly can.

And so, with the inevitable exceptions, Singapore is a short-term city. The questions the investor asks himself is not "Have I here a safe and sound investment?" but "Can I get my money back within five years?"

In the old days, when it seemed British government would continue until the crack of doom, Singapore was considered to be a place where a man stayed long enough to make his fortune before leaving to spend and enjoy it elsewhere. Even if he failed to produce enough wealth to retire to his homeland, he at least sent all he could to his relatives and dependants in India or China or wherever they happened to be. Either way, the wealth that came from Singapore's trade did not stay where it was made, but was dissipated all over the world.

Now, when China is Communist and the accent all the time is on Malayan citizenship and the desirability of people who live here staying here, the future is so uncertain that our wealth still slips through our fingers into foreign, or at least overseas, coffers. Meanwhile, we have to put up with the great tracts of slums, our decrepit public buildings, the acres of rusting corrugated iron, covering beaten earth, which our industrialists like to call fac-

tories, our utterly inadequate public transport system, our open
drains, our stinking pestiferous canals and our tumble-down
shops, shored up at the back and plastered with a façade of new
tiles at the front. What a magnificent boulevard Orchard Road
could have been, if Singapore at the right time had possessed
either the courage or the resources to build a broad, tree-lined
avenue running straight down to the sea. Instead, it consists
today, for the most part, of property that should have been con-
demned twenty years ago, shops that lean at crazy angles, cracked
walls, peeling plaster, faded paint, a mean avenue whose motto
is: "Let us make do with what we have got, for if we build
anything better we shall probably lose it."

This, I believe, is due to the doctrine that has obtained in
Singapore for a hundred years and more: that nothing here
need be permanent. The old reasons for this have now been
augmented by fear of another war and of self-government.

Yet, in spite of all this, Singapore is becoming more of a capital city than ever it was before. It seems to progress towards this
goal in direct relation to the dignity of its skyline. What it is,
precisely, that makes a capital city I do not know. Certainly it
rests in something far more fundamental than an impressive silhouette, or even than mere size. It depends largely on the people
who live in it, what they do and how they do it, who they are
and why they are there. Essentially, a capital city is a centre: a
centre of trade, industry, art and government, a conglomeration
of human beings operating a vast social and industrial machine,
whose importance to the surrounding country is clear and undis-
puted. A capital city must, I think, possess a long history, or a
history at least as long as that of the area of which it is the
centre; it must have a tradition which is the mark of its pride
in its accomplishments. And although Singapore is not yet a
Paris or a Peking, a London or a Shanghai, a New York or a
Tokyo, it makes, in spite of all its inherent weaknesses, steady
progress towards a town of stature. Already its people begin to
believe that they are "citizens of no mean city" and, although
this idea is yet far removed from reality, we can take comfort
in the fact that some, at any rate, believe in it.

In the years to come one hopes to see a great Singapore, a

flourishing, cosmopolitan focal-point of a South-east Asian Dominion which will stand equal with the other great Dominions; a unique Dominion containing within its borders men and women from all over the East who are proud of their home. This great city will not come to pass if it is left to the kind of mentality which covers derelict buildings with fancy tiles, or measures progress by the accumulation of closely-reasoned minutes. It can come to pass only through vision, the kind of vision Raffles had when he founded Singapore and which few of his successors have equalled. Only then will one of the richest cities in the East cease to wear the aspect of a very poor relation.

September 6th, 1954

There is always an approaching Festival in Singapore—Chinese, Christian, Hindu or Muslim, but most often, it seems, Chinese. Now the shops are full of moon-cakes and lanterns, and later this month the Chinese will celebrate the Moon Festival, and we shall see children walking like small ghosts in the dark with lighted lanterns in their hands, some in the shape of aeroplanes, some grasshoppers, and others fat and bloated fish.

When we go into the city during the next few days, we shall inevitably pass Chinese shops where we must bend low to walk under the festoons of lanterns which hang from the roof of the five-foot way. As each day passes, each lantern will become a little cheaper, until, on the day of the Festival, the shopkeeper, standing among the residue of his moon-cakes, will practically give them away.

They tell me that the lanterns are not what they were before the war. I do not know whether this is true, or simply wishful thinking by those who have become convinced that everything was better before the war. All I know is that at this time of year the often sad face of Chinatown takes on an unaccustomed gaiety. The lanterns hang in profusion from a hundred shops, and there is something almost of the spirit of Christmas Eve in England. Always among the swaying lanterns are the children—dirty, unkempt, but smiling children, who know no regular daily routine, but sleep when they are tired and rise when they are refreshed. Often they sleep in the five-foot way, secure under their own particular canopy of lanterns. It is because of the children that the Moon Festival reminds me of Christmas.

There are other similarities: the gay, often lurid decorations; the fat, solid-looking moon-cakes like heavy mince-pies; the feasting and the happiness. And the Moon Festival too, like Christmas, has lost in the towns a good deal of its original religious significance. Often, as with Christmas, it is the children only who make it godly.

The moon of the Moon Festival is that which shines when the harvest has been brought home. It is a moon which brings thanksgiving for the food of the winter that has been safely wrested from the soil. All over the world men celebrate the end of the harvest; the back-breaking toil is over, life, perhaps, for a little while longer is secure, and the bleakness of winter has not yet arrived. In China today I dare say there are philosophies which suggest that whether the harvest is great or small the moon can have had little effect upon the yield of the soil. Equally, I am certain, the ancient wisdom of China must know that the great white ball that has floated across the sky for untold years cannot possibly be without a most astonishing influence. And for this reason I think that the millions of China will continue to turn at this time to the Goddess of the Moon when their government tells them that the success of their harvest has been due entirely to improved fertilisers. I have no doubt that their government is right, but then it would be terribly difficult to give thanks to a bag of fertiliser.

September 7th, 1954

M. took me today to some of the dying-houses in Singapore. They are most of them situated in Sago Street and Sago Lane, in the very heart of the Chinese funeral industry, which, in turn, is in the very heart of Chinatown. Once in those dense, suffocating streets it is difficult to remember that one is in a city that has any connection with the twentieth century. One might be almost anywhere in time except the present day.

A dying-house is aptly named, since it is, in fact, a place to which people retire to die. In the parlance of the notice on the wall of one of the houses I went to, a more polite name is "Sick Receiving House." But whatever the name of the institution, its business is with the dead and dying, and its proprietor deals in this commodity with an astonishingly matter-of-fact air. He might be dealing in tinned food or cigarettes. He has none of the unctuousness of the Western undertaker, and none of the showmanship of the American mortician. He is in business in much the same way as his neighbour who makes coffins, or paper images, or the banknotes of hell. The only difference between them is that the dying-house keeper receives the body before it is dead.

Dying-houses vary. Some are dark caves in the slum-cliff of Sago Street, where those who have lost all hope of living eke out their last few hours, days, weeks, months or even years. As you walk inside you walk, as it were, on to the threshold of this world, to the very brink of the living, and look through the darkness into the world of the dead. The experience might be improved by even the smallest inkling of a vision, but there is nothing to be seen in the terrible blackness but the wide, bright eyes of suffering, and nothing to be felt but the sweaty movement of death. The bundles of persistent life are scarcely distinguishable from the bundles the dying have brought with them. A dying-house is a place of bundles, some living, some dead, and some a little of both. It is a house of hands outstretched and slowly gripping like injured claws; of thin wisps of grey hair pulled back over foreheads wrinkled like screwed paper; of eyes sunk in fleshless faces, peering and staring, always staring through the dust of the halflight; of bony faces bent motionless over pots of food which hands are no longer able to guide to the pursed hole between the hooked bones of chin and nose. Here you can look on death and listen to the beat of the wings of the angel of death; here, also, you can look on decay, the slow, emaciating decay of the human organism, and decay in something still living is infinitely more distressing than the decay which comes after death.

Perhaps the impact of these places would not be so great if we could accept the fact of death. The European, I think, does not accept death at all, not even when he is dying. But the inmates of the dying-houses of Singapore accept it. They sit or lie on their beds and simply wait for it to overtake them. And perhaps it is this attitude which makes the business of dying a much easier process than we of the West find it.

We walked round one of the better houses. The proprietor had no objection, but welcomed us with a gold-toothed smile and pointed the way upstairs. At the foot of the stairs we passed the little bench of spirit tablets with which the owners of dying-houses remember their departed guests, where lamps are kept burning and little offerings of food are placed before each tablet.

At the head of the stairs we entered a large room neatly laid out with iron bedsteads, about half of which were occupied. By the window a bald, middle-aged man half sat and half leaned against his bed, staring dully at the ceaseless activity in the street below. His legs were gigantic and a great pot-belly bulged above his laced-up Chinese trousers. But his shoulders were those of a little boy, wasted away, fleshless, sitting on the terrible hollow that was once his chest. M. suggests that he has beri-beri.

"But isn't it curable?" I ask.

"Certainly."

"Well, then, why doesn't he go to hospital?"

"For one reason or another he does not want to go to hospital. Or he doesn't know there is a hospital. Or if he does, he doesn't know where it is. Or he thinks they will charge him too much. Or he is afraid of the hospital. One of those reasons keeps him from going there."

"And he prefers to stay here and die?"

"That's it."

The conical wreck turns his heavy head and looks at us with his wide, round eyes, and then turns back to contemplate through the window the life he is leaving, one wasted hand resting upon his ballooning belly.

We pass through an archway into another and similar room. Here there are several old women who are, I think, dying of old age rather than from any particular disease. I have never seen such old and fleshless faces. In one corner there is a moving bundle of rags, moving so slowly that for a moment it might be taken for an old blanket thrown over a chair. We go over and find an old, old woman, a woman so old or so worn out that she has shrunk and bent until she is no bigger than a child. Perhaps her body is crippled with rheumatism, or perhaps some other, more sinister agency has been at work. Whatever it is, her limbs will no longer move, except so slowly that their movement is almost imperceptible. And under this filthy blanket, thrown loosely over her squatting body, she is trying to feed herself. I hope I shall never again witness such agony as is caused by the transfer of each greasy morsel from the tin bowl to her mouth—that striving, black hole which sucks avidly when meat approaches it. She eats with her fingers and holds the bowl to her chin, and between the bowl and her mouth she spends perhaps a minute. I think she is also blind, because she does not look at the food in the bowl, but gropes with stiff, bent fingers in the greasy soup for the submerged blobs of meat. Nor does she look at us, or even realise that we are there. Almost everything has ceased to exist for her except the pain of moving.

"How does she come to be here?" I ask.

"Sometimes they bring themselves," says M., "sometimes their relatives put them there. They pay ten dollars deposit when they arrive and thereafter five dollars per week. Food is extra at about three dollars per day. Sometimes they have managed to save the money themselves; sometimes their relatives pay."

"But why, for the love of God, can't their relatives keep them at home to die?"

"Perhaps their homes are too crowded; perhaps they live in conditions so bad that there is no room for anyone to die; perhaps their relatives don't want them; perhaps their relatives think it bad joss for anyone to die in their house, or their room, or their cubicle, or their space, or whatever it is they live in. There are a hundred reasons. But the system is not wholly bad, for many of those who come here to die would die in worse conditions if they stayed at home. The hospital will take those who are sick and try to cure them, but the hospital cannot take those who are simply dying of old age or incurable diseases, for there is barely enough room for the sick, let alone the dying."

We cross to the end of the room by the window, where a prone body covered in a blanket lies tossing in agony. We know of the agony because of the rhythmical groaning which reaches us from below the blanket. Around the bed four sad-eyed blank-faced people sit in silence waiting, it seems, for the end. We go up to the bed and peer over the edge of the blanket at the body of a young man of no more than twenty-two or twenty-three. His face is screwed up in pain, and his breath comes rapidly in little sharp puffs. His eyes are glazed and staring, and if we were to speak to him he would not hear us. A smell of sweat rises from the hot bed and the taut body under the blanket. The sick in the nearby beds seem oblivious to the noise he is making. The four relatives sit like tombstones.

One of the relatives looks brighter than the others, and we ask him who the sick man is. It is his brother. His brother has been in the dying-house for five days, and during all that time he has had a terrible and increasing pain in his abdomen, low down on the right-hand side. He shows us where the pain is. Has a doctor examined him? No. Do they, the relatives, know what is the matter with him? No. Have they ever heard of appendicitis? No. All that they know is that he has been there for five days and they think he must die tonight.

We suggest to the young man that his brother is suffering, quite probably, from a burst appendix. We explain that five days ago there would have been no danger, but that now, perhaps, it is already too late. But, nevertheless, we tell him he must get his brother to hospital at once. The young man seems to agree, although he does not say so. He says that it will be difficult to get his brother to hospital because no taxi will take a man so sick. Moreover, he is not certain where the hospital is. We clinch the matter by offering to take his brother to hospital in our car. This causes him to think for a moment. He goes over to his relatives and discusses the question with them loudly in Chinese while we think of what we shall say to the dying-house proprietor when he finds that we are removing his custom to a rival institution. The young man comes back. He is not a bad-looking fellow, cleanly dressed in a white shirt and trousers. He has, too, a pleasant face—not bovine like the others. He tells us that he thinks that perhaps his brother should go to hospital, but that his relatives do not agree with him. This, however, is immaterial since, he informs us, whatever he or his relatives think, he cannot move his brother until he has asked his father's permission to do so. He does not, at the moment, know where his father is, but expects him to come to the dying-house that evening. He is adamant in the matter: his brother, who is almost certainly dying from an almost certainly curable complaint, cannot be removed to hospital until his father's permission has been obtained. Thus we meet the immovable barrier of ignorance.

I do not know whether the patient lived or died. We hung about in the close room for some time, but the father did not come. After a while we found the laboured breath and the immobile skulls of the dying, the chattering and shouting in the street below and the increasing darkness maddeningly irritating. We came to see that there was little we could do and that we might as well go home.

We clambered down the dark stairway, past the spirit tablets and the flickering lamps, past the coffins lying in readiness on the ground floor, past the proprietor standing in his doorway and wishing us a cheery good night, out into the cluttered stream of people surging endlessly between the black and sightless houses.

It is easy to wax indignant. It is easy to shout that the authorities should do something. But the facts of the matter are that no one who is ill in Singapore and cannot, for one reason or another, be treated at home, is refused admittance to the hospital, and that no one so admitted is made to pay for the services he receives if he is clearly unable to do so. But a man cannot be compelled to go to hospital if he, or his next of kin, refuse. The problem is one of ignorance, a towering, almost majestic ignorance that can be changed only during the course of generations.

Already the battle against ignorance is being won. We were told, later in the evening, that the dying-house trade is not what it used to be. People more and more are going to hospital for treatment, instead of retiring to a dying-house to die. Furthermore, dying-houses lay on, at a charge, the entire paraphernalia of the traditional Chinese funeral. Shops nearby make the paper motor-cars and houses, which are burnt at the graveside so that the deceased may take them with him and thus be well provided for in the next world. Shops nearby also make the joss-sticks and the candles, the paper money, the wreaths and the heavy, carved coffins. The dying-houses lay out the dead, put them in their coffins, and provide facilities on their ground floors for the all-night watch of the relatives and for the ministrations of the shaven-headed Buddhist monks and nuns. The funeral processions form in Sago Street, and the dying-houses organise the business like a military operation. It all costs a great deal of money, and people are beginning to think that perhaps they have been extravagant in their provision for the dead, and that it might be better if they spent less on shepherding the dead out of this world and rather more on escorting the new-born safely into it. They are also beginning to think that perhaps something better can be arranged for Grandma when she is old than an iron bedstead and a blanket in a dying-house. But all these improvements take a great deal of time and until they are made, the dying-houses serve a certain purpose and will survive.

What is far more disturbing than the apparent inhumanity is the undoubted fact that the young man who cannot take his dying brother to hospital until he has found and asked permission of his father; and his relatives who will not have the sick man removed to hospital because they think him better off in the dying-house; and the taxi-driver who refuses to accept as a forty-cent fare a man who is clearly dying because he is dying; and the father who, when his son is on the very verge of death, cannot even contrive to be present; all of them, and tens of thousands like them, are shortly to be given a vote and asked to guide the destiny of our country.

September 8th, 1954

She was a slight, dark-skinned Tamil girl. She stood in the corridor of the hospital holding her baby, a healthy-looking little boy with a tuft of black hair standing up on his head. Like his mother, he had large round eyes. He was a few months old; his mother was twenty-two, and he had two sisters and two brothers. The seven members of his family were supported by the meagre earnings of the father who dug holes in the roads for the City Council.

The girl turned away and walked slowly down the long corridor with her baby, his great black eyes peering sleepily over her shoulder. She walked as though she had no clear purpose in view; at one time she almost stopped as if to turn back. But she went on, through the entrance, and then stood for a moment in the sunlight. I did not see her again.

The doctor said: "I have just told her that if she has another baby she will die. She has a weak heart and another birth will kill her. The last time she was here I told her about contraceptives and how the clinic would tell her all about them and how to use them. But she is a Catholic, and she has been to see her priest and her priest has told her that she must on no account have anything to do with them; nor must she allow herself to be sterilised, for which there is more than sufficient medical grounds. So she will die soon and five, possibly six, young children will be left without a mother to care for them."

September 9th, 1954

Our Indian gardener reminds us of Little Black Sambo. He is so dark that he is almost black, and his dead-white teeth shine like pearls in his innocent yet mischievous face. His name, like that it seems of all Indians in Malaya, is Ramasamy. During the mornings he tramps the countryside for the Health Authorities spraying pools of water with D.D.T. to keep the mosquitoes in check. In the afternoons he works in our garden. Today Ramasamy brought me a letter:

K. Ramasamy,

8.9.54.

Dear Sir,

As I have to make an arrangement for a Tea-party tomorrow at 7 p.m. in the 1st room of R.H.D. QRS. 7¼ mile, Bukit Timah Road, Singapore. I am unable to present your garden tomorrow only.

Yours,

affectionately,

K. RAMASAMY.

September 10th, 1954

This is the story of Ah Lim, told to me in fragments as we walked last night round the Trafalgar Home in Singapore, a vast encampment covering over a hundred acres out towards Seletar. Nine hundred people live in the Trafalgar Home. They are all lepers. Some are children who have been there for a few months only; one dumpy Chinese lady has been there for thirty-five years. The best one can say of the Trafalgar Home is that if this Chinese lady were cured tomorrow, the authorities would have difficulty in persuading her to leave; she likes her life in the Home. The worst that one can say is that there is insufficient money, insufficient labour and insufficient accommodation. This is not altogether the fault of the government, but a part of the picture of post-war Singapore where social services cannot possibly keep pace with the demand for them.

It is not so very long ago that people afflicted with this terrible disease were hidden away by their relatives in the fervent hope that they would die quickly. They were left to rot in back rooms and back alleys. The disease then was not only a terrible thing but a shameful thing, and he who contracted it could expect little sympathy from even his closest relatives. Perhaps in Singapore today there are a few odd cases concealed in this way; one does not know. But the tradition of concealment is dying and the Trafalgar Home can scarcely hold all those who voluntarily enter within its wide perimeter, perhaps for a few years, perhaps for the rest of their lives. In earlier years Ah Lim would probably have been concealed too, in which case she would have died fairly speedily, to the great relief of her relatives. As it was, she was brought to the hospital in the first place by the police, who had found her in the gutter. Her mother had watched her dying for months, but had taken no action; she simply accepted what the Fates had decreed should be her lot. Ah Lim's father had been a casual labourer who during the war had been carried off in one of the Japanese lorries that from time to time careered round the town, picking people at random and taking them away to a mass machine-gunning after the prisoners had first dug their common grave. Ah Lim had two brothers, both very near her in age, neither of them bright, neither of them fitted for anything more mentally exacting than casual labour. Some Chinese boys of eleven or twelve years of age, in spite of their lack of years, could have been of some help to their families in such a crisis. But Ah Lim's brothers were idlers from the beginning, and the family was only kept together by their mother, who hawked sugar-cane water in one of the roads near their attap shelter. Ah Lim would go with her each day and sit by the ramshackle little cart that had been her father's, in the broiling sun and the rain and the dust, and it seemed to her, even in those days, that there was no hope in the world and that she might as well be dead.

She was always hungry and her mother did not like her; these were the miseries, the companions she grew old with in a few short years. Her mother did not like her because Ah Lim was a fierce individualist, a person with a mind of her own, a mind which, unfortunately, was never trained. Her mother, on the other hand, was a dull, apathetic creature who accepted life as she found it. Ah Lim did not accept things as she found them, but, as she had to live with them nevertheless, she found herself frustrated beyond bearing. Her life became one long simmer against injustice, which found an outlet in bursts of violent temper when she would throw whatever was handy at her mother, while her mother, in turn, would shriek obscene imprecations at her daughter. And so they lived through the hot, dead, post-war years, fiercely unhappy and crushingly poor. Ah Lim had spirit, which her mother never had, and with her spirit she might have dragged herself from the gutter. But she was perpetually hungry and, because of the years of hunger and malnutrition, perpetually ill.

Then, in 1952, Ah Lim cut her bare foot on a piece of glass left lying on the ground. It was not a deep cut. It bled a little, and she thought no more about it. A few days later she felt a pain in her foot and a slight swelling around the old cut, which had become red and inflamed. Still she paid little attention, but the pain remained and the swelling grew more pronounced, and when she went out with her mother she was forced to limp. Her mother asked her what the trouble was and Ah Lim showed her the swollen foot. Her mother gave her some ointment in a tiny glass jar. Ah Lim applied the ointment, but it neither eased the pain nor reduced the swelling. She bound her foot in an old rag, and sat in the sun with it throb, throb, throbbing, until she felt that she would become insane if relief did not come quickly.

The next day she stayed at home, lying on the darkened old bed, unable to understand what was the matter with her foot, her mind full of dull, increasing pain until her world became a world of pain, a world in which there was no relief, a world where she learned to live with pain because there was no way to live except as part of the pain, which was everything.

In a few days she was delirious, and it was the delirium that probably saved her from the darkness of the hut and death. The delirium gave her a strength that she did not normally possess, and she flung herself from her bed on to the earthen floor. Her mother urged her back to her bed, but the voice came to Ah Lim through an echoing mist, and although she heard she did not understand. There was nothing but the pain and an urgent subconscious compulsion to leave the house. She dragged herself to the doorway and into the street, and that was where the police found her.

When she was examined at the hospital they saw at once that there was only one way to save her life: to amputate the gangrenous leg at once. It was necessary, however, for Ah Lim to give her consent to the operation, and when she had been quietened with drugs the situation was explained to her. Doctors, almoners and sisters argued and talked with her most of that night, but Ah Lim could not under any circumstance be persuaded to part with her leg. Efforts to find her mother were of no avail; not that she would have been very much help, but there was just the slightest possibility that she would understand the reason for the operation and convince Ah Lim of its urgent necessity. Into the small hours the subdued argument continued, but, the pain deadened with drugs, Ah Lim remained resolute. She did not trust people who wished to cut off her leg. When they told her that she would die if the operation were not carried out almost immediately, she did not believe them. When they told her that she would live, be healthy and happy without her leg, she did not believe them. When they told her that they would remove only a small piece of her leg, she asked them how much, and when they showed her she did not believe them.

It was at this point that Joan entered the story. Joan, whom I know very well, came into the ward almost by chance. Normally she would have been nowhere near it, and today she prefers to believe that some curious dispensation of providence took her to the bedside of Ah Lim. She quickly gathered from the conversation what the trouble was, and she also saw a vision of Ah Lim as she might have been: a striking, indeed, beautiful girl. She noticed first, perhaps, the mouth, the thick yet perfectly-shaped lips, tapering sharply at either end, and now set in a frightened, distrustful determination. She noticed also the rounded chin, and the nose which, like the lips, was thick and flat, yet finely modelled and with sensitive nostrils. She noticed her eyes, now defiant but the more arresting for their fire. She also saw the clear wide forehead on which the black, sweat-soaked hair lay in disarray.

I do not know why these things should happen; all I know is that occasionally two spirits meet and instantly recognise in one another a source of trust and something akin to love. This bond, which none of us may easily understand, was created instantly when Joan and Ah Lim met. When Joan talked to her a cloud seemed to vanish from Ah Lim's countenance, and Joan went with her to the operating theatre. Ah Lim's rotted, stinking limb was removed just below the knee, and Joan stayed with her throughout the operation.

Ah Lim came back into this world in the middle of the following morning. Joan had other work to do and was not able to be present when she regained consciousness, nor was she there when Ah Lim made the first groping explorations to discover where her leg now ended. The creeping, frightened hand did not need to travel far before it reached the great blob of bandages. She had been betrayed. Far more of her leg had gone than she had been led to understand would be taken, and she felt a sickness and a fury greater than she had ever known before. They had lied to her and they had cheated her, as she had known they would; her leg was gone and she wished very much that she could die.

For several weeks Ah Lim could not be induced to speak; she could scarcely be induced to eat. She would lie still in her bed, the slight contours of her body barely discernible beneath the covering sheet, and when people approached her she would turn her face away and remain rigid in her contemplation of the wall until they had gone. Occasionally this resistance to her misfortune would break down and she would sob quietly to herself until she either fell asleep or reacted with some gesture of violence and flung her cup, or whatever else was lying on her locker, at whoever happened to be passing at the time.

Slowly, very slowly, a change came, and Ah Lim began to grow accustomed to the absence of her leg. She found that her sense of balance enabled her to hop successfully about the ward, and she grew proficient in the use of the crutches with which she had been provided. At this time, too, contact was again established between Ah Lim and Joan. It was remarkable that such a close bond of friendship could be established between two people who were able to converse together so little. Ah Lim's Malay was not very much better than Joan's, yet it was the only language they had in common. At best they could express with it only the simplest ideas. But this disability was, of itself, unimportant, since they found in each other something more than could be expressed in speech alone. A kinship was established between them that could only be explained on the assumption that it is occasionally possible to bring a "have" and a "have not" together so that they form something approximating to an integrated whole. In Joan, Ah Lim found someone who could understand and sympathise with her often extraordinary behaviour; someone who regarded her as one of God's creatures, and even liked her. Joan was the only rock Ah Lim had known in a lifetime spent on quick and shifting sand. Ah Lim's feelings were, I suppose, compounded largely of hero-worship, but there is a certain glibness in this explanation, since the differing circumstances of their lives—background, race, colour, creed and economic situation—would in most people render such an emotion impossible.

In turn Joan seemed to find in Ah Lim an embodiment of all that was good in China. And this again was extraordinary, for through no stretch of the imagination could Ah Lim be described as a "good" person. She was selfish to a degree and inordinately bad-tempered. She met her reverses with ill grace, and when she was miserable she seemed determined to make everyone else miserable too. But all this Joan could excuse as being a direct result of the life Ah Lim had been compelled to lead. In Ah Lim, Joan saw the personification of suffering. Perhaps Joan should have been a nun. She had often thought of entering an order, but the dogma of Catholicism provided no solution for her problems. So she did medical and social work among the poor of Singapore and in Ah Lim I think she found a living expression of all that she was working for.

The time came for Ah Lim to leave the hospital. While she had been there Joan had bought her some better clothes, and she dressed on the day of her departure in a flowered *samfoo*. It hung loosely on her spare, flat frame, and the end of one trouser leg was turned up and pinned to the side of her knee. Joan took her home in her car and delivered her to the wooden shanty, where she left her inside the dark little room to await the return of her mother.

And that, Joan might have thought, was that, but it wasn't; not by a long way. Three days later an hysterical Ah Lim was back at the hospital, having been stoned by the neighbours. One of the stones had hit her on the temple, and a dried streak of blood ran down the side of her face.

I should perhaps explain at this point that Ah Lim had two other deformities. One arm and hand were almost paralysed and could be used only in a most rudimentary fashion, and the fingers of the other hand were bunched together in a tight, nearly closed fist. These afflictions had doubtless contributed to Ah Lim's fierce and abiding sense of frustration and antagonism, and when she appeared in her own street again, having lost a leg in the interim and using a pair of crutches to achieve a form of locomotion, there is no doubt that she was rude to the neighbours when they made their inevitable and cruel remarks. Although I do not believe that the neighbours would have stoned her without provocation, I do know that there are a few traditional Chinese in Singapore who would rather see their children crippled with polio than have their legs put in callipers; I do know that many still detest any form of artificial aid to the body and that a person compelled to use crutches is fit, in their view, for two things only—begging or death, preferably the latter; and I do know that in their approach to the physically afflicted the Chinese can be devastatingly cruel. And while, as I say, I have no doubt that Ah Lim was abusive in answer to their jibes, that they should throw stones at her was as inexcusable an act of barbarity as any group of people can be guilty of.

Ah Lim, on arrival at the hospital, steadfastly refused to go away. It seemed that her argument was that since the hospital had deprived her of her leg and given her the crutches, thus making her unacceptable to her own people, it was up to the hospital to provide her with alternative accommodation. In the end Joan took her to her own house, where she gave her a bed and provided her with food. In return she was to help with the housework. This idyllic state of affairs lasted for just three days; the stump of Ah Lim's leg began to give trouble and back she had to go to hospital. Ah Lim's flesh, through years of malnutrition, did not heal easily, and before long it became apparent that even more of her leg would have to be removed. Again the pantomime of persuasion ran its tedious course and Ah Lim only agreed—as everyone knew she would—when Joan had talked to her for hours. When the operation was over, there was again the same silence, the same refusal to eat, the same apparent absence of a will to live.

But again Ah Lim recovered. Her leg was now removed well above the knee, and only a thin stump of thigh, no thicker than a man's forearm, was left. She refused to use her crutches, and hopped about like an undernourished sparrow, perpetually raging against discipline, society and the world. She had never learned to control her emotions and easily abandoned herself to fury. But the strange thing was that, however much she might cheek the hospital staff, no one actually disliked her. Ah Lim, in spite of her manifold shortcomings, possessed an enviable ability to get away with murder.

Low Tide—Bedok, Singapore.

Singapore River.

Chinese Grave, Singapore.

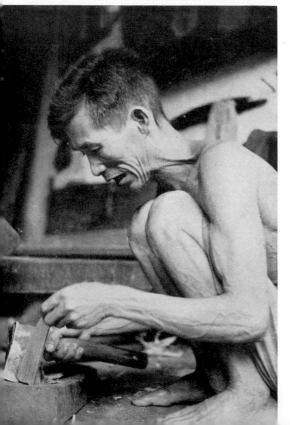

Coffin-maker, Singapore.

Joan came to see her every day, brought her presents and saw that she had everything the hospital could provide. She was fitted for an artificial limb, and when this arrived it was Joan who helped her to practise until she could walk without assistance. It was also Joan who arranged for Ah Lim to work in the hospital and to be trained in needlework and, in spite of her paralysed arm and her deformed hand, Ah Lim achieved an astonishing proficiency as a seamstress.

Perhaps this period of her life was the happiest that Ah Lim ever knew, or is likely to know. She was now twenty-two. She had work, friends, a comfortable bed and a sense of security. Joan would take her out in her car in the evenings, and in those few months Ah Lim saw more of Singapore each evening than she had seen in the whole of her life. They would go to the cinema and sometimes to the Chinese theatre. Ah Lim began to lose some of her resentment against the world; she was growing up quickly, gaining self-respect and confidence, and when she had her hair permed she looked almost sophisticated. Life was so good that Ah Lim herself felt that it could not last, and in this she was proved correct. But no one, possibly, could have imagined that Ah Lim's honeymoon, as it were, would end so drastically.

One day she showed Joan a sore that had developed on her arm. Joan showed it to a doctor at the hospital, who showed it to another doctor, who called in an expert, who lost little time in diagnosing leprosy. It was left to Joan to tell Ah Lim. When Ah Lim learnt the truth she ran screaming from the hospital and flung herself under a passing car. By the grace of God the driver knew what he was doing and swerved sufficiently to miss the prostrate body. Then there began a most undignified chase all over the hospital and its grounds in pursuit of the distraught, hysterical Ah Lim, who twice more attempted to commit suicide by trying to throw herself down stairways. In the end she was caught, injected and driven in Joan's car to the Trafalgar Home.

There she is, of course, still. When we called the other evening, we had to wait until she had finished bathing. As we waited outside her ward, we were surrounded by chattering women with healed but eaten faces. One woman, who was only able to move about on her bottom, made several circuits of the group, but finally despaired of obtaining a view and made off to her bed.

Then Ah Lim came, her hair still retaining vestiges of the last permanent wave which Joan had given her. She was shy, I think, because I was there, and alternately twisted her deformed hand in her *samfoo* and played with her loose and hanging stump. I could see in the semi-darkness that she was almost beautiful. Her conversation consisted largely of a complaint that the authorities had been too long in returning her artificial leg, which had been taken away for alteration. Joan said that she would see what she could do. The other women looked at Joan as she spoke, not understanding, and wondering what it was that made this strange white woman come so often to see Ah Lim. Ah Lim also told Joan of a recent visit from her mother, who came to the Home occasionally. Apparently all her mother had to say when she came were further variations on the theme of the disgrace that Ah Lim had brought upon the family.

We stood for a moment in the gathering darkness. Then we said "Good-bye," and Ah Lim said "Good-bye" and flapped her paralysed arm in a travesty of a wave, still playing with the stump of her leg with her other hand. For a moment I thought she was going to cry, and then she didn't. She simply turned and hopped away into the darkness.

We walked to the gate and, as we drove away, the little leper children standing round the gate shouted after us "Good-bye," and then added for some strange, quite unaccountable reason, "God bless you."

September 11th, 1954

I have just read Laurens van der Post's remarkable story, *A Bar of Shadow*, and I found the spectacle of the typical Japanese Imperial Army brute almost unendurable. Trained through years of war and semi-war to despise the Japanese military barbarian, it is disconcerting to find, quite suddenly and unexpectedly, an explanation of his being and behaviour which seems, at once, to hold water. And to find oneself sympathising with the brute Hara and understanding something of *his* motives and trials is an unusual experience. Here, for once, a writer has put forward a reason for the horrors of Japanese occupation, instead of simply describing the horrors as he knew them. Here, at least, a writer has made the Japanese, to some extent, comprehensible, has to some extent explained the utter contradiction of the Japanese met in Japan today and those who ravaged most of Asia during the war:

"Yes! He explained Hara had never expected anything except death of some kind in the war. In fact, in an unconscious way, perhaps, he had even longed for death. I must please not be too sceptical, but try and follow what he was trying to say with intuition rather than with conscious understanding. This was the other half of what he'd been trying to say in the beginning. It was most important, most relevant and the one foundation whereon his understanding either stood erect or fell. . . . He had always felt even when he was in Japan that the Japanese were a people in a profound, inverse, reverse or, if I preferred it, even perverse sense more in love with death than living. As a nation they romanticised death and self-destruction as no other people. The romantic fulfilment of the national ideal, of the heroic thug of tradition, was often a noble and stylised self-destruction in a selfless cause. It was as if the individual at the start, at birth even, rejected the claims of his own individuality. Henceforth he was inspired not by individual human precept and example so much as by his inborn sense of the behaviour of the corpuscles in his own blood dying every split second in millions in defence of the corporate whole. . . .

" 'I shall never forget one night in prison,' Lawrence continued, picking up yet another thread of our prison yesterdays, and weaving it as if it were something new and freshly made into this pattern of Hara in his mind until my heart was heavy that so much should remain for him apparently immune to time. 'Hara sent for me. He had been drinking and greeted me uproariously but I knew his merriment was faked. He always behaved like that when his heart and mind were threatening to join in revolt against his long years of exile from Japan. I could see that the drink had failed to blur the keen edge of

nostalgia that was like a knife-stab in the pit of his stomach.
He wanted someone to talk to about his country and for some
hours I walked Japan from end to end with him through all
four of its unique and dramatic seasons. The mask of cheerful-
ness got more and more threadbare as the evening wore on
and at last Hara tore it from his face.

"Why, Rorensu," he exclaimed fiercely at last. "Why are you
alive? I would like you better if you were dead. How could an
officer of your rank ever have allowed himself to fall alive in
our hands? How can you bear the disgrace? Why don't you
kill yourself?"

" 'Yes, he asked me that too once,' I interrupted, more with
the object of letting Lawrence know how closely I was following him than of telling him something he didn't know. 'In fact,
he taunted us all so much with it that in time the Koreans
picked up the habit too, but what did you say in reply?'

" 'I admitted the disgrace, if he wished to call it that,' Lawrence replied. 'But said that in our view disgrace, like danger,
was something which also had to be bravely borne and lived
through, and not run away from by a cowardly taking of one's
own life. This was so novel and unexpected a point of view to
him that he was tempted to dismiss it as false and made himself say: "No! no! it is fear of dying that stops you all." He
spat disdainfully on the floor and then tapping on his chest
with great emphasis added: "I am already dead. I, Hara, died
many years ago."

" 'And then it came out, of course. The night before he left
home to join the army at the age of seventeen, that is after
nine months in the womb and sixteen years and three months
on earth, he had gone to a little shrine in the hills nearby to
say goodbye to life, to tell the spirits of his ancestors that he
was dying that day in his heart and spirit for his country so
that when death came to claim him in battle it would be a
mere technicality, so that far from being surprised he would
greet it either like a bosom friend, long expected and overdue,
or merely accept it as formal confirmation of a state which had
long existed. To hear him one would have thought that this
bow-legged boy, with his blue-shaven head, yellow face and

shuffling walk, had gone to report to his ancestors his decision
to enter one of the grimmer monastic orders like the Grande
Chartreuse, rather than to announce his banal intention of
joining a regiment of infantry. But you see what I mean when
I say the end too had been foreseen?'

"I nodded silently, too interested to want to speak, and
Lawrence went steadily on. Even that evening in prison Lawrence was conscious of a content, a sort of extra-territorial meaning to the moment that did not properly belong to it. It was as
if Hara's end was drinking his wine with him, as if far down
at some inexpressible depth in their minds the ultimate sentence was already pronounced. Looking back now, he found it
most significant, that towards the end of the evening, Hara
began to try his hand at composing verses in that tight, brief
and extremely formal convention in which the popular hero of
the past in Japan inevitably said farewell to the world before
taking his own life. He remembered Hara's final effort well:
roughly translated it ran:

When I was seventeen looking over the pines at Kura-
shiyama, I saw on the full yellow moon the shadow of wild-
geese flying South. There is no shadow of wild-geese returning
on the moon rising over Karushiyama tonight.'

"'Poor devil: as I watched and listened to him trying to
break into verse, suddenly I saw our roles reversed. I saw as if by
a flash of lightning in the darkness of my own mind that I
was really the free man and Hara, my gaoler, the prisoner. I
had once in my youth in those ample, unexacting days before
the war when the coining of an epigram had looked so con-
vincingly like a discovery of wisdom, defined individual freedom to myself as freedom to choose one's own cage in life.
Hara had never known even that limited freedom. He was
born in a cage, a prisoner in an oubliette of mythology, chained
to bars welded by a great blacksmith of the ancient gods themselves. And I felt an immense pity for him. And now four
years later, Hara was our kind of prisoner as well and in the
dock for the last time, with sentence of death irrevocably pronounced.'"

September 12th, 1954

Potter has just bought himself a new, low-priced English motor-car. He took delivery a couple of weeks ago. He has been nursing the engine as the instructions direct, not exceeding 40 m.p.h. until a thousand miles have been covered. He has now travelled six hundred miles; the first three hundred impatiently, anxious to give the car its head; the second three hundred apprehensively, wondering whether the car is sufficiently robust to withstand the strain of a thousand miles.

He told me all about it today, this fat, fiery, little man, utterly intolerant of fools and of all that is shoddy. He works in insurance and spends his time persuading an ever-dwindling number of prospective insurers to buy what an ever-increasing number of insurance companies have to offer. Perhaps it is the rigours of his employment that have made him bad-tempered—and he *is* bad-tempered—and, bearing this fact in mind, I am surprised that he still has his new motor-car, and has not yielded to what, in the circumstances, would have been a perfectly understandable temptation—to set it on fire on the premises of the agents who import this fine Product of Traditional British Engineering Skill.

The first seed of doubt was sewn in Potter's mind when the accelerator fell off. As far as Potter could remember there was no mention in the art-paper Instruction Book about a removable or detachable accelerator. The mishap occurred in the middle of particularly dense traffic while he was negotiating an island and, not being a particularly nimble man in a motor-car, he was for the moment flummoxed beyond the point of doing anything intelligent in a purely mechanical sense. As might be expected, the car, with an idling engine and yet still in top gear, jolted to an ignominious standstill, with all the traffic in the world blowing its hooters behind it.

Now, as I have said, Potter is not a nimble man, and the problem of examining closely the accelerator pedal, which lay in an indeterminate position beneath his feet, was an acute one. He thrust his fat thighs apart and attempted to peer between the narrow opening thus revealed, but he found that the steering wheel obstructed both his vision and the downward movement of his bullet head. He leaned heavily to the left in his next manœuvre, so that he was, in effect, lying across the front seats, but this time his vision, already impaired by the rush of blood to his head, was again obstructed, since his legs would no longer open at all, being jammed together between the raised tunnel that runs the length of the floor, presumably housing a quite immense transmission system, and the underside of the dash-board.

By this time Potter, feeling incredibly foolish and becoming increasingly aware of the hell that had been let loose behind him, began to grow a little hysterical. He heaved himself to an upright position, pushed his foot into the space where he had a notion the accelerator pedal used to be, pulled the starter knob, and was astonished to find the engine roar into life and achieve in a split second a fantastic number of revolutions, which would have been harmful even to a car that had completed its running-in period, let alone to one that had scarcely begun its life. The whole car chattered and shook as though an explosion and disintegration were imminent. Meanwhile, Potter dug away with heel and toe in very much the same way as a Rugby footballer prepares a position for the ball. But nothing was achieved, and by this time the revolutions of the engine were beginning to set up counter-harmonics in the body, and it is possible that Potter's finally switching off saved his vehicle from total ruin only in the very nick of time.

He flung open the door and struggled off the seat. His feet found the roadway and he gave himself a tremendous push to bring himself upright—a feat which he almost accomplished. It was particularly unfortunate, however, both for Potter and for the company that manufactured the motor-car, that the stout ribbon compounded of rubber and rolled upholstery which nor-mally ran along the inside of the body, above the doors, should have chosen the few preceding minutes to become detached from its moorings in the centre, but not at either of its ends. The result was that the murderous, rubbery loop caught the en-raged Potter squarely across his windpipe.

For a second Potter thought someone had assaulted him and,

tensing all of his not inconsiderable muscles, he threw his weight into a great disengaging lunge. The loop came away and hung forlornly round his neck, attached at each end to a remnant of roof upholstery. Had any man, at that moment, been foolish enough to remain within striking distance, Potter would quite certainly have killed him. He wrenched the ridiculous loop from his neck and flung it away from him in a gesture of enraged despair. He felt a mad impulse to kick his car, but at that moment a Malay policeman appeared, and from the look on his face Potter knew that he was going to suggest that together they pushed the gleaming Product of Traditional British Engineering Skill to the side of the road. Potter simply said:

"You can ask Mr. Bloody . . . of Messrs. Bloody . . . to shove the bloody thing away."

With these inspiring words he stalked away to the nearest telephone to tell the agents to fetch their "bloody heap of tin," as he described it, away.

The damage was easily repaired, and for a few days the car ran without further trouble. Then, as Potter was driving home one evening along Orchard Road, he suddenly discovered that not only was the car riding with a pronounced list but, although the offside front wheel appeared to be normal, the nearside wheel was riding the road in much the same way as that of the front roller of a traction engine. Again the car went back to the garage, this time with a jammed shock-absorber. Potter, ever so slightly, was beginning to lose faith.

A succession of trifling deficiencies revealed themselves in the next two or three days before the final, major failure. He found, for instance, that the air scoops forming a part of both front windows, which obstinately refused to remain open when in contact with even the slightest of light airs, served their purpose admirably when the car was travelling almost flat out backwards. Then the clock stopped, seemingly for ever. This was followed by Potter's discovery that a greyish patch was spreading like a creeping stain all over the pristine paint of the boot. Then the petrol gauge stuck permanently at "empty." Potter practically lived in the agents' garage, making everyone, including himself, utterly miserable.

Then the great fiasco occurred. Potter and his wife went into town one Saturday afternoon—they lived just over six miles from the centre of the city—to a fête that was being held to raise funds for an addition to the Chapel they regularly attended. Potter is a pillar of the Chapel and—for his sins or his virtue, I do not know which—had been placed in charge of a sideshow, which consisted of two No. 7 irons, four old golf-balls with split covers and eight empty paint drums. The object of the exercise, for which participants paid twenty cents, was to lob the golf-balls into the paint drums from a distance of some twenty-odd feet. Potter toiled away through the hot sun of the afternoon and by six p.m., when the fête officially closed, had netted the useful amount of thirty-seven dollars and eighty-three cents. Being, as I have said, a pillar of the Chapel, he and his wife naturally stayed behind to help clear up some of the appalling mess of ice-cream cups that littered the Chapel grounds, and generally to arrive at some rough estimate of the day's takings. By the time he got away it was half-past seven and dark. He was last seen leaving the Chapel hall in a cheerful mood, after promising to see his colleagues of the afternoon at early service the following morning, and, having thanked the caretaker, who was still struggling with the mountain of ice-cream cups, he made his way, with his wife, to his parked vehicle. As they got into the car the threatened thunderstorm began to break, and fat drops of rain splashed on to the film of dust which covered the bonnet. The car started easily enough, the lights snapped on and Potter, his wife and his car moved sedately away towards the traffic lights. When they reached them the tropical downpour was in full spate. Potter closed the windows and changed into bottom gear as he waited for the green light. The lights changed and as they moved off, Potter was just about to ask his wife, a stumpy, docile woman with short little legs and no lap, where she supposed the extra three cents had come from when, with a furious yanking at the frail contraption attached to the steering column with which, previously, he had been able to shift the gears of his car, he announced:

"It's stuck! The bastard's stuck! Stuck solid in bottom bloody gear."

After this, Potter's language became more or less consistently unprintable. He pulled into the side of the road and wrestled with the gear lever, letting the engine race for fear it would stop. The rain lashed down in torrents outside, and in the heat of the closed car Potter began to sweat, as dying men sweat in doomed submarines. It was soon apparent that nothing less than a sledgehammer would move the lever out of bottom gear, and he set off on the tedious five-mile journey at ten miles per hour in bottom gear, a gear so low that in the normal course of driving it was seldom necessary to use it. The windows steamed to a grey opaqueness and he found it necessary to clean the window screen regularly with a duster as rivers of water streamed down it. He hunched himself over the wheel, concentrating desperately on keeping the revolutions down to the maximum recommended by the manufacturer, and trying, at the same time, to see through the rain that swirled towards him in the beams of his headlights.

He was well out on Holland Road when he noticed that his trousers were wet. At first he discounted the evidence of his senses, but the sensation of wetness about the thighs increased to the point where it could no longer be ignored. He dropped an exploratory hand from the wheel and was astonished to find his trousers soaked. As he felt about in the steaming darkness, he encountered a particular spot where a steady drip, drip, drip of water fell on to the back of his hand. Even as his hand remained there, he could feel the steadily increasing tempo of the drops that were shortly to become a constant flow, and he said what no chapel man should ever say :

"Jesus Christ Almighty!"

He thrust his bottom forward on the seat so that he could open his legs to allow the water, which seemed to emanate from his corner of the windscreen, to plunge between them. But then he thought of the water ruining the carpet and so he closed them again, and his hands gripped the steering wheel like twin vices as the chilly water seeped between the pressed flesh and crept by capillary action to the seat. Then he thought of the stain coming out of the upholstery and ruining the seat of his best trousers, so he lifted himself, like a man in a trance, from the seat so that his head bumped the roof. The full force of his weight pressing against the back of the seat caused the seat to slide suddenly backwards off its runners, and this precipitate shock caused him to accelerate fiercely, which displaced the position of his seat even farther. His reflexes were slowing down perceptibly, so that he only thought to remove his foot from the accelerator when he had lowered himself to the seat, which had grown wetter in his absence. Meanwhile he was dimly conscious that not only were his shoes filling with water but his point of vantage in the car was now so low and insecure that he could no longer see over the dashboard, and the steering wheel was now so far away that he could only reach it with the outstretched fingers of one hand. The situation was not helped by his wife, who was quickly becoming demented and recalling the days when they travelled everywhere by bus.

Potter was now beyond caring, but he made one last despairing effort. He managed to grasp the steering wheel and haul himself from the seat, which had now assumed a sideways position, so that he could squat in the still-increasing cascade, one leg thrust forward to the accelerator in the manner of a Russian dancer, the other doubled excruciatingly beneath his ponderous body.

It was only a matter of time before the muscles of his tortured thigh bunched up in cramp. He had known that they would and, because he could think of no way of escaping the ordeal, he passively awaited its onset, hoping that they might reach home before it arrived. The first pangs hit him when they were two hundred yards from their gate. There was no alternative but to shoot the afflicted leg forward so that he was, in effect, sitting on the wet floor of the car, the steering wheel far above him, his wife staring down at him in anguish, sweat pouring from his every pore. The car ground harmlessly into the mud at the side of the road just by the sixth milestone.

When the spasm had passed, Potter began to cast around for ways and means of removing his vehicle from its impasse. The first thing he tried was the gear lever.

At the lightest of touches it moved obediently and silently into neutral.

September 13th, 1954

The everlasting argument which revolves about the prospect of self-government for Malaya continues without respite. At the clubs, in the bars, at dinners and luncheons all over the land, the conversation, sooner or later, drifts to self-government. Some are against it, others are for it, almost no one nowadays questions its inevitability. Self-government is the supreme issue consuming every political party and the long-term problem of every commercial interest.

Last night it was another of those purely European dinner-parties whose sole advantage, in this cosmopolitan land, is the opportunity that any racially exclusive congregation presents, of letting down, as it were, its own racially exclusive hair.

Fernald is one of those dogmatic people who is quite certain that there are very few answers which he, personally, does not know. This is particularly apparent when the subject approaches self-government. He was our host and it was he who set the ball rolling. His wife for many years now has agreed with everything Tom Fernald has said, not because she has always understood him, but because she has found it much easier to agree than to go to the trouble of wondering why she has disagreed. She has developed a remarkable facility, which many European women in the East seem to develop quite easily, of relating the most far-reaching world events to the minutiæ of her own domestic affairs. In a flash she is able to strike an analogy between Communist belligerency off Quemoy and the off-hand manner of her local greengrocer, and will readily undertake to prove the essential unfitness of Malayans for self-government by reference to the fact that Ah Han, her cook, will not, until told, clean under the sink.

Tom Fernald's guests, apart from myself, were a well-fed professor from an Eastern University, who was there, it almost seemed, by accident, and who was the only complete cynic amongst us, and his wife, a most serious-minded young woman, half her husband's age, who made up in earnestness what her husband lacked in faith. I think the Morrisons must have been an unhappy pair, since neither saw anything in the same light as the other, with the result that a tension existed between them which was noticeable even at the dinner-table.

A man by the name of Napier was also there with his wife. I had not met them before, since he had but recently arrived to take up an appointment in Government service. It was a responsible position and it struck me at once that Napier was of a stature insufficient to fill it. He was essentially a little man whom someone had inflated, with almost disastrous results, and I could not help but suspect his pushing, voluble, little wife who, for some unaccountable reason, had dyed her hair a curiously patchy shade of blue. The Napiers were out to impress, playing a game at which they had long ago become adept, and it was apparent that they confidently regarded themselves as being, all things considered, on the winning side.

Finally, there was Julia Ashcroft, a beautiful, level-headed creature of pronouncedly leftist views. She was a journalist, and stood above her local fellows as a man towers over a mouse. Say what you like about Tom Fernald, he certainly mixed his guests. It was Tom Fernald who started it. He said:

"I have tried for a long time to believe in a united Malayan nation, but the more I think of it the more impossible of accomplishment it seems to me to be—at least in our time, or even in this century—unless we are in control."

Freda Morrison was at him in a flash. "Why we? Why not the Chinese or the Malays?"

"For a variety of reasons, Freda. Firstly, because we had faith in the future of Malaya and took it over when it was a morass of warring Sultanates. We pacified it, administered it, defended it and made a prosperous country out of a peninsular consisting largely of jungle. Secondly, because practically everyone in this country who has made a living out of anything but piracy and padi-growing, has made it simply because we first created the conditions necessary for him to do so. Thirdly, because, in bringing Chinese and Indians here to do the hard work because the Malays either would not or could not do it, we created an artificial state—and artificial growth, if you like—which, when British power is removed, must inevitably collapse. Fourthly, and finally—although I could think of more reasons—because if we leave this country it will not be the Chinese as such, nor the Malays, who will take it over, but Communism."

Julia Ashcroft spoke: "Do you admit the proposition that it is improper for one race to rule another, especially when that rule was founded on, and has been maintained by, the threat or use of force?"

"I think I would allow the proposition, yes."

"How, then, will you reconcile it with what you have just said? Surely you will not deny that our rule *has* been based on force?"

"Of course our rule has been based on force, although I would prefer to use the word strength. But we are not living in an ideal world, and for this reason, perhaps, our actions cannot always be ideal. I object to self-government on several counts—some of which I have given you—but the most important are these: Malaya is an artificial growth which cannot survive as we know it today without the greenhouse-like protection of British power and, however big you build its navy and its army, it can never, never, in this world, defend itself."

"I quite agree," said Napier.

"And anyway," Mrs. Fernald said, "you only have to look at Indonesia to know what will happen when we have self-government."

"Or Burma," added Mrs. Napier. "Fred and I came through Rangoon on the way here and the place was like a pig-sty."

"Dreadful," said Fred, "absolutely dreadful!"

"But everybody in Burma who matters is happy," Morrison put in. "The only people who matter are the politicians, and for the first time in their lives they're enjoying power, wealth, privilege and position. You mustn't allow such a plebeian and old-fashioned thing as a consideration for the people to affect your judgment."

"I think there is something in what you say," Tom Fernald said. "Just about the only people who clamour for self-government in this country are those who hope to have a hand in running the show when we are gone."

Julia Ashcroft spoke again:

"Is there any reason why Malaya should not be independent and yet be defended as it is today?"

Fernald answered:

"No reason at all: but nor is there any guarantee that an independent Malaya will allow itself to be defended."

"In which case one might reasonably suppose that it might not wish to be defended?"

"One might indeed."

"In which case you wish to thrust your protection on people who do not desire it?"

"That is the conclusion I have come to."

"Now tell me how your policy differs from that of the Communists. Tell me how you differentiate between a Malaya you want to save from Communism and a South Korea the Communists wanted to save from Syngman Rhee and the Americans."

"Simple," said Morrison. "Malaya would appear to be worth saving. Anyone who tries to save South Korea from anything wants his head seeing to."

"Do you have to be so cynical?" his wife asked.

"All right!" he answered. "I would be inclined to vote for an agency that set out to save Malaya from being saved."

"Saved from what?" asked Julia.

"From itself, from Communism, from China, from us—anything you like—but I feel we ought to deal with these things one by one."

"Isn't this getting a little far from self-government?" asked Napier.

"Not in the least," replied Fernald. "It's all part and parcel of the same problem. It is indivisible. I read the manuscript of an unpublished book the other day in which the author set out to show the immediate desirability of self-government for Malaya. He took four hundred and seventy-three pages to do it, and said not a single word on the question of defence—either from within or from without. It would be as intelligent to write about Beethoven without mentioning music!"

"But don't you see," said Julia, "that you are asking us to spawn a nation of slaves? I don't mean slaves in the old-fashioned sense, but in the sense that none of them, ever, under your dispensation, can become anything but subjects of a perpetual British rule. If you try to apply such a theory, you will find that it must in the end, in practice, break down. In fact, we might take as an axiom the impossibility of the perpetual rule of one people over another. Surely you must see this; the whole history of the world supports what I say."

"But I have not spoken of perpetual rule," protested Fernald. "I have simply suggested that at the present moment talk of self-government is criminal, since it can only lead to the greatest unhappiness this country has ever known."

Morrison said: "Now, Tom, even I protest. On what possible basis can you make such a statement—unless you are simply worrying about your business?"

"In Malaya there are over five million people," Tom Fernald answered, "who are largely either Chinese or Malay. The members of these two peoples are almost equal in number. The Malays came here centuries ago by 'natural' means. Nobody quite knows where they came from or why they came, but when we arrived here they were the people of this country. They had effectively hounded the poor, bloody aboriginal almost to death, and had become the effective owners of the land. Then the Chinese came. Some came before we did, but most of the settlement, encouraged by us, has taken place in the last hundred-odd years. Now just consider: would you, if you were in a position similar to that of the Malay, easily forget this fact? Suppose, for instance, the Germans had won the last war and had immediately brought to England fifty million Japanese—the analogy is apt, since, in the same way as the Chinese work harder than the Malays, so the Japanese would have worked harder, for longer, and for less, than the English—what would have been your reaction? Would it not have been one of bloody-minded resentment against the Japanese for coming, and the Germans for bringing them? Of course it would. And how long, if the English and Japanese retained their racial identity within the same country, would it take the English to forget their resentment? The answer is never, never, never in a thousand years and, in the same way, the Malays will never forget theirs. It would be a different matter if

The New rising above the Old in Singapore.

Prostitution Alley, Singapore.

they inter-married. But they don't. And so far as I can see, they never will."

"One doesn't see why they should, of course," said Morrison. "But you're uttering heresies, you know. Did not Templer himself say that no man could do a greater disservice to Malaya than to increase the divergence of the races of Malaya? And that is exactly what you're doing now."

"I must say I agree," chipped in Napier. "Self-government *must* come. I do not see that anything one does or says can prevent it."

"Oh, shut up, Fred," his wife said testily. "You've only been here five minutes and he's been here for years."

"Tom," said Julia, "I will do you the credit of believing that in what you say you are sincere, and that you say it because you are concerned with the happiness, prosperity and well-being of Malaya. I do not for one moment deplore your motives! I admire them."

"Thank you, Julia. That, I fancy, is more than Morrison there would admit."

"Hear! hear!" said Morrison's wife.

"But the inescapable facts of the matter seem to me to be these: here we have a country which, however it came into being, wherever its people came from, what they do and why they do it, and whatever the racial antagonisms that exist within its shores and boundaries, is subject and tributary to a foreign and alien power. That rule has lasted now for well over a hundred years. It may indeed last for another hundred years—I don't know. But of one thing I am certain: it cannot last for ever. The reason it cannot last for ever is because, in spite of the peace, prosperity and security it has brought, it is fundamentally wrong. The rule of one country by another is a question over which we fought Germany and over which we have just fought China in Korea. That is why every development that is brought forward in support of Colonialism, when every move that, even by mere antagonistic imputation is calculated to perpetuate the present order, has no effect whatever upon a remorseless disintegration of the world which Raffles, Farquhar, Clifford and Swettenham believed in implicitly and without question. I believe that this disintegration is taking place, not only because that which is being destroyed was often harmful or selfish, but because it was, and is, wrong. This being so, we must accept the inevitability of self-government and, having accepted it, try to prepare the people who want it for their responsibilities. The important point is, Tom, that this thing cannot be evaded on grounds of expediency, any more than we can stop the sun rising tomorrow morning."

Morrison's wife broke the short silence that followed this declaration.

"I do so agree. It seems to me that you have put your finger on the very heart of the matter. We have become so used to looking upon ourselves as an unqualified benefit to the human race that it always comes to us as a bit of a shock to find that people would often rather live their lives without us, and that, however deplorable their new lives in our view will be, they will find them preferable to the old order."

"Can't you see all the little darlings," said Morrison, "living their delightful, twisted, corrupt little lives, each living in happiness on the rake-off he gets from his neighbour? In a moment I shall cry."

"You are all wrong," said Tom Fernald, "all terribly pathetically and, since we are all being so frank, so wickedly wrong. We have all of us contributed to the Malayan Frankenstein. It was created largely to extract rubber and tin from Malayan soil. On the end of this appendix of Asia is an abscess called Singapore which was created to tap the line of wealth that ran between East and West, and later to ship the wealth out of Malaya and to ship the consumer goods and machinery of production in. At the beginning of the last century the city in which you now live was steaming jungle. The city, like the life we know today in Malaya, was created—created, I say—out of raw nature, because the rest of the world wanted rubber tyres to run its motor-cars on and tin to put its food in. To this end millions—yes, millions —of people were brought from all over the world to extract, process, transport, pack and ship this wealth of Malaya. They came from China and India, from the Indies and Western Europe. Then, having brought them all here, under the defenceless noses of the helpless Malays you say, 'O.K., chaps, make yourselves into a nation.' Do you honestly think that this can be accomplished in ten, twenty, thirty, fifty years? Or even in a hundred years?"

"What about America?" asked Napier.

"God preserve us!" answered Morrison.

"Yes, what about America?" echoed Mrs. Napier.

"As the Americans would say, Mrs. Napier," Fernald answered, "that's a pretty good question. But the difference between Malaya and America is largely this: the Americans outnumbered the Red Indians by thousands to one. The Red Indians were so few that in the long run they scarcely mattered. But in Malaya the indigenous people still compose approximately half of the total population. And, I suspect, the indigenous people, to this day, still see no reason why anyone else should be in their country besides themselves. And I can't say I blame them."

"But do you agree," Julia persisted, "that we should do everything possible to prepare them for self-government?"

"If you really want to know what I believe, I'll tell you quickly, and then we must have coffee. I believe, on the one hand, that self-government can be the doom of Malaya and, on the other, that the government of Malaya as we know it today is an institution that cannot be indefinitely prolonged. I believe that in a self-governing Malaya, where all men have equal political rights, the Malays must inevitably perish or, at best, become a depressed and possibly oppressed segment of society, calling hopelessly on an impotent Indonesia. I believe also that in a self-governing Malaya, where all men have equal political rights, the Chinese must inevitably, through their numbers, drive and energy, gain control of the country and, this being so, must inevitably strengthen their connection with China and, in time, become a part of the Chinese Red Empire. I therefore believe that the only sane policy is one of self-government with conditions, and these conditions, whatever they are, must provide for three things: the maintenance of external defence, the maintenance of internal security and the maintenance of a free and equal society of Malays, Chinese, Eurasians, Indians and Europeans, until such time as these five main groups begin to think and act as one. And I think the time when this happens will never come. But, if you really want to help Malaya, I suggest you set to work to devise the machinery whereby these conditions can be imposed. It may be that you will find that they cannot be imposed. And that, indeed, is the tragedy as well as the heart of the matter."

His wife was quick on the uptake.

"Shall we have coffee in the other room?"

September 14th, 1954

It is extraordinary how quickly a person gains and loses friends in Singapore. Almost as soon as he has come to know anyone, he or she goes on leave, or is transferred to some other place, or resigns and goes home. Or it may be that the person he knew was in Singapore but temporarily, anyway. The turnover of residents in Singapore is astonishing. It is a place where a man gains a great many acquaintances and a remarkable number of charming, but regrettably absent, friends.

You go to the airport or the Harbour Board to see them off and somewhere among the parting thoughts is the intention to write, an intention in which no one quite believes. More often than not no letters follow or, if they do, at most one, or perhaps two, and then these friends drift out of your life very much as leaves fall from a tree in winter, to be blown goodness knows where.

Life in Singapore can quickly turn you into a most accomplished "see-er off-er." We spend hours sitting about at the airport waiting for 'planes either to leave or to arrive, and we know every inch of the Harbour Board wharves, where we have stood patiently in the blazing sun for a ship to arrive at a certain hour, only to find it arriving anything up to several hours later because of the apparent modern impossibility of human movement divorced from the army of little men who must first stamp meaningless pieces of paper with meaningless rubber stamps.

We are even adept at meeting people we have never seen before, and with an almost infallible insight we are able to spot the character walking across the tarmac or struggling down a sloping gangway who, quite clearly, is expecting to recognise someone whom he too has never seen before. People in such a situation wear an easily identifiable expression: tense, preoccupied, shaded over with a deliberate quirk of recognition, rather like an Einstein on the verge of a new theory of relativity.

"Mr. Smith?" you ask. And he, not to be outdone, replies: "Mr. Jones?" Contact is made, and while you talk you forget that the other is not in the least what you expected.

We have grown accustomed in Singapore to letters from other parts of the world which say: "The Possingtons are coming to Malaya, or Singapore, or are passing through Singapore, and we have given them your address," or "You remember So-and-so at school? Well, she married a man who raises donkeys, and his brother is coming to Malaya to study the market." And they will have given him our address too, and once more we find ourselves pounding out to the airport and hanging round for hours while his ridiculous aircraft trundles round the sky, using up its petrol because it has a flat tyre. It has happened so often that we no longer complain, and if someone started tomorrow a Society for the Abolition of Letters of Introduction we doubt if we would join, since it is still pleasant to see a new face from England.

September 15th, 1954

Heard today a new story from Brompton. There was a new Christian Church established somewhere up country, and a Tamil vicar was placed in charge of the vast parish. In the gentle course of time the Bishop called to see him, and they discussed at great length the project of producing a hymn-book entirely in Tamil. The Bishop suggested that the vicar might spend the long country evenings putting his excellent knowledge of both Tamil and English to the service of God by translating into Tamil all the well-known English hymns. The vicar readily agreed, and set to work the following day.

When next the Bishop arrived on a tour of inspection he found lying on the vicar's table an enormous and splendidly bound volume.

"What is this?" he asked.

"The new hymn-book, my Lord Bishop."

"Is it really! Is it really!"

"Yes! Here, you see, is *Onward Christian Soldiers* and here *While Shepherds Watched* and here *Rock of Ages!*"

"Wonderful!" said the Bishop, "really wonderful."

The vicar beamed with extreme gratification.

" 'Rock of ages, cleft for me,' " murmured the Bishop. "Tell me," he said, "how would you translate that line from the Tamil version back into English?"

The vicar placed his steel-rimmed spectacles on the end of his nose and peered at the page.

"Very old stone," he said slowly, "broken for my benefit."

September 16th, 1954

Curiously enough, another hymn story—this time from Sam Pickwick, concerning Africa, where he was attached to a Christian mission. The hymn the Yoruba had been singing since the days, almost, of Livingstone was *Ride on, ride on, in majesty.* Then a bright young Yoruba came along to point out politely that what they had really been singing all these years was "Get on your horse, get on your horse."

September 17th, 1954

Dinner at Fatty's. I do not know his more formal name since I have never heard it used; for as long as I can remember he has been Fatty, and so he will remain.

Fatty has a restaurant in Albert Street, a street of Chinese and Indian restaurants, where it is possible to eat an incredible variety of food at almost any hour of the day or night. Fatty's, we reckon, is the best, or so we judged several years ago, since when he has become a habit with us and it may well be that he is now no longer the best. But we have been going to him for so long that a change now would be too great a wrench. All I can say is that if other Albert Street restaurants serve better food than Fatty, then it must be very good.

Each restaurant in Albert Street employs the quaint Chinese

custom of cooking its food in the gutter. Perhaps, for this reason, it tastes better. I am told that the cooking destroys the microbes that doubtless congregate in Albert Street in their millions— which is perhaps as well, since we go there often.

The restaurants are little two-story shops. We can, therefore, sit either upstairs or down, but I fancy that upstairs is considered more formal and probably results in a slight, extra, concealed charge in the final bill. If we can secure the upstairs window-seat in Fatty's, we can look down on to Albert Street with its row of cooking stalls stretching into an infinity of cooking smoke. It is one of the more remarkable sights of Singapore. Each stall, with its tattered tarpaulin cover, is brilliantly lit, illuminating the sections of pig, fowl, duck, fish, octopus and miscellaneous offal strung up for inspection and the neat little heaps of vegetables, mee, fruit, rice and bean and bamboo shoots. Behind each stall are the braziers with their great elliptical pans in which the food is placed, stirred, turned and tossed to the accompaniment of billowing clouds of smoke which swirl round the naked bulbs and then float skywards, leaving behind a lingering, pungent aroma that incites acute hunger.

Behind one of these stalls, almost hidden by a curtain of pork strips, and often disappearing in an uprush of smoke from his matchless cooking, stands Fatty. Most of the day, and most of the night, he stands there in the sizzling hiss of his frying-pans, like a fat, smoky, ebullient devil.

Fatty is not so much fat as simply chubby. Perhaps the name Fatty partly arose from the khaki shorts he wears, which clearly were made for a man of very much greater proportions. They begin just above the bulge of his buttocks and end somewhere near his ankles. I have no doubt that he finds himself more comfortable when dressed in this way, since it allows the whole convex curve of his stomach, encased within a tight but flimsy T-shirt, complete freedom of movement. It can expand when he smiles, oscillate when he laughs, and contract as deep-seated rumblings fight their way upwards through the enveloping darkness to emerge as exquisitely controlled belches.

"Good evening, sir. Good evening, mem. What you like? Sharks-fin soup?"

He knows that we always start with sharks-fin soup. He not only knows what *we* always have, but also what hundreds of others who patronise his restaurant always have, and in this way alone he is superior to the many European restaurants and hotels in Singapore, which, although they regard themselves as being rather better than Fatty's, would not, with one notable exception, recognise a person twice, let alone remember what he eats, even though he eat there every day for twenty years.

"Then some prawns, maybe, or chicken mushloom?"

"What is this?"

"Porkskin, sir."

He takes down a strip of the parchment-like meat, lays it on a wooden block and chops off two small pieces with an enormous chopper. He then hands the two morsels to us in his fingers and there is no alternative whatever but to eat them.

"Very good, but let's have chicken and mushroom."

"Yes, sir! And Anchor beer?"

Fatty then sets his minions to work, and within five minutes is placed on our table a steaming bowl of sharks-fin soup, which, as everyone knows, is the food of the gods.

I think Fatty must be very wealthy, since his restaurant is never empty, and I am sure that he never spends any money, either on himself or on the restaurant. The cost of the food he serves and the wages of those who serve it, plus a trifling amount for fuel, must be his only outgoings. He has no need for clerks and cashiers, since he carries his balance-sheet in his head, and I have seen him add up the bill for a six-course dinner for thirty-odd people, with drinks extra, by astonishingly accurate mental arithmetic. He accomplishes these feats of calculation largely by counting dirty plates and empty bottles. In some ways Fatty is a genius.

But, in spite of his own frugal habits, I fancy he lusts after just one expensive fling. The other evening he told me that it was his ambition to go to London and, when pressed, admitted that he was tempted to go next year. I asked him what he wanted to do in London. It appeared that more than anything else he wished to ride in a London underground train.

September 18th, 1954

It is extraordinary, in this market-place of the East, how difficult it sometimes is to buy an elementary item of personal
equipment. I do not think I differ greatly from other average
males, certainly not in the simple requirements of headgear,
but today I have enquired at more than a dozen shops for a cap,
a cloth cap, a cap with a peak, a flat cap, an ordinary cap, a cap
for the head, in short, a cap, and on each occasion would have
been greeted with considerably less astonishment had I asked for
a Virgin-form brassière with which the men's outfitters of Singapore seem largely to be stocked. I was shown Homburgs and
topees, trilbys and berets; at one establishment I was offered a
curious cloth contraption with a green celluloid peak, on which
was printed in large, gold letters the legend "Fu Lung Shing,"
the meaning and purpose of which evaded both myself and the
shopkeeper. It seemed wherever I went that the only garment
remotely approximating to the common cap was a half-leather,
half-cloth creation with a peak like the lower lip of a pelican,
giving one the appearance of a cross between Babe Ruth and a
Bethlehem steelworker. At one outfitter's shop, which proudly
calls itself "*the* man's shop," I was offered everything from a
beer mug to a brass garden fountain.

And so I have been driven to the conclusion that it is impossible to buy a cap in Singapore and since, on the equator, one
appears ridiculous in any of the more conventional forms of
headgear, I shall probably end up by wearing a turban, an
article of which, I am sure, there is no shortage. After all, one
can always buy a dress length or two from the men's outfitters.

I remember recently experiencing similar difficulty when I
wanted to buy a plain wooden cigarette box for use on a plain
wooden desk. Again I toured the entire city. Certainly it was
impossible to complain of a shortage of cigarette boxes. The
shortage was simply of plain wooden ones. There were cigarette
boxes which slid cigarettes out of twenty cigarette-sized holes
when the lid was opened; cigarette boxes got up to resemble
television sets, so that when the lid was opened a succession of
coloured pictures of gross-bosomed girls in indelicate postures

appeared on the screen; cigarette boxes with flashing lights; cigarette boxes which played everything from *The Bluebells of Scotland* to *Yokohama Mama*; I was even shown an elaborate, highly-coloured box made from the wooden foundations of the old Waterloo Bridge, but that anyone could possibly want a plain wooden cigarette box was beyond the belief of the proprietor of every shop I entered. I cannot even begin to provide a reason for this extraordinary state of affairs.

September 19th, 1954

Chong's wife has had another baby. The baby is a boy and has three sisters and two brothers. Since the mother had pre-natal care, and since the child was born in the Kandang Kerbau Maternity Hospital, it is unlikely that either of them will die. If Mrs. Chong's six children all grow up healthy, as they probably will, and marry, as they almost certainly will, and have several children each, as they quite certainly will if they are able to have any at all, and if each of these six children produces an average of four offspring, and if this process is continued over several generations, Mrs. Chong will have 24 grandchildren, 96 great-grandchildren, 384 great-great-grandchildren and 1,536 great-great-great-grandchildren, and all this ponderous increase will take place in less than one hundred years. That is how the population of Singapore grows.

Before the first world war the population of Singapore was about 300,000. After the same war it was 400,000. It passed the half-million mark before the 'thirties, and after the second world war it stood at 900,000. Today it is almost 1,200,000. According to the present rate of increase, with immigration into the country practically stopped, it will reach 2,000,000 in less than twenty years.

What are all these people going to do? Where are they going to live? How are they going to be educated? No one knows.

At the present moment primary schools can take pretty well every child reaching primary school age. But if the Education Department is to be able to go on doing this, it must provide from 35,000 to 40,000 new places each year, indefinitely. How many

schools do you need to accommodate that many children? How
many teachers do you need to cope with nearly 40,000 new children every year? How can a city a tenth of the size of London
cope with the economic burden when most of its citizens are
poverty-stricken to begin with? And which line should the government take? Should it try to educate everyone imperfectly;
give them a six-year course and spew them into the world, unless they are bright enough to go on to a secondary school, at the
age of twelve? Or should it select and educate the only children
it can afford to educate—that is, the brightest? And while
either course is found to be necessary, is it possible for Britain to
claim that she is doing her best for her overseas possessions? Is
it possible for Britain to have an easy conscience over Singapore
when her own children go to school until they are fifteen, while
a good many of Singapore's children are thrown back into the
slums at the ridiculous age of twelve? It seems to me that Singapore's problems are just as much the concern of Britain as they
are ours.

But this is not the whole story; in six years' time 20 per cent.
of the population of Singapore will be of primary school age.
One person in every five will be a small child attending primary
school. Even today over half of the population of Singapore is
under twenty-one.

The Singapore annual report for 1953 says:

"With a young and virile population rapidly reaching maturity there will be a cumulative effect upon the birth rate and the
phenomenal increase will continue."

Ten thousand men every year come on to the labour market
to seek employment in an economy that is not expanding at the
same rate as the population. If the building of houses continues
at the present rate—which is just about as fast as the public
and private building resources of the Colony will allow—insufficient houses will be built to keep pace with the growing population, let alone to rehouse the tens of thousands who already live
in appalling squalor.

It is a problem which, on the surface, would appear to be insoluble, but if an answer is to be found at all it must be found
in either of two directions: either there must be a phenomenal

increase in Singapore's capacity to produce wealth, so that it may be able to house, clothe and feed its population; or some means must be found of putting a stop to the present reckless proliferation of the human race on this tiny island not much bigger than the Isle of Wight. The first direction is doubtful, because the prosperity of Singapore does not altogether depend on the people of Singapore but almost entirely on the likes and dislikes of the rest of the world, which, in turn, are subject to all manner of unpredictable influences. The second direction is also doubtful, because so many people believe it ethically wrong even to look that way. But those are the alternatives, and no reasonable person can deny that the answer, or as much of the answer as will ever be found, lies in an amalgam of them both.

In Singapore there is a body known as the Family Planning Association, which attempts to deal with the problem of the production of unwanted babies. They have many enemies— ignorance, superstition, tradition, male selfishness and the Catholic Church. The Family Planning Association and the Catholic Church are at perpetual loggerheads, and the local press seize avidly on every statement of their respective views and thus fan even more the merrily burning fire of mutual dislike and distrust.

The Family Planners say: it is unjust that children should be brought into this world when it is beyond the capacity of their parents to feed, clothe and care for them properly; when it is beyond the capacity of government either to house or to educate them: when it is necessary for them to live out their lives in the black holes of Chinatown. They say that it is unjust for women to die young or, at any rate, to grow old while they are still young, because they must go through life almost permanently pregnant, because neither they nor their husbands know of any way of preventing the continual, ruinous creation of life. They say that it is wicked to bring unwanted babies into the world to live in cubicles where T.B. is endemic, where sanitation is non-existent, where overcrowding has reached a stage which animals would scarcely tolerate. They point to the thousands and thousands of women who turn to the abortionist, who are permanently injured by the abortionist, who are sometimes killed by the abortionist, and say that this is the greatest wickedness of all, which only education in the principles of Family Planning can prevent. They say, in effect, that children who cannot be properly cared for in a decent home should not be born at all, and there is much truth in this belief.

The Catholics, on the other hand, are implacably opposed to the ideas of Family Planners, but I am continually astonished at the slackness with which they present their views to the general public. I have no doubt that there is nothing slack in the way their priests dissuade their flock from listening to the arguments of the Planners. I have no doubt that the discipline in the Catholic ranks is of a very high order. But I cannot understand why it should be that their pronouncements in public are left largely to the ill-educated youths of the Catholic Young Men's Association, or to devotees unable to grasp the essential difference between abortion and contraception, between licentiousness and planning. These stupid young men and silly young women do a great deal of harm to the Catholic cause.

Faced with the appalling problem of the rising population of Singapore the Catholics say, in fact, "The Lord will provide." It is idle to point in answer to India or China, and to say that the Lord has not provided there, since an American in America, or an Englishman in England, or even a Chinese in Singapore a hundred years ago would have argued on the same lines—that the country could not possibly support the growing numbers of its people and that something, swiftly, must be done to stop them growing.

The Catholics also say that it is wrong to prevent conception when all the biological evidence suggests that conception *should* take place. There is some sense in this too, since the opposing argument most frequently brought forward, and perhaps the only practical opposing argument that *can* be brought forward, that if you perpetuate life, remove famine and prevent disease you destroy a balance which can only be rectified by a corresponding decrease in births, is equally unprovable. Neither can be proved right or wrong. Both views, logically, are equally tenable or untenable according to one's own persuasion.

Again, the Catholics say, if all these people need schools, houses and other essentials of modern life, then provide them;

nothing is impossible providing the will is there. And this argument, too, is unanswerable, since there is the evidence of two world wars before us to show the incredible amount of energy and wealth that *can* be released once the magnitude of the need is appreciated.

But the one argument that the Family Planners have which seems to me to be quite unassailable is the one that refers to the mother. If, by the failure of society to provide a mother with a means of preventing the conception of a child she does not want, of preventing the gradual disintegration of a thing of beauty— her body—into a bedraggled sack of tired bones and flesh, of preventing her from undergoing a succession of pregnancies which in the end will maim and kill her, of protecting her from a life of almost perpetual pregnancy imposed upon her by a dominant male whose only claim to superiority resides in muscles stronger than hers so that he may compel her submission—if, by this failure, we think we are carrying out the will of God, then we shall surely pay for our insufferable conceit.

September 20th, 1954

I was so struck with a sign I saw this morning in Raffles Place which drew attention to "The —— Studio" where, it appeared, one could be photographed in "Six different positions for only $15.00," that I found myself examining every sign I passed during the rest of the day.

I am now convinced that a whole book could be written on Singapore shop signs, which would not only in itself be a most entertaining document but would also be an exhaustive guide to what the people of Singapore do for a living. Perhaps the most compelling aspect of the subject is the extraordinary variety of merchandise with which one shop seems able to deal. One shop announces: "Grand selection of nylons, gowns, carpets, pyjamas, teasets, dinner-sets, musical boxes, suits and shirts, and other ready-made goods." This particular shop is not a large department store but a poky little shop, and that it can announce such diverse and arbitrarily chosen commodities as musical boxes and suits suggests to me that inside their premises they must have a great many more items, extending even to teapots and quails, than those listed on their signboard. Perhaps the random choice of articles is deliberate. Perhaps by bracketing nylons and dinner-sets they seek to draw attention to the infinite variety of their wares. Or perhaps the items listed are simply their best-selling lines—in which case it is difficult to see how a shop which has developed, say, a profitable trade in gowns can turn with a natural equanimity to the forceful marketing of musical boxes. But I imagine they know their business better than I do.

There is another company which tells the world that it is engaged in *Advertising and Construction*. This is odd, for I have never known an advertising agency to add building to its activities. It may be that it builds buildings and then advertises them until they are sold. This, of course, is a mild form of cheating for, by the same process, each time I advertise my car for sale I am in the advertising business.

Wherever one goes in Singapore one comes across the same keynote of diversity: "Dealer in sport-shirts, chappels, provisions, toilets, perfumes, sweets, news, cigars and cigarettes." What on earth are chappels? And is there not something odd in the mixture of sweets and toilets? Is it possible that on asking for a certain brand of sweets which the proprietor of this astonishing shop does not have, he will ask whether he can interest you in a toilet, or in the latest nineteenth-century gothic or Primitive Methodist chapel to seat five hundred?

Then, another curious aspect of the Singapore retail trade is the number of people actively engaged in making and selling wooden ladders: "Maker of mosquito nets, mattresses, cushions, wooden ladders, ironing-boards and camp-beds"; or "Barber chairs, ladders and canvas beds"; or "Manufacturers of wooden tong, canvas bed, canvas shade, ladder, desk, chair." Quite apart from a natural curiosity to know what constitutes a wooden tong, one wonders where the connection lies between camp-beds and ladders. Are the beds these people make so high that a ladder is needed to reach them? Or can it be that a man who has spent years making camp-beds invariably becomes, at a certain point, obsessed with a terrible urge to make ladders as well?

There is only one generalisation that can be made about Singapore shops: not one of them deals in one line only. There are always at least two, and between them the casual observer is most unlikely to perceive the slightest connection. Take, for instance, the case of eyes and piles: "Specialist for eyes, piles and other weakness" or "Amazing cure for eyes and piles" or "Eyes and piles specialist. Cures without operation."

Notice the insistence that eyes are things, like piles, to be cured. If one accepts the suggestion that one is likely to be better off without both one's eyes and piles, then perhaps it is possible to draw a tenuous line of relation between the two afflictions. But not otherwise. It is so difficult to discover the truth of the matter without risking a permanent injury, but does the practitioner, having examined the patient's eyes, say: "Now, if you wouldn't mind bending down a moment, I will have a look at your piles" or does he, having examined the patient's piles, suggest that he buys himself a pair of glasses?

But even more disturbing is this third, sinister and unmentionable "weakness." If a man has weak eyes and weak piles, what else is likely to be weak—except perhaps his faith in eyes-and-piles specialists? Is this third weakness something that only arises when one is landed with both eyes *and* piles? Could it be an eyes-and-piles neurosis?

Clearly this is a field for immediate scientific investigation.

September 21st, 1954

Chong Nam is a printer and spends most of his time sitting at a little polished table gazing through the open front of his shop at the busy dusty street beyond. Always you will find on his table a glass of cold Chinese tea, over which he has placed a smooth circular piece of wood specially made for the purpose. Perhaps several hours earlier, when the tea was first placed there, the wood may have served, albeit inefficiently, to keep the tea warm. Now it can serve only to keep it clean. Occasionally, very occasionally, he will sip noisily at the tea, always carefully replacing the little circle of wood immediately afterwards. But he never seems to finish his glass of tea, and that is why, whenever

Mourner at Chinese Funeral, Singapore.

Malay House, Singapore.

Malay Boys.

you call on Chong Nam, he will have a half-empty glass of tea before him on his little polished table.

The only other item of equipment with which Chong Nam's desk is furnished is an abacus, on which his fingers can fly like those of a pianist, flashing the little beads first up and then down, miraculously producing an answer, it seems, from nowhere. There are many printers you can ask to estimate for a certain piece of work who will take the material you give them and pore over it for days, consulting tables and costs and graphs, and laboriously, after a great period of time, producing the figure you require. Chong Nam can do all this in his head. Only when the estimate required is especially complicated will he use his abacus, and he may be relied upon to produce a figure which, having regard to his costs of production, is as accurate as any more scientific methods could make it.

Chong Nam has white hair, which is unusual for a Chinese, and it is still so wiry that it stands out horizontally from his head on either side, giving him a curious, thatched appearance. He wears a white shirt which hangs down outside his striped cotton trousers. The stripes on his trousers are very broad and blue so that they resemble pyjama trousers, and I have never known Chong Nam to wear anything else.

Behind his desk are ranged his printing machines, which clatter away continuously above the squeak of the Rediffusion speaker which keeps his workers happy. There is not one of his workers who can honestly be said to possess an adequate grasp of the English language, and yet they are each engaged in printing practically nothing else. How they do it is a mystery.

Today I went to see Chong Nam to ask him to quote for printing a book. It was not a very big book, and it could not conceivably have been of a less political nature. But the first thing Chong Nam said was: "Before we can print anything in book form we must ask government permission."

Now this, to begin with, is untrue. Chong Nam can print whatever book he likes so long as it is not subversive, libellous or obscene. The fact that Chong Nam was badly informed on some aspect of government regulations did not surprise me in the least. What surprised and disturbed me, assuming Chong

Nam's belief in the existence of this regulation forbidding him to print anything in book form without government permission, was the complacency with which he was clearly prepared to put up with it. To me, and to most other Europeans I know, the very suggestion that one must ask the Government's permission to say, write or publish *anything*, is entirely outrageous. One's whole being revolts at the very preposterousness of the idea. But not so Chong Nam's. This, he believed, was what the Government had said, and that was the end of the matter. He would comply. He would acquiesce in an outrage which tens of thousands of men throughout the world have died at the barricades to prevent.

I wondered how it was that a successful businessman and a reasonably intelligent man could apparently maintain such an attitude. If he thought and acted in this way, how would the thousands of unsuccessful, unintelligent citizens of Singapore think and act when confronted with a similar problem? Do they, in fact, watch a city-state moving rapidly towards democracy and self-government without the foggiest idea of what is implied by the words? Would they tolerate without complaint the thought-controlling mechanisms of the totalitarian police state? Perhaps they would. Perhaps that is what, after all, they will get. Chong Nam will make a most able Commissar.

September 22nd, 1954

L. says that the trouble with this government is that it always thinks of twenty reasons why a thing should not be done before it will admit to even one reason why it should. The principal exception to this rule is, of course, the Income Tax Department, which the government was determined to have in spite of the numerous and entirely valid arguments which were brought forward to prove the impossibility of its functioning fairly.

The other day I was talking to a Chinese architect who has recently designed a magnificent new building that is to be erected on our waterfront. I forget how many stories it is going to be, but something like fourteen or fifteen. I asked him if there was any technical reason why a building thirty to forty stories high should not be erected on the same site, and he stated that there was none. "Why then," I asked, "do builders stop commercial accommodation at less than twenty stories? Why did one company have to go to the extent of hiring lawyers to plead their case when they wanted their building to be eighteen stories high? If the land and the foundations will take the weight—and you say they will—why not build buildings that will compare with those to be found in other parts of the world? Why must we always have midget skyscrapers instead of the real thing?"

He said, with a great deal of derision in his voice:

"The Government has a plan—or rather the City Council has a plan—which they call the Master Plan. This Master Plan concerns itself with densities—densities of people working, and densities of people living, in particular areas. If you put up a thirty-story building on Collyer Quay the density of people working there will be far too high and the roads and approaches to it will be inadequate to deal with the load."

"But," I said, "land is scarce in Singapore. Before we are really old men the population is going to double itself and, even if there *is* enough land to scatter the city all over the island, I don't think it's a good idea. We shall spend all our time travelling miles from office to office."

"I agree," he answered, "I agree with you entirely. But they have their Plan and they mean to stick to it. We can build car parks out over the sea. We can build a railway which would circle the suburban areas and which would not take many years to pay for itself. We can widen the roads in a hundred places. But they won't allow these things because they have their Plan and everyone must conform to the Plan."

I can see very clearly what my architect friend means, and I can also see the point of view of the City Council. Between their views is a world of difference. There was a time when no one would dream of stopping a man or a company from putting up a building which could be as high as he cared to make it. The only concern of Authority was that it should not fall down. In consequence, cities grew and became Londons and New Yorks, Chicagos and Berlins, where the great thing was that men should be full of energy and ideas and faith in the future. And if the density of people became too great in particular areas, then the problem was tackled and railways and subways were built that could carry the people in and out of the crowded areas at unprecedented rates. It may not have been a lovely city that arose in such circumstances, and the amenities of travel provided may not have been of the most comfortable, but at least it was a vigorous city, a city where men crossed their bridges only when they came to them, for the simple reason that the thought that they might be unable to cross them never entered their heads. The men who built these cities were men with a boundless faith in themselves and their abilities. They had little time for plans, which would probably have been all wrong, anyway.

What a contrast if you compare this with Singapore today! If a man wants to build higher than anyone else, he must go out into the jungle and build it where it will be of no use to anyone. If he wants to help create a skyline that men will look at in wonder, he will not be allowed to do so because his ideas do not fit the plan of the men who are versed only in theoretical planning and do not understand the aspirations of a young and growing city.

It is not, after all, I suppose, particularly important that we shall never have a building exceeding twenty stories. The problem is greater than a mere consideration of the cubic capacity of buildings. What is important, I think, is the hedging about of men with vision by plans made by men who derive their vision from text-books. There is something infinitely awe-inspiring in a great building. It is no accident that they are for the most part found in America. In Singapore you will find the same spirit that inspired the men who built America, and if you try to fence them in with plans and regulations you will injure not only them but also their city. Singapore today is threatened with many dangers, and different people would give different answers if asked to list them. But few, I think, would omit the spectre that confronts us at every turn : the cold and lifeless hand of militant bureaucracy.

September 23rd, 1954

The perpetual problem of the Malay Sultan, a historian recently said to me, has been to establish himself on a river at a position sufficiently far downstream to enable him to exact tribute from all who use the river as a form of egress to the sea, and yet sufficiently far upstream to preclude the danger of a rival tapping this remarkable source of wealth before him.

It is wise for those who would successfully enter the higher social strata of Singapore society to take pains to master the details of at least one subject of universal interest, but of which the people they are likely to meet may be relied upon to know nothing. The very wise will take the precaution of having several such conversational aids in reserve which they may utilise at a moment's notice, the particular aid used depending entirely upon the nature of those people present. An aid may vary in substance from a knowledge and plausible appreciation of modern art, through the marital defection of Mr. and Mrs. X which you alone know about, to an intimate picture of the private life of whoever at the time happens to be in the news.

It is astonishing, on those now not so rare occasions when we have a great musician in Singapore, how many people feel themselves qualified to find fault with his performance. One did not previously recognise that they had any knowledge of music at all until, either verbally or in print, they show themselves able to pass, without visible effort, entire judgments on the performances, successively, of Gieseking, Kentner, Campoli, Goosens, Arrau and others. The most staggering instance of conceit occurred at the recent impeccable Arrau concert, when an acquaintance of mine, whom I had not previously suspected of even liking music, walked up to me and said: "Quite good, isn't it?"

September 24th, 1954

Philip Nelson is a European I have known now for a number of years. He has been in Singapore a long time and he is likely

to remain as long again. He likes Malaya and he likes his work
—he is an executive in a Chinese company—and to all intents
and purposes he is a Malayan, a man who is ready to give his
loyalty to Malaya. He plays his part in the community, does
valuable work both in and out of his office, and is prepared to
raise his children in this country as Malayans. He does not
suffer from any kind of colour or racial complex or prejudice,
and he would have been delighted if his son could have been
educated in Singapore at an English school—an English school
in Singapore or Malaya meaning a school attended by all races
but where the medium of instruction is English.

His son has now reached the age when work at school begins
to grow more serious and when some thought must be taken for
the morrow. Accordingly, Philip Nelson, as he told me last
night, went to see the headmaster of one of the better secondary
schools in Singapore to ask that his son might be admitted. His
son then was coming on to seven years old and this particular
school is one where children are educated from the Primary level
right up to Post-School Certificate classes. I think Nelson would
have been willing to leave his son there until the time came for
him to go either to work or to a University. His son, however,
was not admitted on the extraordinary grounds that he was
European; on the grounds that, if there is a greater number of
applicants than places, the school must give priority to the Asian
child. Philip Nelson did not follow the headmaster's line of
reasoning, but he was obliged to accept it nonetheless. So he is
now making arrangements to send his son to a boarding-school
in England.

It would be untrue to say that it was impossible for Nelson to
have his son educated in Singapore. Almost certainly one English school or another would have taken him. But Nelson was
not convinced that *any* of the other schools were up to the standard he required, nor did he wish his son to be the *only* European
in the school to which he was sent—which almost certainly
would then have been the case. The importance of the episode
resides in the reason given by the school's *European* headmaster
for not admitting the boy : he was European.

But this is not the end of the story of racial discrimination in

Malayan education. There is another aspect far more important than that revealed in the matter of Philip Nelson's son. This lies in the field of vernacular education. Wilson Harvey, another acquaintance of mine who is keenly interested in the problem of Malayan education, became most indignant about it the other day. This is roughly what he said, although I have filled in a certain amount of detail to make the story complete:

"In Malaya and Singapore there are, roughly speaking, two types of schools and in both of these two types there are many subdivisions. Basically, however, there are English schools and vernacular schools. In English schools the medium of instruction is English and the pupils are drawn from every race that lives in Malaya—except, almost wholly, from the Europeans. In vernacular schools the medium of instruction is the language of the pupils attending each school. There are therefore three types of vernacular schools—Chinese, Malay and Indian—all of which, necessarily, are racially exclusive. This is the way education has grown up in Malaya and probably it is educationally sound: the parent, providing he is able to pay (in certain cases), is able to choose the type of school at which he would most like his child to be educated.

"The problem is not, however, so simple as it may seem. A Malay child is educated at a Malay school entirely at government expense. A Chinese is educated at a Chinese school almost entirely at the expense of the Chinese community—although government grants-in-aid to Chinese schools have recently greatly increased. A child at an Indian school is educated largely at government expense, while the parent who wishes his child to be educated at an English school has to bear some of the financial burden in the form of fees.

"The discrimination does not, however, end even here: not only does the source of finance vary between different types of schools but so also does the amount. In primary schools an analysis of expenditure reveals that it costs nearly twice as much to educate a child in an English school as it does to educate a child in a Malay school, and about forty per cent. more to educate a Malay child than it does to educate an Indian child. This is not because education in one language is necessarily more expensive than education in another, but simply because more money is available to certain schools, either through the medium of government or through the people who support them.

"Traditionally the Malays of Malaya have been protected. They have received free education and a priority in government posts as a measure of return by the British Government against the losses they have sustained through the arrival in their country over the last one hundred and fifty years of an almost equal number of Chinese. Traditionally, too, the Chinese have been left to their own devices, and if at any time they felt a need for education it was up to them to provide it for themselves. This was all very well in the old days, when they could be told that they came to Malaya on the terms of the Malayan Government and that if they did not like what they found here there was, after all, a frequent and efficient shipping service back to China. Times have changed, and it is impossible to suggest to a Chinese who was born in Malaya, whose father, grandfather and, possibly, great-grandfather were born in Malaya, that he go back to China. It is becoming equally impossible to tell the Malays that their education is free and that therefore they should be thankful, when they see that every other form of education except Indian has more money spent on it per pupil. In fact, education in Malaya has become a total anachronism in its present form.

"The Malayan schools system is a product of an administration which people generally are agreed must ultimately end or at least be modified out of all recognition. To try to hasten the day when a measure of self-government is brought about, without, at the same time, hastening to an equal degree the day when education in Malaya is brought more in tune with the times, is futile. It is extraordinary that the present administration of Malaya should devote such a wealth of its time and money to persuading people who have come from all over the world to live in Malaya, to accept Malaya as the object of their first loyalty, to be faithful citizens of a country that has become their homeland, when, in the matter of education, some children are treated as first-class and others as fifth-class citizens. As long as the present inequality of educational opportunity exists, Malaya can never attain a status of independence that is worth tuppence. If it still exists when Malaya becomes independent, then the electorate will alter it themselves. Because they will be inexperienced in these matters and will then still be intoxicated with the dangerous wine of Independence, they will try to effect the alteration overnight, when the very essence of the problem is, and always will be, one that is susceptible only to gradual change. When the electorate attempts to carry out an instant educational revolution in a country which even today is only half-educated, a struggle will begin between the different racial communities to obtain the best for their children. And no question that is likely to arise in the new Malaya will generate more easily the latent racial feeling and prejudice that may yet be the curse of this country. There will be the question of the medium of instruction, and the Chinese will doubtless want this to be Chinese and the Malays will want it to be Malay. There will be the question of the re-allocation of children among available schools, and it will still be found that it will be impossible to educate rural Malay children, particularly in the overwhelmingly Malay states of Kelantan and Trengganu, other than in the attap-thatched, concrete-floored shelters in which they have always been educated, where every class in the school can see and hear every other class. There will be neither the money nor the teachers to form the new schools, and if the question is left until self-government, the Malays can rest quite assured that they will *never* get any decent schools. Neither, for that matter, will the Indians.

"If there were any indication today of a realisation of the paramount importance of this matter, then concern over it would not need to be so acute. But there is no indication whatever. There has been much talk of National schools for several years now, but it is difficult to see what has been done so far. The solution is no nearer than it was ten years ago, and meanwhile Malay children sit in their mud huts chanting the Koran, while Chinese students in Singapore riot and throw bricks at the police because the Government requires them to register for National Service, which cannot possibly take up more than three hours a week. And in the English schools one has the slightly ridiculous situation of the immediate descendants of Kwantung peasants striving for a pass in the Cambridge School Certificate. It would be no more ridiculous if school children in Leicester or Leeds sat each year for the Peking Diploma.

"Educational plans in Malaya must, it seems to me, be based on two fundamental assumptions. In the first place they must provide as speedily as possible for universal, elementary, free education, and in the second place parents must retain freedom to send their children to whatever type of school they prefer. The medium of instruction in the free, elementary schools must be English. There can be no question about this, since if there are to be National schools the medium of instruction must be a language to which half of the population of Malaya will not immediately and violently object—as the Malays would object to Chinese, and vice versa. Given National schools which will breed loyal Malayan citizens, there must also be given a common language, and although it is possible to find numerous objections to this language being English, it is possible to find far more and even stronger objections to its being either Malay or Chinese. Then, in these National schools, a second language must be taught, not as French is taught in schools in England, but as a dual, equal language which the student will be able to use as easily as English. This language will be that which the student speaks in his home. Thus the Malay child will study Malay, the Chinese child will study Chinese and the Indian child will study whatever Indian language he wishes to study which, in most cases in Malaya, will be Tamil. If a parent does not wish his child to study this second language but to study science, for example, instead, then the pupil will have a right to ask for this facility.

"This will provide for the system of free, elementary education. Parallel to this system, different communities can set up privately as many schools as they wish and, provided that they measure up to certain minimum educational standards laid down by government, they can teach in whatever language they like. These schools will receive considerable grants from government, which will cover a fair proportion of their expenses, but there will remain a balance to be made up by the parent in the form of fees. In other words, if a parent requires for his child an education which differs from the type provided by the country of which he is an enfranchised citizen, then he must pay for it. The important thing is that the payment must never be prohibitive.

"Educationalists will probably reply that this is precisely what they have in mind. In this case, I wish to God they would get on with it."

September 25th, 1954

We walked down the long rows of wooden beds. Those who were able struggled to their feet and squatted on the edges of their beds, their brown, long-nailed toes curled round the wooden bed rails so that they looked like rows of ancient crows, too old and too tired to move any more. There were perhaps thirty beds on either side of the long, low, black-raftered room, and as we walked between them sixty pairs of eyes followed us, hollow eyes, set in deep, grey sockets, round and vacant eyes, watching yet not wanting. As we walked down the length of the room sixty heads turned slowly as they would at a game of tennis played in excruciatingly slow motion. Gnarled hands picking at flaked skin, a toothless, bobbed welcome, a palm rotating rhythmically on the scarred stump of an amputated leg—these were the only movements. Otherwise, in this long house of decay there was silence, a dark and musty silence, lit by bright tunnels of sunlight that splayed in patches on the whitewashed walls.

We walked to the end of the room where a man with a completely shaven head sat like some hideous doll on the shined planks of his bed. His clothes were many sizes too big for him, and it was in some way clear that this was not because they had previously belonged to someone bigger than he was, but because he himself had shrunk within them. He had shrunk in some half-living, half-dying process that left behind the mummified appearance of the heads the Amazon pigmies shrink and wear strung from their waists. Within the loose sleeves were arms little thicker than the bones that formed them, and ankles protruded like the stick-limbs of a scarecrow. And as I looked at him, slyly with a deep sense of discomfort, the long, bubbling choke of a tubercular patient echoed down the corridor of beds. No one heeded the dying sound of dying; the shrunken little man still looked at us, and on the bony structure of his face there appeared, for a tiny instant, for so short a space of time that I wondered whether what I had seen had really occurred, a ghost of a ghostly smile.

We went out into the sunshine and walked down a white-washed cloister to another, similar room. Here the patients were women, and I had brought Ah Wong, a relative of our houseboy, to see his aunt who had been reported dying. Again we walked down the lines of human agony, between the ranks of dead-white, flat-white faces, young faces that still were beautiful, faces that in the extremity of life take on a new goodness, and the old and creased and crumpled faces that merged into bald and irregular scalps like broken eggs. We came to a bed which had planked wooden sides, inside of which, as though in a coffin, lay the withered old body of a woman, wrapped in the rags she had worn when she first came to this place. Her hands were tied by rags to the sides of the bed and she was scarcely conscious. The great cancerous growth, like a huge, loosely covered cricket ball, stuck out from the side of her face so that one felt sick with a horror of life and of where life could lead and end and die. Had one plucked at the growth it would have come away in the hands as a loose currant will come away from the surface of a bun. It looked so easy to remove. But no doctor had ever seen it until a few days previously. And in this hospital there were two doctors to five hundred patients. And most of the patients were dying.

It was a hospital run by the Cantonese community in Singapore. A small monthly charge is made and food is provided for those still well enough to eat it. Both Western and Chinese treatment is provided, but because the staff is so pitifully small it is impossible adequately to administer it even to those who could benefit from it. But the Cantonese people have given money to the project and it is growing quickly. Recently they have added new, modern wings and also a maternity section, but the problem remains the same, the problem that recurs again and again in Singapore: however fast you build, although you end up with more buildings, more expense, more staff and more equipment, you collect, in the process, even more people for whom your still limited resources cannot provide.

For the most part patients in Chinese hospitals in Singapore are there because they are beyond cure and have no one to look after them at home. They go there, in fact, to die. Conditions at the Government Hospital are such that, in general, a patient is discharged when he is either made well again or is dying. If he is dying, the hospital will probably make an arrangement with a Chinese hospital for him to be admitted there, provided he is Chinese. The Chinese hospitals take these dying patients, not only because it is a part of their purpose to do so, but because the General Hospital, in return, takes their surgical cases.

That is why my walk through the old wards of the Cantonese Hospital was so distressing.

September 26th, 1954

I went to see Bessie Lim today, who lives in a small house in a terrace of houses at the back of Lavender Street. She was sitting at her window on a hard chair with her two legs resting on a box. The legs are encased in irons and she cannot walk. All day she sits by her window making sophisticated stuffed toys. Her only companion is her seven-year-old daughter who does most of the housework.

Eight years ago Bessie was young and pretty. She married what seemed to be a reasonable young man, and within a year she had a baby. She would doubtless have gone on having many more babies had it not been for polio, which she developed shortly after her child was born. Very little could be done for her and she became paralysed from the waist down. She could not even control her bladder.

She was taken to a Christian Mission hospital, where she remained for four and a half years. She was discharged on crutches which enabled her to make a most unsteady way from one chair to another: her sole means of livelihood an ability to make stuffed animals. Her child, who had been looked after by relatives, came back to her and, with the help of the hospital, she obtained a small house in which they could live. Her husband long ago had left her, since in her condition she could be of no use to him!

She had not been in the little house long before she was taken off to hospital again where they diagnosed tuberculosis. The tuberculosis was so bad that they had to remove an entire lung. Again she was discharged and again she took up toy-making in her little terrace house. Again her daughter came back to live with her.

Then she got tuberculosis in the remaining lung, but by some special dispensation of Providence it was possible to cure it this time without surgery. Again she returned home.

Yesterday, when I called, her table was piled with the toys she is making for Christmas, each one sewn into a little Cellophane bag. On her table she has piles of the felt she uses, the stuffing for the animals and a much-thumbed, paper-bound copy of the New Testament. Her daughter, who is very pretty, now goes to school. Bessie may live for many years yet. She may even see her daughter married.

September 27th, 1954

Arrived at the office twenty minutes late due to a traffic jam in Orchard Road. Four times a day we fight our way to and fro through a deluge of traffic, and from the hastily snatched, eight-o'clock breakfast to the welcome six-o'clock tea we are in a hurry. We go to bed late and we get up late, and because we get up late we never seem to catch up with ourselves until, worn out, we throw ourselves on our beds at night. Even in our recreation we are in a hurry, and we have to break the speed limit to arrive at the cinema in time for the big picture.

In the office the telephone shrills incessantly, and just as we are sitting down for tea the home telephone rings and for a moment we feel homicidal and would like to fling the contraption into the flower-bed, torn from the wall by its malignant roots.

Even at the week-end we are still in an indecent hurry, tearing out to the beach or tearing back from the beach. We even have to drive dangerously to get the children to Sunday School on time. All this, and the tropics too!

I think, perhaps, we have all gone slightly mad.

The other day I was reading a book by a traveller named John Cameron who came to the East about a hundred years ago. He wrote about his journey and he called his work *Our Tropical Possessions in Malayan India*. He paints a vivid picture of the European daily routine of those days, a picture which bears not the slightest resemblance to our routine today, but which, as you will see, had a great deal to be said for it.

"To give a correct idea of the everyday-life of the European it is necessary rather to distinguish between the unmarried and the married, than between the man of narrow and the man of extended means. Most of the bungalows, as I have before mentioned, are about two miles from town; nearly all, at least, are within hearing range of the 68-pounder gun on Fort Canning, the discharge of which each morning at five o'clock ushers in the day. This is the accepted signal of all old residents to start from bed, the younger, however, usually indulge in an extra half-hour's slumber. Still, six o'clock generally sees all dressed and out of doors, to enjoy a couple of miles walk or ride through the lovely country roads, in the delicious coolness of morning, before the sun's rays become disagreeably powerful.

"The air at this hour is of that temperature which may be described as a little colder than cool, and it has a sharpness which I have experienced only in the early mornings of tropical countries, or on a frosty day at home. A slight mist, too, rises from the ground, that, whether it does in reality lend any measure of coolness, certainly by association gives a frosty aspect of nature. Indeed, I have often, when setting out on my walk at sunrise, been positively startled by the resemblance of sharp frost. All over the grassy patches of lawn, on the shrubs and bushes and on the roadside hedges, a species of spider work their fine cobwebs upon which the dew is caught and held in minute pearly drops, giving exactly the appearance of hoarfrost; add to this, the rising mist, the sharp air and the red sun just showing his upper limb of clouds, and the illusion is tolerably complete. I may remark that, throughout the year, there is barely thirty minutes' difference in the hour of the sun's rising. In June and December it dawns about a quarter-past five, in March and September at a quarter to six.

"I have already partly described the appearance of the country or suburban roads, but if beautiful at any time, they are certainly much more so during the first two hours of morning. The rich, green, wall-like bamboo hedges which generally line those parts of the roads which border the various residences, sparkle with large drops of dew, and from many of these that have been newly clipped may be seen shoots of over a foot in height, the growth of a single night. The trees, which are almost all evergreens, have also their large leaves wet and glistening with the refreshing moisture. Here and there, too, a strip of jungle-covered land is passed, from which breathes forth the last fragrant airs of the night blossoms. Everything living seems to share the vigorous freshness; the birds that are hushed in shelter during the midday heat now chirp and carol forth their short and musical notes.

"Nor are these morning walks always given over to solitary commune with nature. At no other hour of the day are the roads out of town so lively with Europeans. One can always depend upon picking up a companion, and getting and giving all the little gossip of the night before; or more seriously discussing the last China or Europe mail news. During these walks, too, may be encountered pretty nearly the entire rising generation of European parentage—the heirs and heiresses, to be, of Singapore's merchants, who with their ayahs or native nurses are sent to 'makan-angin'—literally, 'eat' the morning air.

"Than this practice of exercise in the early morning, there is, perhaps, none to which the inhabitants of Singapore are more indebted for their singularly good health. It has an effect quite opposite to fatigue; and whether it be considered as a corrective of the previous evening's dinner and its accompaniments or simply as a means of bracing up one's nerves for the day's labour, it is invaluable. Most people limit their walks to two miles, or about half an hour; but this is by no means a rule. Some go as far as four, five or six miles in a morning; these are the early birds who start at gun-fire sharp, and they are in the minority. I know one gentleman, now nearer seventy than sixty years old, who is out of doors at five each morning, goes a round of six miles, and comes back to his tea at about half-past six. He has

The 'Royal' Sampan, Kuching. Government House beyond.

Sarawak Cathedral.

Tweedledum and Tweedledee, Johore Bahru.

State Offices, Johore Bahru.

kept up this practice during forty years of residence, and has
reaped his reward in still robust health, strong nerve, clear head,
and a yet lively enjoyment of the good things of life.

"During the training season for the races, it is at this hour
that the horses are taken their rounds, and the course then forms
to a great many the limit of their walk. As early as half-past four
the syces or native grooms are up preparing their horses, and
start a little after gun-fire for the course, a distance of about two
miles. At sunrise the horses commence to go their rounds, and,
as they wait their turns, it is generally half-past six before all
have been exercised. As the distance is to most a tolerably long
one, the stewards provide tea on the course, so that it is altogether a very favourite resort for about six weeks before both
the spring and autumn meetings. Very little training takes place
privately, but still some horses have occasionally been met returning from the course before daylight. The Malays, however,
have a superstition connected with this 'moonlight training,'
which is not favourable to it. A few years ago an owner, anxious
to test his horse's strength and speed in secret, had him taken to
the course about two o'clock in the morning; some Malays who
lived on the borders of the course saw the horse saddled, mounted
and started. He went round, they aver, once, twice, thrice gaining in speed each time; the fourth time he passed like a bird,
the fifth time like lightning, and the sixth time nothing but a
blast of wind went by. Certainly the horse was never seen on
the course again, and so the Malays think he must have been
translated into the spiritual world, where both horse and rider
are still going their rounds with undiminished velocity.

"On coming home from these morning rounds, the custom is
to get into loose, free and easy attire, generally *baju* and pyjamas.
A cup of coffee or tea, with biscuit or bread-and-butter and
fruit, is then consumed, and the next two hours spent in reading, writing, or lolling about on the verandahs which front each
apartment of a house. I have said reading, writing, or lolling
about; but, more correctly speaking, the time is devoted to a
combination of the first and the last. In the daily avocation of
most, the pen is pretty actively handled; and unless at mail
times, or by those of a literary turn of mind, it is seldom taken

up out of office. Reading is generally accomplished in the extremely reclining posture for which the verandah chairs of Singapore are so admirably adapted; and no doubt a deal of 'Quiet contemplation' must be gone through in the same attitude, in fact, perhaps, more than is generally conceded. The *dolce far niente* has its charms here as well as elsewhere, and what is more, it has a good excuse.

"At half-past eight the breakfast dressing-gong or bell is sounded. A gentleman's *toilette* in this part of the East is not an elaborate one, and half an hour is ample time for its completion. The bath is its chief feature. Attached to the dressing-room of each bedroom in almost all houses is a bathroom, with brick-tiled floor, containing a large bathing-jar holding about sixty or seventy gallons of water. The orthodox manner of bathing is to stand on a small wooden grating close to the jar, and with a hand bucket to dash the water over the body. This is by no means such an unsatisfactory method as to the uninitiated it may appear. The successive shocks to the system which are obtained by the discharge of each bucketful of water seem to have a much more bracing effect than that of one sudden and continued immersion. Every gentleman has his native boy or body-servant, whose sole duty it is to attend upon him personally. While bathing, these boys lay out their master's apparel for the day; so that on coming from the bath a gentleman has little trouble to get himself attired. As to shaving, the process is generally performed by itinerant Hindoo barbers, who for the small charge of a dollar or a dollar and a half per month come every morning round to the residences of their customers. The charge is so small, and the saving in trouble so great, that almost all avail themselves of the convenience.

"The universal breakfast hour is nine o'clock, and when the bell then rings the whole household assembles, and should there be ladies of the number this is the first time of their appearance. Singapore breakfasts, though tolerably substantial and provided with a goodly array of dishes, are rarely dwelt over long, half an hour being about the time devoted to them. A little fish, some curry and rice, and perhaps a couple of eggs, washed down with a tumbler or so of good claret, does not take long to get through and yet forms a very fair foundation on which to begin the labours of the day. After breakfast the conveyances drive round to the porch or portico and having received their owners hasten in to town. No matter how many may reside together, each bachelor has generally his own 'turn-out'; and for half an hour every morning the two bridges leading across the river into town present an endless string of these rather motley vehicles— by no means an uninteresting spectacle. On the whole, both the private conveyances and horses of Singapore are creditable to it, though the same cannot be said for the miserable pony hack-gharries that are let out on hire. A large number of horses are brought up from Australia, not less I should say than a hundred each year, and all find a sale at what must be remunerative prices. None are ever exported again, and where they all go to it is difficult to conjecture, for the European population who chiefly make use of them increases but slowly, and yet horseflesh is not subject to greater mortality here than elsewhere. The climate seems to agree well with them; they grow fat and sleek and live long, though they can scarcely go through the same amount of work as in their native country; each horse has its groom and grass-cutter, and probably the additional attention they receive compensates for the exhausting temperature.

"Arrived in town, ten minutes or a quarter of an hour are usually spent in going the rounds of the square to learn the news of the morning. These commercial square gatherings are quite a characteristic of the place and of the community, and whatever channels they may open to the flow of local gossip, or it might even be scandal, yet they are so far useful that they serve the purpose of an open-air and non-commercial exchange. Differences of position are in most cases left behind in office, and all meet here on a footing of equality, or if there is any ascendancy at all it is that which is obtained by the readiest wit or perhaps by the greatest measure of self-assurance. As scarcely a day passes without the arrival of a steamer with news from England, China, India, or from some interesting point in the neighbourhood, there is always ample material for an animated exchange of ideas and information on leading topics, whether they be European politics, the war in America, the position of affairs in China, the combined action at Japan, the affairs of India, Java, Borneo, the administration of the local Government, or the condition and prospects of the adjacent markets.

"This sort of congress takes place between the first arrival in town and ten or half-past ten o'clock. At that hour business has commenced and continues in full force till tiffin time, or one o'clock; and certainly it is gone through in quite as smart and active manner as at home. The climate, though it may produce a greater langour in the evening, has apparently no such effect during the day. There is not much out-of-door bustle; but still when occasion requires the folks post about the square under the midday sun at a lively pace and with apparent impunity.

"Tiffin time does not bring the luxurious abandonment to the table which it does in Java; people in Singapore are more moderate in their indulgence yet some show of a meal is in most cases made; a plate of curry and rice and some fruit or it may be a simple biscuit with a glass of beer or claret. Half an hour's relaxation too is generally indulged in, and as the daily newspaper comes out about this hour, there is a goodly flocking either to the exchange or the public godowns in the square for a perusal of it.

"Two o'clock is the exchange hour, and though I do not think there is really much intercommunication on commercial subjects, yet as a rendezvous and a place where the leading men of the mercantile world can have an interchange of ideas even on irrelevant matters, it has the good effect of promoting and maintaining a more general intimacy than might otherwise prevail. Unlike the chamber of commerce, from which it is distinct, the exchange as a body assumes no political influences, and it thus no doubt saves many a humiliating experience which it has fallen to the lot of the former body to encounter. The exchange is rather distinguished for its hearty and mixed co-operation in all that tends to ameliorate or enliven the condition of life in the settlement.

"Business hours are not particularly severe, and by half-past four or five o'clock most of the mercantile houses have got through their work. But only a few proceed direct home at this hour; the greater number, at least of the younger members of the community, resort to the fives-court or the cricket-ground on the esplanade. The former is an institution of long standing in Singapore; as far back as thirty years ago it was erected, and at no time since then has the interest taken in the game subsided. On the contrary, about two years ago it was found necessary to build another court out at Tanglin about two miles from town in the vicinity of the residences, so greatly had the number of members increased. The game is well known at home and I need not describe it further than to say that it is a kind of rackets, but that the hands, instead of bats, are used to play up the ball and that consequently the exercise is much more severe. It is really surprising, in a temperature seldom ranging at the hour the game is played below 82°, to see those who have gone through a fair day's work at the desk come here and doff their vests, coats and shirts to an hour or an hour and a half of about the most severe exercises in which it is possible to engage; and this too in an unroofed building with the rays of the sun if not directly beating down, at least reflected in fierce glare from the whitewashed walls. And yet medical men attribute the extreme good health of the residents to this continued exercise indulged in, begun by the morning walk at sunrise and ending with cricket or fives at sunset. Cricket is of course precisely the same game in Singapore as it is at home.

"But there are two evenings in the week when the whole European community may generally be seen upon the esplanade, whether or not they be fives or cricket players, and these are band evenings, generally Tuesdays and Fridays. The band, which is that of the regiment on the station at the time, or from one of the men-of-war which occasionally visit the port, plays on a raised mount on the centre of the esplanade green. The chains which protect the green on ordinary occasions are on these evenings let down, and carriages, horsemen, and pedestrians are alike admitted to the greensward. Gathered round the band in a tolerably broad circle are the beauty and fashion of the place. The ladies, to whom almost all the other outdoor amusements are denied, partake at least in this, and though the ruddy glow of the colder latitudes has fled from most cheeks, still there supervenes a languid softness which is more interesting and perhaps more beautiful. The pretty pale-faced European children too may on these occasions be seen tripping about in playfulness a little less boisterous, but quite as cheerful as is witnessed at home. The band plays from half-past five till half-past six, at which hour it is all but dark, when the carriages make for home in a long string, gradually falling off one by one as the various residences are reached.

"Except on band nights, however, most of the commercial and all of the official world retire home a little before six o'clock. Arrived there, probably a glass of sherry and bitters will anticipate the refreshing process of dressing for dinner. A slight difference as to dinner hour prevails; some dine at half-past six, some at seven; the former however is the time most commonly adopted. There is one advantage here which is too seldom to be found in other parts of the world. Whatever may be the hour, a clockwork regularity and punctuality is observed, and this is not with respect to dinner only, but with respect to all other meals. No doubt this regularity also has its share in the maintenance of the good health of the European community.

"Dinner in Singapore is not the light airy meal which might reasonably be imagined from the nature of the climate; on the contrary, it is quite as substantial a matter of fact as in the very coldest latitudes. The difference is not that the substantials are fewer, but that the luxuries are more numerous. Indeed the every-day dinner of Singapore, were it not for the waving punkahs, the white jackets of the gentlemen, and the gauzy dresses of the ladies, the motley array of native servants, each standing behind his master's or mistress's chair, and the goodly display of argand lamps, might not unreasonably be mistaken for some more special occasion at home. Soup and fish generally both precede the substantials, which are of a solid nature, consisting of roast beef or mutton, turkey or capon, supplemented by side-dishes of tongue, fowl, cutlets, or such-like, together with an abundant supply of vegetables, including potatoes nearly equal to English ones grown in China or India, and also cabbages from Java. The substantials are invariably followed by curry and rice which form a characteristic feature of the tables of Singapore, and though Madras and Calcutta have been long famed for the quality of their curries, I nevertheless think that those of the Straits exceed any of them in excellence. There are usually two or more different kinds placed on the table, and accompanying them are all manner of sambals or native pickles and spices, which add materially to the piquancy of the dish.

"During the progress of the substantials and of the curry and rice, the usual beverage is beer, accompanied by a glass or two of pale sherry. The good folks of Singapore are by no means inclined to place too narrow restrictions on their libations, and it has been found in the experience of older residents that a liberality in this respect conduces to good health and long life. Besides this the American Tudor Company keeps up a tolerably regular supply of ice, and as it is sold at three cents, or less than $1\frac{1}{2}d.$ per lb., it is within the reach of all, and is an invariable adjunct to all beverages.

"To curry and rice succeeds generally some sort of pudding or preserve, but sweets have not the same temptation here as at home. Very good cheese however is obtained in fortnightly supplies by the overland steamers, and, as good fresh butter is always to be had, this part of dinner is well enjoyed, accompanied as it is by no illiberal allowance of excellent pale ale. But it is in the luxuriance of the dessert perhaps more than anything else that the tables of Singapore are to be distinguished, and it is little wonder that it should be so; for there is no season of the year at which an abundance of fruit cannot be obtained. Pineapple may be considered the stock fruit of the island, and one or two splendid specimens of these generally adorn the table. There are plantains, ducoos, mangoes, rambutans, pomeloes, and mangosteens; the latter fruit is peculiar to the Straits of Malacca and to Java, and so great is its fame that to India or China no present or gift from Singapore is more acceptable than a basket of them. It is of a somewhat singular genus; it is round, of the size of a small orange, is covered with a thick woody purple bark in place of rind, which has to be cut or broken off, and inside are the snowy-white cloves of the pulp, sweet and with a very delicate flavour, unlike anything else I know of. But though dessert generally makes a finer display than any other part of dinner, it is not that to which most attention is directed. A cigar and a glass or two of sherry after the ladies are gone, and dinner is over.

"Many of the residences have billiard-rooms attached, in which case the usual custom is to retire there after dinner. Where no billiard-room is within reach, a chat on the verandah, a little meditation, or perhaps a book passes the hours pleasantly enough until bedtime. And as dinner is seldom over before eight o'clock, and the usual hour for rest is ten, it is not a very long interval between them that has to be disposed of.

"As I have remarked before I think it is to be regretted that the people of Singapore so determinedly set their faces against every sort of entertainment which does not include a dinner. I am quite sure that much of the after-dinner time, that is under the present system in a manner thrown away, might be more agreeably, and at the same time more profitably spent, if the custom were to set in that people should meet occasionally after dinner, and pass their evenings in the same sort of social intercourse as is usual at home, and in most other parts of the world.

"Such is the every-day life at Singapore. It is true I have taken rather an uncommon method of describing it, and one which might be thought more to become the pages of a journal or diary, than a book such as this, but it appears to me that by thus detailing the various acts of the day as they succeed one another, I shall have carried out more effectually the object I have in view, and presented a clearer picture of the nature of the European's life there to the people at home, than had I confined myself more to generalities."

September 28th, 1954

Edward Gibson-Harris was one of those men who had stayed too long in the East; he had arrived at the point of no return. Occasionally, from force of habit, he would speak of England as home and would even, from time to time, repair to that country for a holiday—for leave, as he termed it, again from force of habit—but when he returned to the East he came home in a far fuller sense than when he arrived in England. Few men reach the point of no return; none may mistake it when it is upon him,

and most of those who do reach it are content in their acknowledgment of the inevitable.

They do not stay to die in the East for profit, these men who
forsake the bonds of country and of race; nor do they stay for
the comfort, the convenience or the ease of living that can be
theirs, but for a far deeper purpose which even they themselves
cannot properly explain. They achieve, it almost seems, a sort
of serenity through harmony with their environment, an environment that, to their compatriots, remains adamantly foreign but
which to them becomes part of the very essence of their existence.

Edward Gibson-Harris was such a man. He came to the East
as a young man fifty years ago and spent most of the succeeding
years in China. He was a "China Hand." He was part of a system
that made the economy of 450,000,000 people tick in time with
the twentieth century. Perhaps he and his system and those
others who administered the system failed; perhaps the system
was wrong, perhaps the motive was wrong, perhaps the best part
of Gibson-Harris's life was devoted to a cause that was wrong
from the beginning; but nothing could be wholly wrong that
had within it the elements of the love and regard that Gibson-
Harris had for China and her sons. He understood China and
the Chinese—not in the way that journalists profess to understand, but with the quiet comprehension of a country. He did
not deal in non-existent abstracts such as "the Chinese mentality" or "the oriental mind," but with people, many people, people
whom he knew and comprehended as one Englishman will com-
prehend another.

During the war he was interned in Shanghai, where he was
inconsiderately, but not brutally, treated by the Japanese. He
rejoined his firm in Shanghai when the war was over. For the
next few years he watched with growing dismay the fall of a
country, a people and a system. He was in Shanghai when the
grey Communist waves swept through the streets of the great
city, and although he acknowledged the horror of the depriva-
tion that had produced the Communists and the often worthy
motives that inspired them, he perceived also the poison that
percolated through the channels of their minds and grieved for

the China that was no more. The New China had no use for him, and eventually he came to Singapore where he took a job with the Government.

Fortunately for me, he was one of the people I met when I was in Shanghai immediately after the war. We met several times, and then my ship sailed and we lost touch until I saw him, many years later, in Prince's in Singapore. There he sat, as large as life, a pink gin before him, relating to his incredulous guests a no doubt incredulous story of China which neither they nor anyone else in the room was in a position to dispute or deny. He was, if anything, a little fatter round the waist but otherwise unchanged, erect and immaculate, the smile that always played on his lined, sun-beaten face still there. The occasion became, as I remember, a very jolly party.

After that we met regularly until, quite suddenly, he died. His death was caused, it seems, by a weak heart which no one, least of all himself, had suspected. He left behind him very little: a large number of books, many of them in Chinese, a number of pieces of porcelain which he had managed to salvage from the wreck of his home in Shanghai, and the modest furnishings of a small and inconvenient flat. His bank account yielded practically nothing when the expenses of his burial had been met. But although he left behind him few material possessions, he is not without a permanent memorial: Gibson-Harris's legacy to his friends was his stories, stories of the East that he had gathered over half a century and which none could tell so well as he.

This brief summary of life has served to some extent as an introduction to the story I wish to tell, but more importantly it is an introduction to the man who originally told it to me. A part of every story rests for the hearer in the personality of the teller, and this one is incomplete without a knowledge of the man who was, in fact, its author. He related it as a gospel truth and I see no reason to assume it otherwise—indeed, the records of Singapore essentially confirm its probability—but as fact or fiction it is a memorial to a man I admired above all other men I knew.

We were sitting on the tiny balcony of his flat, which looked over the carpet of light that was Chinatown at night. We had just finished dinner and he was pouring me a more than adequate brandy.

"You were talking," he said, "of fortune-telling. You know, there is nothing a Chinese likes to hear so much as an accurate prediction of his own fortune."

You could always tell when Gibson-Harris was about to embark on a story; there was always an air of authority in the introduction that silenced his company. We lit cigarettes and I waited for him to continue.

"In China, and in the numerous nearby countries that the Chinese have colonised, as much by accident as by design, fortune-telling is a principal sport. The outlook of a Chinese on life in general is for the most part fatalistic and there is nothing strange, therefore, in a predictable future; everything has been ordained beforehand and, provided the teller of fortunes is able by whatever means he possesses to glimpse the pages of the book in which the future is recorded, few will question the inevitability of his prognostications. The Chinese tends to look a little askance at the idea of Man in control of his destiny, and is inclined to lay far more store by the unequivocal assertions of the horoscope than by the mysterious ways and whims of a quite unpredictable Almighty. And, of course, there is a lot to be said for this belief as, indeed, there is a lot to be said for most of the things the Chinese believe; after all, there can be few pleasures so satisfying, so rewarding, as a *good* horoscope which each succeeding day more clearly proves correct. Consider, for example, the acute bliss of observing a quite inevitable million dollars accumulate with mathematical precision in one's bank account! —or the sweet heaven of contentment with which one might set about the business of winning a score of beautiful and quite inevitable mistresses!

"Before the war, when I was in China, I passed through Singapore many times—usually on my way to or from Europe—and whenever possible I would contrive to stay for a week or two. In this way I came to know a number of the local inhabitants, most of them, of course, Chinese. It was my custom to stay at the old *Europe* hotel—which used to stand where the Supreme Court stands today—and one night as I sat in the bar a somewhat tipsy

Chinese came over and flopped into the chair beside me. I remember the occasion particularly well because one does not often see a Chinese in such a condition except at one of their riotous dinners.

" 'Good evening,' he said, after gazing at me solemnly for two or three minutes.

" 'Good evening to you,' I answered. 'Good party?'

"He simply nodded his head and then appeared to fall into a deep sleep—except that his eyes remained open. He had an extraordinary babyish face, even for a Chinese; it was completely round and as smooth as a baby's bottom. Not a line, not a crease, not a hair disturbed its almond-coloured smoothness. His mouth was a little pressed button of a mouth, rather like a woman's, and his chin sloped away to a smooth, fat, rounded neck. You will perceive that his appearance was curious; it was surmounted by an abundance of black hair plastered down flat and smooth so that his head became an almost perfect sphere. His eyes were of the customary Chinese aspect but almost hidden by the light reflected in his rimless *pince-nez*. His body was as globular as his head and his white duck suit was stretched tightly round the tyres of fat that encircled his body. He was, indeed, a most curious specimen.

"Suddenly he heaved himself upright and peered at me through his thick glasses :

" 'I'm a millionaire, you know,' he said in a squeaky voice.

" 'Oh?'

" 'Yes! But money means nothing to me. Nothing! I don't care for money. Some of us have it and some of us don't. I have it. You don't. Pity!'

"He was silent for a moment, lost in his own thoughts—or lack of them. Then he continued :

" 'You know what my friends call me? Hm? Humble Lee! Humble Lee they call me!

" 'Humble, that's me. I'm a millionaire. Can't help making money. But I'm still an ordinary guy underneath. Ring me up some time. Just ask for Humble Lee. Come and see me. Any time. Look, here's my card. Come and see me in my seventeen-bedroomed seaside bungalow. Just ask for Humble Lee, that's me!'

"He pulled himself to his feet, bid me a civil but alcoholic good night, and rolled away and I saw him no more during my stay. But having met him under such extraordinary circumstances, it was not possible easily to forget him. I finished my drink and took myself off to bed. I left the next day.

"A couple of years later—it was somewhere in the late 'twenties—I came through Singapore again. I still had the gilt-edged card he had given me and almost as soon as my ship docked I set about the business of finding out all I could about my odd little friend. My task was not a difficult one. Peter, the barman at the *Europe*, gave me most of the information I wanted.

"It appeared that P. H. Lee—for that was his name—had been a more than usually successful dealer in rubber. His company had grown, was trusted and respected, and the wealth of Mr. Lee had grown as the company had expanded. Then three years ago P. H. Lee had been told his fortune—I never knew by whom, but the man, at any rate, must have been a most forceful personality—and the effect upon P. H. Lee had been both immediate and unusual. A man who had previously spent almost his every waking hour at his business suddenly ceased to attend his office more than once a week. Each task that he himself had previously performed was delegated to his lieutenants. He ceased to take any interest whatever in his business and left its entire management in other hands. And that, for a Chinese, was most peculiar.

"It appeared that the fortune-teller had foretold that Humble Lee would live a life of quite unusual prosperity on one condition and on one condition only: that he should at once start building and never for a moment stop! It mattered not, apparently, what was built nor where or how it was built—the essential point was that the simple process of laying one brick upon another should be rigorously continuous. Come boom, come slump, the massive piles must rise remorselessly!

"Our towkay consulted his architect that same night, and the work to which he was to dedicate the rest of his life began the following day. First he built a gigantic palace of a place that stood upon several acres of valuable seaside land. It was this house that had been finished the day I first met him in the bar of the *Europe*, and it was its completion that he had been celebrating. This was the seventeen-bedroomed bungalow to which he had invited me.

"Having gleaned all this from Peter, I set about finding P. H. Lee. Although I had not seen him for two years, and then only for one brief period, I knew that I would have no difficulty in remembering his face. Whether he would remember me was a different matter. Peter told me that his bungalow was on the East Coast Road, so I took a taxi out beyond Katong. And there, sure enough, I found it.

"The view from any of the windows of the seventeen bed-rooms was clearly peerless; the great lawns were impeccable and the stone lions that flanked the long drive had obviously been regularly scrubbed. The house itself was predominantly green in colour, with green tiles on its many sloping roofs, and was built in what, for those days, was an exceptionally modern manner with a liberal provision of cantilevered terraces. But there was a strange air of desertion about it and I could see no sign whatever of occupation.

"I paid off the taxi and walked up the concrete driveway. As I approached the ornate teak front door, half hidden behind a screen of wrought bronze, a pleasant-faced boy came out to meet me. He was neatly dressed in white trousers and a high-buttoning white coat, and he greeted me civilly enough.

" 'Good afternoon, Tuan.'

" 'Good afternoon. Is Mr. Lee in?'

" 'No. He no come here, now. But please come in.'

"I went inside, into the great unlived-in house that echoed emptily to my footsteps. It was furnished almost entirely in artificial leather and chromium. Doubtless conforming to Humble Lee's conception of comfort, style and modernity, the room into which I was shown resembled nothing so much as the saloon bar of a recently opened roadhouse on the Great West Road.

"I questioned the boy—who appeared perfectly prepared for me to stay for a week if I chose—and he told me that the only occupants of the house, apart from the standing army of ser-vants, gardeners and watchmen, were occasional individuals who had happened to meet the owner when in an expansive, generous and possibly mellow mood.

"As the boy talked in his almost perfect English, I could see Humble Lee again as I had encountered him two years ago. To those who knew him he was doubtless a joke; but he must have invited many to his house who knew him not at all. They would take this friendly, rotund, vulnerable, ridiculous little man seriously and turn up expectantly at 'Ocean View,' only to find Ah Kee, the boy, to welcome them instead of their genial acquaintance, who, at that time, under the secure protection of his own astonishing star, would be engaged in a further fantastic building project. Some would go away in a huff. Others, more sensible, would take what the immaculate Ah Kee offered them and spend a delightful and luxurious week-end entirely at the expense of someone they scarcely knew.

"I neither stayed nor went away in a huff, but returned to my hotel where I quickly became immersed in matters of business. I was unable to find another opportunity of calling on my odd little friend before I left, and until I again returned to Singapore I almost forgot his existence.

"It was something like three years before I returned, but this time I spent six months in the Colony attached temporarily to our Singapore office. It was during this period that I really came to know P. H. Lee.

"During the first three years Humble Lee built four houses, each one a little larger, a little more hideous and very much emptier than the one before. In the course of their construction he formed the opinion that builders as a race worked both too quickly and too well, since had they not worked with such a will the previous house might, mercifully, still have been under construction, and had they not worked so well he could, conceivably, have been already building upon the ruins of the first. The continual acquisition of more land, by the time the fourth house was completed, was one of Humble Lee's more urgent problems, a problem that sent him on a quest for the design of a totally unfinishable house—unfinishable, that is, in his lifetime, even if he lived to be a hundred. He soon found what he thought to be the answer, and during my more than usually lengthy stay in Singapore the fabulous project got under way.

"He had purchased a large, hilly plot of land far away from town and off the main road beyond Bukit Timah Village. The plot consisted, in fact, of one large rounded, tree-covered hill which rose perhaps one hundred and fifty feet above the surrounding ground. On the very pinnacle of this hill Humble Lee erected a comparatively simple house in which, as soon as it was habitable, he took up residence. It was fashioned in the Chinese style with delicately curved roofs and with a little half-covered courtyard in the centre, and from this most becoming point of vantage Humble Lee devoted himself entirely to the supervision of the army of workmen who toiled daily at the lower levels. I quickly learnt of this, his latest venture, and as soon as I had settled down to a routine of work I went to call on him. From the foot of the hill a concrete road had been laid through the appalling confusion of builders, coolies, cement mixers, tractors, lorries and mountains of bricks and bags of cement, to Humble Lee's eyrie. I found him at home, as I knew I should, seated at a small blackwood table on which was spread a prodigious pile of plans and drawings. I do not think he remembered me—although he affected to—but once I had introduced myself and described the occasion of our only previous meeting, he seemed genuinely pleased to see me. He gave me a chair and asked the servant to bring Chinese tea. In the intervening years he had not changed a scrap. He was still a round little ball of a man, good-natured and hospitable, and his face still the smooth moon I remembered so well. And that afternoon he told me the whole story.

"It appeared that the fortune-teller had gone rather further than I had previously understood. Not only had he said that Humble Lee would live to a great age and remain prosperous if he spent the remainder of his life engaged in the continuous erection of buildings; he had also prophesied that if Humble Lee once stopped building, if only for so much as half a day, then he would certainly die almost immediately, a financially ruined man. I grasped now far more clearly the most compelling motive behind my friend's eccentric behaviour. He told me that although he had scarcely been near his office for several years, those he had put in charge of his extensive business had proved completely reliable and had, indeed, accomplished for their ab-sentee employer a more than considerable expansion of business. It was well known in local commercial circles that Humble Lee could not go wrong; what his company did today, its competitors did tomorrow.

"He then told me of his plans for his present building project. On all sides of the hill leading up to his own solitary eminence he was going to build caves, statues, animals, trees, birds and fishes. He was going to illustrate in concrete and plaster the Chinese classics as well as contemporary Chinese life. He was going to have models, in fact, of everything that came into his head. Although he obviously looked forward to seeing the sides of his hill sprouting their curious adornment it was my impres-sion that his chief satisfaction lay in the belief that he had found something that would exercise his constructional ingenuity in-definitely. He liked his little unassuming house, and enjoyed pottering about among the concrete mixers. As far as he was concerned, he was set for life.

"During my stay in Singapore I went out to see him several times and always found him at the inevitable blackwood table at which we always drank the inevitable Chinese tea. Each time I called, the work of covering every square inch of the hillside had progressed a little farther. First of all he lined the road leading up to his house with trees. They were not, I should point out, ordinary trees, but trees whose trunks were reinforced plaster painted brown and whose leaves were delicately wrought metal, painted green. To the workmen and craftsmen who fashioned them, they were works of art; to the passer-by who did not come too close, they appeared sufficiently realistic to pass as the real thing; and to Humble Lee, they were the joy of his existence.

" 'Look,' he said to me, 'just look! Good, eh? See! just like real trees. Better! Better than real trees! They don't make a mess when their leaves fall. Just a coat of paint and they are new. Very clever! You like them?'

"It was then that I first began to notice in Humble Lee a some-what unnatural enthusiasm for his task. Before, I had known a man who had believed implicitly in his horoscope and had acted accordingly. As things had turned out, he had acted quite rightly. At first he had shouldered his burden of building with a slight air of fatalism, resigning himself, not altogether unhappily, to the inevitable. Then the process of building, igniting in his mind a spark of interest, had become a hobby, and Humble Lee had clearly enjoyed his hobby. Now, with the ridiculous trees, it was becoming much more than a hobby, almost, it seemed, an obsession. But the next time I saw him he seemed quite normal and I rather forgot my earlier disquiet.

"Again I left Singapore and returned to Shanghai, and by the time I next passed through it was clear that war was approaching in Europe. Here, in the Far East, Japan was already on the march. I think I stayed for a week, it may have been a little longer, but it was a period in my life that I wish never to live again.

"As had become my habit, after settling into my hotel I motored out to Monkey's Hill, as it was called, to see Humble Lee. It was a Sunday afternoon and I thought that little work would be in progress. On arrival at the ornate entrance to the drive, I was met with a most extraordinary scene. Around the entrance were clustered ice-cream vendors, food stalls, soft-drink merchants and the usual roadside haberdashers. Humble Lee's little residence was still perched on its eminence, but now entirely surrounded by gigantic slopes of stone and plaster work. And over the entire hill trudged and clambered numberless Chinese in holiday mood.

"I parked the car with some difficulty in the overflowing car park provided, and walked up the long hill to the house through a scene of the most incredible complexity and animation. The sides of the hill had become veritable cliffs of coloured concrete cut into ledges and criss-crossed with winding steps and steep pathways. The ledges bore red, blue, black and yellow effigies of every character that ever besmirched the honourable annals of China. Women were shown being flung naked and screaming into cauldrons of bubbling, boiling oil, and whole tracts of tunnelled concrete were set aside as subterranean chambers of horrors. Men were depicted in the process of disembowelment, their red and bleeding entrails festooning on to the floor, and bloody, decapitated heads rolled in splendid profusion. Striding over the incredible, almost endless vista, were gigantic lizards with human heads and misbegotten humans with crocodile heads. Other obscene creatures, half animal, half human, were shown locked together in orgiastic dances. Every animal known to man was shown in most unnatural aspects: toads with great misshapen feet, bloated snakes in the act of swallowing goats and sheep, dragons of fantastic length coiling and squirming from chamber to chamber. Wolves leapt out of the concrete with splintering spears thrust through their gushing stomachs, and huge, green crabs with human heads fed obscenely on human remains. Running through this appalling accretion of nightmare statuary were the twin accents of cruelty and the admixture of the human with the animal. Just below the summit of the hill was a depiction in the grand manner of the mass execution that took place in China after the Taiping rebellion when Tung Wang, the Eastern King, was beheaded with twenty thousand of his men. There were two hundred executioners and that made one hundred heads apiece. For every ten heads they received extra pay of one ounce of silver, and not one unbeheaded body was left of the twenty thousand and their king. It was a day of carnage such as even China had rarely known and Humble Lee's artist and designers had done full justice to the scene.

"As I entered the little red-painted gate that gave entry on to Humble Lee's terrace I knew that something was wrong. The blackwood table was still there but it was empty, and an atmosphere of neglect had settled on the usually neat and spotlessly clean house. Whenever I had called before I had found it in apple-pie order, with nothing out of place: now it was unkempt and dirty, the home of a man who no longer cared.

" 'Lee!' I called.

"There was no answer.

" 'Lee!' I called again, louder.

"This time there was an answering shuffle from within the house and a man I scarcely recognised came to the door. He was thin, almost emaciated, and the soft smoothness of his face had been replaced by a sallow expanse of fine wrinkles. For a moment he appeared not to recognise me, and then, fleetingly, there appeared on his lips a hesitant shadow of his old, warm, friendly smile.

" 'Hello, Lee,' I said.

" 'Hello,' he answered in a low, slightly tremulous voice.

"He made no move to suggest that I might come in; neither, I fancied, did he want me to go away. We simply stood and looked at one another, I with mounting uneasiness and he with no visible reaction at all.

" 'Are you ill?' I asked, when I felt I could no longer delay the necessity of saying something. 'Is there anything I can do for you?'

" 'Yes,' he answered after a long, long pause, 'I am ill. But there is nothing you can do for me.'

"Just then he swayed forward as if he was going to fall. I sprang forward to save him and found myself standing with Humble Lee in my arms. He seemed to have no strength left and leaned his whole, but by now insignificant, weight upon me.

" 'Take me inside,' he said.

"I led him as best I could into his house. He was able to walk with slow, shuffling steps and at last I got him to a chair, into which he flopped exhausted.

" 'I knew you would come,' he said. 'I knew you would come before the end.'

" 'What on earth is the matter, old chap? You must get some-one to look after you. You've been doing too much. Can't you leave here for a few days?'

"He shook his head, and at once fell into a fitful sleep. I looked about the filthy little room. Clothes, builder's debris, plans, books, drawings, eating and cooking utensils were strewn in con-fusion, simply dropped where they had last been used. Over everything lay a film of dust. Curtains, chair covers and rugs were alike filthy and greasy. Clearly no effort had been made to clean the room for months.

" 'Did you see the monkey?' asked Humble Lee, so suddenly as to make me jump. 'Did you see it?'

" 'No, I saw many things, but I did not see the monkey!'

"Humble Lee giggled quite suddenly, and then sat as quiet and expressionless as before.

"For the first time that day I began to feel afraid.

" 'Look out of the back window,' he said. 'Go on, look!'

"I walked over to the window which faced the front door and which looked down the slope of the hill on the opposite side to the drive. It was just the same, a great sloping expanse of coloured concrete, populated with hundreds of outrageous figures. But there was one difference. Towering above all else was a gigantic monkey. It must have been a good thirty-five feet high, with a great grinning ape's head looking directly towards the house. Someone had painted it in a most realistic manner so that behind the sharpened white teeth could be seen the cavernous red mouth. Its great arms were raised above its head as though it were about to grasp a branch that was not there.

"I gasped, not so much as a result of my first sight of the monkey alone, but because, I think, it was the last straw, the final horror in acres of horrors. Quite clearly my old friend Humble Lee was mad. I stared for a moment at the great brute, at its muscles standing out in relief from the stone anatomy, and then was called back to the problem of the moment by another sniggering giggle from the old man in the chair.

" 'Do you see anything odd about it?' he asked.

" 'No, what?'

" 'Look again, look very carefully.'

"Again I heard the foolish, irritating giggle. I turned back to the great beast. Apart from its ridiculous size and the patent fact that it was made of painted stone and plaster, I could see nothing that appeared different from the real thing.

" 'Look at the hands,' suggested Humble Lee.

"I saw that, in spite of the great bulk, the enormous height and the undoubted fact that it probably weighed several dozen tons, the hands were delicate and shapely. They were also curiously paler and had no painted hair upon them. Then I realised that the hands raised to the heavens to grasp the invisible branch were human hands.

" 'Come away! Come away!'

"It was Humble Lee shrieking the words. I spun round and found him staggering to his feet.

" 'Come away. Get away from the window.'

"I moved swiftly across the room to where he was standing, gesticulating wildly. I grasped him under the arms and shouted:
" 'Stop it. Stop it, do you hear? Stop it at once.'

"It was like dealing with a hysterical woman. I had acted instinctively, not pausing to think, and I believe I shook him as one would shake a bawling child. Gradually the fear and the sudden energy passed from him and his body grew limp in my grasp. I lowered him gently to the chair, where he sat with his head thrown back, sucking in each breath as though it were his last.

"I crossed over to the window and looked again at the hideous ape. To see that dreadful grinning countenance every time one looked out of one's window was enough to make any man demented. From the lower slopes of the hill came the chip, chip, chip of the stonemasons' hammers and the steady drone of the holiday crowds as they slipped and clambered over the bright concrete. The sun was reddening and lowering in the western sky, and the shadow of the ape was lengthening, creeping towards the house of Humble Lee. Inside the house there was no sound except the regular, sucking breath of the owner.

" 'Have you any drink in the house?' I asked.
"He shook his head.
" 'Are you getting any proper food?'
"Again he shook his head.
" 'You know, you can't stay here tonight. You're sick. Let me take you into town and I'll get a doctor to look at you.'
" 'No! No! Leave me here! I'll be all right in a little while.'
"His voice was almost a whisper.

"I went into the filthy little kitchen and looked around for some cups. After a good deal of hunting I found an old saucepan and started to boil some water. Further exploration under the piles of unwashed debris revealed a packet of tea. Trying to boil water in a saucepan over an electric hot-plate is a lengthy business, and by the time I returned with the two cups containing a somewhat indifferent brew, Humble Lee appeared to be asleep. I shook his arm and he opened his tired eyes and even smiled. He took the cup gratefully.

" 'Now, then,' I said, after a moment's pause, 'tell me all

about it. Tell me what is wrong. Maybe I can help you.'

"He smiled again. 'No. You can't help me. Nothing can help me now. It is simply a question of time.'

" 'What is just a question of time?' I demanded impatiently.

"He looked at me for a moment.

" 'My death,' he said.

" 'You're being melodramatic, Lee. What do you mean?'

"There was a long pause and he put his hands to his face. Then he drew aside his fingers so that he could look at me between them.

" 'I stopped building,' he said slowly.

" 'Oh rubbish! No one believes your silly old tale except yourself. You're driving yourself crazy for nothing. Look, let me take you away from here. Right away. You've been surrounded by this dreadful concrete so long its sending you . . .'

"I stopped myself and did not finish the sentence. I could see the half-mad, half-terror-stricken expression returning to his face. Then again it subsided.

"Over the next half-hour he told me what had happened. One day, it seemed, when he had been out inspecting the work in progress, he had slipped on some wet concrete and rolled half-way down his hillside. When they picked him up he was unconscious and he had stayed that way for almost two weeks. By a miracle he had broken no bones, but he had received a terrible blow on his head that had all but killed him. According to his doctor there was absolutely no reason why he had not died—the wound in anyone else would certainly have been fatal. But to the consternation of his doctor, Humble Lee survived. He had been terribly concussed and there was no longer any question in my mind, that although the injury may not have killed him, it had quite certainly affected his brain.

"It had been, as far as I could gather, a combination of circumstances. In the first place he himself was away; in the second, his foreman, too, was ill; in the third, it was one of Singapore's numerous public holidays; and to cap everything it rained the whole day. Those workers that had turned up went home at midday, and the customary eight hours' work between eight a.m. and five p.m. had not been performed, as the fortune-teller,

I learnt, had said it should. The fortune-teller had been quite definite on this point, and the routine of several years had therefore been destroyed.

"After the discovery of this dereliction of duty Humble Lee had almost killed his foreman and had sacked every worker involved—but not before he had hired a fresh batch and put them to work with redoubled fury. And then it was that Humble Lee began to be afraid of the great ape he had created. The hour of his greatest fear was each evening, when its shadow fell across his window. As he told me this the room grew slowly darker.

" 'It's here,' he said.

"Again I crossed to the window and looked out. What I saw chilled me to the marrow of my bones. The ape stood stark against the red sky, outlined in dead black silhouette, the angry flames of the dying sun playing round the roughened plaster and concrete that in brighter light resembled the hairy coat. And most terrifying of all were the hands, the disproportionately small hands, the smooth, deformed, hairless hands, black against the livid, cloud-shot sky. I shuddered and as I watched it seemed, almost, as though the hands moved.

"As I turned away from the dreadful sight, Humble Lee screamed. He was back against the far wall, his bloodshot eyes almost starting from his head. He appeared to be struggling with something I could not see, something that was forcing back his head, something that was preventing him from breathing. He could not scream again, but simply grunted like a pinned wrestler.

" 'Get out,' I shouted. 'Get out, for Christ's sake, get out.'

"I sprinted over the darkened room and made to lift him bodily from the ground. I got one arm round his legs and the other round his middle. His body was rigid, rigid like a poker. I heaved and threw myself toward the door. But Humble Lee's body was fixed to the spot on which it stood. I pulled like a madman, but something far stronger than me was holding it there, tortured and immovable. At last I let go and rushed to the door and on to the terrace and yelled for help. Voices answered from below, and when I was certain help was on the way I ran back into the house, shouting at the top of my voice to give myself false courage.

"I found the body of Humble Lee slumped in an untidy heap on the floor. Kneeling down, I felt for his pulse in the skinny wrist. Then I put my hand to his open mouth. There was no life left in Humble Lee.

"Later that night, after the ambulance had been and after I had returned to the hotel and had a meal, I telephoned the hospital to see what they could tell me. I spoke to the house surgeon who said that their examination of the body showed quite plainly that Humble Lee had been strangled.

"I had endless interviews with the police. If you were to inspect their files you would probably find that the case—it became quite a case—is still open, filed and forgotten perhaps, but still unsolved. By then, of course, I believed implicitly in the power of fortune-tellers and it came as no surprise to me when, a week after his death, Humble Lee's great business foundered and died mysteriously, even as its creator had died."

September 29th, 1954

Huggins has been astonishing me with some tales out of school. He teaches English in a Singapore school, and claims that a fair proportion of his Chinese pupils are Communist sympathisers. When the Cathay Pacific airliner was shot down off Hainan, their immediate comment was to ask what the airliner was doing there. It would not have happened, they felt, if it had not been flying so close to China or Chinese territory; therefore, why did it not keep clear? The barbarity of the crime did not, it seems, occur to them.

Whenever he talks to his class about British achievement in Malaya or Singapore, a necessary aspect of the history lesson, supercilious smiles will develop on the faces of certain boys. And if he stops to question them they will trot out claptrap about Colonial exploitation and the down-trodden proletariat.

The interesting point of this, however, is that it is simply another instance—and they are legion—of an identification of Communism with Chinese Nationalism in the minds of many

young Chinese in South-east Asia. China has gained in the last
four years an immense prestige among young Chinese. She has
emerged as a power to be reckoned with, and they will support
that power whatever the political system that brought about the
change. Young Chinese, quite naturally, are pro-Chinese. Because
they are pro-Chinese they are, almost of necessity, pro-Com-
munist. I do not know which of these two aspects of the same
problem bodes least good for Malaya. As one of Huggins's pupils
said to him the other day: "Why should we worry if the Communists come here? They are our own people, they are Chinese
—why should they harm us?"

September 30th, 1954

Dinner at the Tanglin Club. The company was most representative: a judge, a doctor, a foreign correspondent, a social worker
and a government servant. The conversation was as good as any
to be found at a Singapore dinner-table. The food was excellent.
And yet, on the only two occasions I have crossed the threshold
of the Tanglin Club, I have been unable to avoid a sense of em-
barrassment. Perhaps it is merely conceit to wonder why the
numerous members of the club are not also similarly troubled.
Yet, I am, nevertheless, astonished that so many Europeans are
able to enjoy themselves in the Tanglin Club, so often and with
such an absence of inhibitions.

If they find that the decoration of the barn-like structure is, in
fact, pleasant to the eye, I have no wish to cross swords with
them. If they find the music of the village-hall dance-band sooth-
ing to the ear, then again I am content that they should enjoy
the pleasure it so clearly gives to them. The point that I fail to
see, however, is the need for a club, in the twentieth century, in
Singapore of all places, that considers, when a new member is
put up for admittance, not whether he is decent or indecent, nor
whether he is honest or a crook, nor whether he is English or
foreign, but whether or not he is white. I find it extraordinary
that anyone should worry about the colour of a man's skin. It
seems to me to be as sensible to form a club of those who have
blue eyes or bow legs.

If, of course, one produces this argument in Singapore, one is told that it is perfectly natural to wish for the society of one's own people. Is it? I know so many Europeans for whose society I do not wish in the slightest degree. One is also told that the Chinese have their exclusive clubs and that so do the Indians, and that it is therefore unfair to pick on the European clubs. My answer to this is that the Chinese and the Indians, in forming their exclusive clubs, are just as stupid as we are. Simply pointing at similar institutions does not make any one of them any more desirable.

I feel that the Tanglin Club, and all the other racially exclusive clubs—as, for example, the Chinese Swimming Club—are outcrops of communalism and that someone, surely, must deplore them. If Singapore is to survive as a cosmopolitan city, and if the Federation is to survive as an independent entity, then this communalism must first be killed. People may not like this, but it is one of the prices of survival.

That is why I dislike the Tanglin Club. I do not dislike its members—many of them are my friends. I, too, am able to enjoy myself more among Englishmen than among men of other races. But the few activities that take place in Singapore based on the colour of a man's skin, the better it will be for all of us. We are no more guilty of them than the Chinese; they, if anything, are more guilty. But we, at least, if we are to believe in the policy of our own government, should know better.

October 1st, 1954

I began this book by stating the position of many Malayans in relation to Communism. I tried to show that we had become so sickened with brutality that we no longer held the slightest brief for either the creed or its followers, that we recognised only the presence of sadistic killers in the Malayan jungle and that there was nothing to do with such people except to shoot them before they shot us.

When we saw our papers this morning, we read of one of the most bestial crimes ever committed. I do not know to what extent the incident was reported in the press overseas, but I do not suppose it received any more prominence than any other item of Malayan news. But I want the world to know of this crime: the fact that the world will never know of it, or, if it does, will almost certainly forget it, is as great a tragedy as the crime itself. Here, in harsh detail, is the essence of Communism. Here, in bold relief, is the core of the evil that is Communism. Here is not the economic theory nor the social philosophy nor the political system, but simply the men who form the ranks of Communism, the men who earn the approbation of Moscow and Peking, the men who would rule Malaya and shape the destiny of its people. Here are the men we must fight, from one end of the world to the other, if we are to survive as human beings. I quote verbatim from the *Straits Times* of today's date. The passage will repay some study.

"Terrorists exacted a hideous revenge yesterday against a village councillor, Mr. Yap Poh Kok, by slashing his fifteen-year-old son's head off with a parang. Another son, aged eleven, gave the *Straits Times* an eye-witness account of the murder.

"The bandit's revenge was complete in Chinese eyes, for by killing his son, the bandits struck even more deeply at Mr. Yap than they would have done if they had murdered him instead.

"A terrorist produced a Communist 'black-book' and crossed out Mr. Yap's name. Then he gave a casual order for the brutal murder of the son, Yap Boon Hoi, two miles from the Selangor-Negri Sembilan border town of Sepang.

"Yap Boon Hoi's younger brother and two friends watched in horror as two other terrorists seized the boy and bound his wrists behind his back.

"The boy's frantic screams for mercy were cut short as one of the killers slashed eight times at his throat with a parang until his head dangled by a thread of flesh.

"Before the laughing terrorists left the murder scene one of them kicked at the boy's lifeless body.

"'This was a ghastly, brutal and senseless murder which has incensed the people of Sepang,' an official spokesman said today. 'The boy had never given information to the police or helped them in any way. He was not even known to the police. This outrage against an innocent lad is a typical example of the ferocious, sadistic and merciless tactics of the terrorists.'

"When the *Straits Times* reporter visited Sepang new village today, he found a sad-eyed little boy who had seemingly aged far beyond his eleven years.

"While his widower father and three remaining brothers and sisters stood with him in the yard of their tiny house, Yap Eng Kim gave an eye-witness account of his brother's murder.

"With an expressionless face and speaking with his voice barely above a whisper he told how he, his brother and two friends were gathering firewood at about 11 a.m. when three armed terrorists appeared.

"Yap Eng Kim recognised one of them as Lim Kim, an ex-Sepang villager who entered the jungle three years ago and hated Yap's father because he was a councillor. Lim asked Yap Boon Hoi where his father and eldest brother were.

"The boy replied that they were both at home in the village, whereupon Lim accused him of being an informer.

" 'It is false,' denied the boy, bursting into tears.

"Ignoring his pleas for mercy the terrorists tied the boy's wrists together and told him they were going to kill him with the words: 'Your father's name is on our wanted list. That is enough for us.'

"While Lim stood to one side and crossed Yap Poh Kok's name from his revenge list, which included photographs of intended victims, one of his accomplices grabbed the boy's hair and forced his head back to expose his neck to the third terrorist, who hacked viciously with his parang until he had almost severed the boy's head.

"Then the killers left, warning Yap Eng Kim and the two other boys not to move until they were out of sight.

"A vigorous follow-up operation has been mounted against the gang, who are believed to form part of the strong 3rd Independent Platoon operating in the area."

What price co-existence now?

October 8th, 1954

It is a business trip and no time can be wasted. It is a journey by road I have made many times before but which never loses any part of its attraction—Singapore, Kuala Lumpur, Ipoh, Penang, Ipoh, Kuala Lumpur, Singapore—a round trip of a thousand miles accomplished in four, roughly equal, daily instalments. Cho, our salesman, is coming with me, but I shall leave him in Kuala Lumpur and pick him up again on the way back.

He arrives at the house at seven o'clock and we are ready to go. As the Jaguar XK120 pulls out of Holland Road and into the Bukit Timah Road—the main road north which, if you follow it for long enough, through, in its later stages, river-beds and landslides will lead you eventually to Bangkok—it is raining slightly. But it is insufficient to warrant our putting up the hood, and if we do not actually stop, most of it flies over the top into the spray cloud that will follow us until the roads are dry.

At seven o'clock on a wet morning in Singapore it can be cold enough to make you wish you were wearing a jacket. The sky is a sheet of grey, the sort of sky that will often clear by nine o'clock so that you wish it were still covered by its wet, weeping blanket of cloud. At seven o'clock, too, the Bukit Timah Road is full of lorries, lorries going north to the Federation and lorries carrying workers to the factories that are still springing up all the way to Johore Bahru. During the last year a good deal of this road has been converted into a dual carriageway. We can now reach the Causeway in about five minutes' less time than previously, but it is still a slow business weaving in and out of the strings of lorries.

We leave Bukit Timah Hill on our left. Bukit Timah Hill has a flat top where prisoners-of-war spent months levelling the summit to receive a Japanese war memorial. After the war the memorial was blown up with high explosive. All that remains now is a wide avenue leading to the top which is used for the Singapore Motor Club Hill Climbing events, and the steps that carry you up the last fifty feet to where the memorial used to be. I think perhaps it would have been better to have left the memorial where the Japanese put it, since a memorial which reminds us of our defeats can be no less useful than one which commemorates our victories. On the right, high above the granite quarry, the wet, tangled trees of Singapore's only remaining piece of jungle stand tightly packed under the low, drab sky. Most of Malaya is still like that small area: hills standing in high ranges, hills merging into other hills, hills rising precipitately from the plains and sweeping down to the sea again, and all of them covered in the deep, green mantle of the endless Malayan forest, bursting upwards in a million explosions of tight foliage.

Now we see the Straits of Johore over the mangrove on the left, beyond the single-track railway which also ends in Bangkok. The surface of the sea is flat and grey, like a dusty mirror, its surface cracked by a distant police launch. The engine noise of the car ricochets unevenly from the drawn-up queue of lorries, British lorries with local bodies, all loaded to within an inch of the regulation height. There must be almost a hundred of them, and the first fifty have probably been there all night, their drivers sleeping under their tarpaulins, in order to obtain an advantageous position in the queue. The reason for the queue is the Customs inspection at Johore Bahru which the lorry-drivers have to undergo before they can enter Malaya. Here they even go to the length—or did until the other day—of taxing joss-sticks to pay for the war that is still called an Emergency. We from Singapore, secure in our supposedly inviolable tradition of free trade, look with undisguised superiority upon the Federation's petty taxes. Travelling from Singapore to the Federation is like moving from some twentieth-century Utopia to mediæval China, where a man had to pay tax before he could move from A to B. But the Federation *has* to raise the money, and taxing toothbrushes, exercise-books and potted plants is one way of raising it. Meanwhile, someone has to pay for the fleets of patient, idle lorries.

The police at the Singapore end of the Causeway do not stop us, but we know we shall have to stop at the other side. The Causeway is a narrow road, set down on rocks in the sea, bounded on the left by a low wall and on the right by the railway track and an enormous pipe bringing much of Singapore's water supply down from the hills of Johore. At one time there was a good view to the right, along to the Naval Base, but now, unless you climb on to the top of your car, you can see nothing but pipe.

I should not care to be a Customs officer in any country, since everyone to whom he speaks must resent him. "Anything to declare?" he asks. And although you answer in the negative, he still wants to search your luggage. Not only does he pry into your private effects, but he does not appear to believe you when you say, in effect, that you are not carrying diamonds, guns or opium. It becomes intensely difficult to remain patient, especially if he finds in your luggage a bulging file of book jackets. Book jackets, I have found, if carried in sufficient numbers, will throw the most experienced Customs service into instant confusion. They cannot understand why any person should want to carry with him several book jackets. And you can see the questions running in succession through their thick and puzzled heads: subversive? Communist? obscene? In the end they give up and let you go.

We drive slowly through the narrow streets of Johore Bahru, which is situated at the very tip of Malaya. It is a pleasant little town, running along the edge of the placid Straits, dominated by the Johore State office, practically the only building in the whole of Malaya which seems successfully to combine the virtues of Eastern and Western styles of architecture. It is impossible to describe it except as a subtle, yet massive, mixture of the Taj Mahal and the Shell Mex building on the London Embankment. The Sultan of Johore, on the rare occasions when he is in Johore, lives in Johore Bahru's other effective building, Bukit Serene, a vaguely Spanish house, and yet not Spanish, with a green tiled roof. We pass it on the right, on the outskirts of Johore Bahru, standing majestically on its eminence, looking down the sweeping green slope to the sea.

It is then that the long, gruelling drive to Segamat begins. Johore is perhaps the dullest state in the Federation. Its scenery is unspectacular, consisting of little but undulating forest, rubber, pineapples and oil palms. The road, which, as roads go, is not a bad road, winds among the plantations for a hundred miles and more. Segamat is the first place of any size you come to, and that is only a big village. There are smaller villages every five miles or so, which are now enclosed in barbed-wire fences, at whose entrances and exits are road blocks guarded by armed policemen.

A great many people in Malaya live behind barbed-wire fences. They need permission to go outside the fence, and any-one wishing to go inside is required to give a fairly convincing demonstration of the fact that he is not a Communist. In par-ticular, the movement of food is prohibited without a special licence, since one of the most effective ways of beating the bandits is to deny them the food which at one time they collected, and still to some extent collect, under pain of death, from the vil-lagers. It might seem odd that anyone should starve in the Malayan jungle, an area where vegetable growth is more spec-tacular than, perhaps, anywhere else on earth, but it is so. The jungle does not grow the kind of food men need to stay alive and fit.

When we pass through Ayer Hitam, a village some sixty miles from Johore Bahru, the sky begins slowly to clear. Our average, which we check every fifteen minutes, is below forty miles per hour, for we have wasted too much time at the Customs shed. As the sky clears the air becomes warmer, and as the air becomes warmer the cockpit grows hotter. Every time we work up to a decent speed we have to drop right down to thirty for a sharp bend where the road probably still follows an old estate track, or where it has gone all the way round a water-course, because, when it was first built, it was cheaper to go that way than to build a bridge. Now they have bulldozers all over Malaya carv-ing arrow-straight new roads through the jungle and over the ruins of the old. In the long run it is perhaps worth the millions of dollars that are being spent for traffic to be able to move faster and more smoothly. But for the present I cannot help thinking that schools, hospitals, health services and housing are more im-portant. In what way is a country helped if, when it shows the foreigner its beautiful roads, most of the people who use them still live in slums?

Then we are in Yong Peng. If you drive through Malaya it is like driving through a history of Emergency. Yong Peng was at one time a notorious bandit area. Now it is safe to walk about again without expecting a bullet in the small of your back. Templer was responsible for the cleaning up that took place around Yong Peng, and if, in the process, he put the villagers to considerable inconvenience, I do not think that they all objected. The people of Malaya are like drug addicts. They can only rid themselves of the monkey on their back if they themselves will help. Most of the time they are too ignorant or too frightened to help. Sometimes they have not the will-power to resist what, for the moment, is stronger than they are. Eventually, either they are killed, or someone like Templer comes along and rids them of their killers. Then they are, I think, in most cases, thankful. But if only they had shown in the beginning some elementary sense of solidarity as Malayans, a thing which, more than any other quality, Malayans lack, the task would have been so much simpler.

Yong Peng consists of little more than a single street with dilapidated "shop-houses" on both sides, although some new ones have been built in the last few years. It is a grim little scab of semi-slum in the midst of the rubber, and there must be something wrong with a country when these tiny spots of squalor spread like a rash across its face. It is not *all* the fault of capitalism and colonialism and exploitation as some would have us believe. It is caused equally by profits and wages being remitted over decades to China and India. And if there is one single thing which towers in importance above all else, which an independent government of Malaya must accomplish, and accomplish quickly if it is to survive, it is the prevention of the remittance outside Malaya of money earned in Malaya, until sufficient capital is produced to allow of a margin for overseas investment. Most of the people of Malaya will not like such a ruling. But if they want self-government they must put up with it.

By the time we reach Yong Peng our average has risen to forty-three. Now we begin to move, and for long stretches we are able to put the speedometer to 100 and keep it there. The morning is turning hot and the temperature gauge rises steadily. There is still very little else but rubber.

A peculiar feature of rubber estates is that as you pass them they seem simply to be collections of similar-looking trees. It is only when you look at them from particular directions that you see that the trees have been planted in the neatest possible rows and that it is possible to see between the rows to the other side of the plantation. Through the dark corridors of trees you can see a glimmer of light at the other end. The light comes from the gap between the plantation and the jungle which is ready to creep over the man-made rows the moment man's back is turned. The jungle is like that. It is like a creeping sea, swallowing everything in its path. It is kept at bay by hacking and cutting at its tentacles, burning them, and even poisoning them with chemicals. But whatever is done to stop its growth, nothing succeeds unless repeated indefinitely. The power of the jungle is seen on the old roads that have been abandoned now that new ones have been built, where the thrusting grasses and shrubs have broken up the stones and asphalt as a pneumatic drill would break them. The only difference is that the jungle takes longer and possibly does the job more thoroughly. Everything in Malaya has been wrested from the enveloping power of the jungle, and to the jungle it will all return if man ever loses interest in the fight.

Now we can see our average speed climbing steadily—forty-five, forty-six, forty-seven, forty-seven and a half, forty-eight, forty-nine. Then we are in Segamat just before achieving an average of fifty.

Segamat, again, is little more than a large village. It boasts the first Rest House encountered on the road north from Singapore, and little else. These are splendid institutions, run by government, which provide food and rooms at remarkably cheap rates. For most of the year their rooms are fully booked, but to the Malayan traveller they perform the function of the public-house in England: we can always get a drink and something to eat that is wholesome.

In the old days, when the main Malayan north–south road was almost as dangerous as any other in Malaya, I always parked the car outside the Segamat Rest House facing the opposite direction from that in which I was travelling. I had the idea that if the bandits were sufficiently well organised to have their spies in Segamat looking out for what, in those days, was something of a rarity, a road-using European, and ready to signal their friends in the jungle when he was about to approach their no doubt well-concealed position, there was about one chance in a thousand of fooling them in the matter of direction. Looking back now, those silly ruses seem a waste of time. But four years ago, when my constant fear when travelling was a burst tyre on a deserted road, they made me feel better. Once, near Segamat, I did have a puncture, and the Segamat area, even to this day, is not considered particularly safe. As I wrestled with the intractable hub-cap and wheel-nuts I had the oddest feeling between my shoulder-blades. It is in the back that a Communist strikes by instinct.

Today we do not stop at Segamat. We have passed its modest collection of houses within a minute. The next landmark in the long drive in the sun is Gemas, where we cross the State border and the railway line. For some miles now we have been following the railway line closely, and sometimes on these trips you can see fleetingly one of Malaya's Puffing Billies—a not very robust-looking engine hauling an enormous string of carriages, at an average speed between Singapore and Kuala Lumpur of about twenty miles per hour. To travel in Malaya by train is often more satisfactory than travelling by air, since it is possible to board the train in Singapore in the evening, have a good dinner on board, a drink or two at the bar, and retire to an air-conditioned sleeper for the night, to be woken next morning at seven o'clock to a peaceful breakfast before arriving in Kuala Lumpur at eight. In the old days the traveller would lie apprehensive in his bunk wondering whether he had, after all, picked the wrong day and whether he could expect bullets in his bed at any moment. In those days the bandits took their target practice on passing trains and at least once a week would derail them. Now the trains run unmolested.

When we reach Tampin our average speed since leaving Singapore has risen to fifty-one. We shall be able to hold this average to Kuala Lumpur, but shall not be able to improve upon it. From now on, the road is more difficult. It twists and turns, and the first faint beginnings of Malaya's backbone become visible on our right. This backbone of hills travels right up to the north and exceeds in places seven thousand feet. It is wholly covered in trees and for the most part is impassable. Those in Malaya who travel the hard way, on foot, as troops and bandits, can take several months to cover a few hundred miles of this kind of country. The Communists, in particular, have made some quite remarkable journeys through deep jungle. Today they have a startlingly efficient courier service that covers all of Malaya, and all the couriers' journeys are made without the aid of roads. What endeavour gone to waste!

There is scarcely a cloud in sight. On the horizon ahead there is a group of rising white thunderheads; otherwise the sun burns in an empty sky. It bakes our arms, grown soft in air-conditioned offices in Singapore, and already they have turned a bright red. For a few days we shall have a healthy tan, but before a week has passed we shall be as pallid as ever. Tropical sunburn fades quickly.

Now we are approaching Seremban through a succession of fearsome bends on which we leave far too much of the tread of our tyres. Seremban is a pleasant town, neatly laid out and clean. At one end there is a park and a placid lake; the people who live in Seremban are very proud of their little town. Nothing spectacular ever happens there. Very little occurs that can in any way disturb the peace. It is the capital of Negri Sembilan— although you would not think it possible that it should be the capital of anything—and some of its people find employment in the State offices there. The remainder of the inhabitants derive their wealth for the most part from shops which sell the essentials of life to those in the surrounding countryside.

From Seremban to Kuala Lumpur is thirty-odd miles and by car it takes perhaps forty minutes. Out of Seremban we climb the first steep hill we have met since leaving Singapore, and drop down the other side round a series of hairpin bends. Shortly afterwards we cross the State border and are in Selangor, the capital of which is Kuala Lumpur, the Federal capital.

Kuala Lumpur is the first night stop and the first town we come to which can truly be called a town. Kuala Lumpur is growing, visibly, month by month: more and more new buildings are going up, roads are being widened and every day the traffic in its streets becomes denser. When we switch off the engine outside the Caxton Press it is 11.55. We have taken four hours and fifty-five minutes to cover two hundred and fifty miles, an average of about fifty-one miles per hour.

There are two kinds of European in Malaya : those who know everything and those who do not. The former may usually be assumed to be the more recent arrivals. This evening I dined with members of this former category.

Basically, I think, the Petsons are nice people. I would not accuse them of miserliness, greed, hate or jealousy or, indeed, of any of the more common vices. On the contrary, they are kind, hospitable, upright folk. But their besetting sin is a quite astonishing capacity for believing themselves always in the right. This would not be so distressing if it were possible, instantly and effortlessly, to prove them wrong. But one has been in the East too long to be dogmatic and certain about anything any more, and one's weakly protesting suggestions are swept away in a Petson avalanche of half-assimilated fact. Further, everything they say is a half-truth. A glimmer of the truth has shone before their confident eyes, and upon the evidence of this fitful light which many people cannot even see, they build a whole philosophy, neither wholly right nor wholly wrong, but simply half-baked.

They have lived in Malaya for six months and the whole of that time they have spent in Kuala Lumpur. They have seen little of the country and have scarcely met its people, and yet they know the answer to Malaya's every ill. This evening the argument began over the Chinese students in Singapore who attend certain Chinese schools. The teachers in these schools, if they ever exerted any influence over their students, which is doubtful, have now lost it to Communist agitators. If the students do not wish to register for National Service, which will take up a few hours of their time each week, they seek a solution in public demonstrations which end with their throwing bricks at the police. Then they lock themselves in their school for days on end and defy everyone, including their teachers, their parents, their Governors and the police, to enter. When they are brought before the courts for injuring policemen with bricks, they whine and talk about injustice and issue ridiculous manifestos and hire itinerant Q.C.s to defend their wretched cause. And many of the good people of Singapore throw up their hands in despair and say, "Why in the name of God did these Chinese students and their futile parents and teachers ever leave China? Why, if they want to throw bricks, do they not go and throw them in China? Why, if they think China is such a wonderful place, do they not go there and stay there and leave us in peace?" And as soon as they have said this the citizens of Singapore realise that they have said something which at best only contains an element of truth. But not so the Petsons. They would have the ships commandeered tomorrow to transport all dissatisfied Chinese back to China, without any further delay.

That is how the conversation started. Then, by some devious means which I now forget, it arrived at what they consider to be the essential uselessness of all Chinese.

"You say that when we were running around in woad they had invented printing and gunpowder, that they were cultivated and civilised, that they wrote poetry and painted beautiful pictures. But what have they done with these gifts? Can you name one single accomplishment of the Chinese nation that is less than a thousand years old? They have failed, utterly, to make any material progress whatsoever. And unless you have material progress, other forms of progress are difficult, if not impossible.

"Now, if you want to understand the Chinese in Malaya you have to remember that they want the best of both worlds. They want to remain Chinese, and retain their Chinese loyalty, and cling to the silly, useless culture they are always talking about. At the same time they want everything the West can give them without accepting any of its responsibilities. They want our Western education, our Western technical know-how, our Western ideas and our Western thought. They want our machinery and our superior organisational ability.

"Because of this, you have the situation that exists in Malaya today. This situation can be summed up in these words: The Chinese want everything we have to give and they want it for nothing. They want the peace and prosperity of Malaya without becoming Malayans; they want the freedom of Malaya without ceasing to support the Communists; they want to defeat the Communists in Malaya without lifting a finger to help; they want the help of the British against Communism and yet will not cease to owe their allegiance to China—and so on, inconsistency rampant, fence-sitting *par excellence.*

"Just look at the Chinese! What can you do with a people that claims an ancient cultural heritage and cannot even build a bicycle properly? Look at their customs! Look at the old women you see hobbling on their tiny, cruelly deformed feet, who, when they were young girls, suffered almost unendurable agonies, while not a single Chinese male who demanded this pain was prepared to take time out to invent an aspirin!"

And so we went on—or so Mrs. Petson went on. So much of what she said contains the element of truth that makes refutation so much more difficult than if she were wholly and clearly wrong. But I liked her remark about aspirins, all the same.

October 9th, 1954

I left Cho in Kuala Lumpur after lunch today and set out for Penang. It was raining before I reached the outskirts of Kuala Lumpur and the canvas hood leaked as all canvas hoods do. The sky was black with grotesquely burdened rain clouds.

As soon as it leaves Kuala Lumpur the main North Road winds through hills that are for the most part still covered in jungle. They were at one time dangerous, but now they contain the Templer Park where the people of Kuala Lumpur can spend their Sunday mornings in peace. After I had topped the pass and began to drop down the other side, the rain began in earnest. It rained as it can rain only in Malaya. As you drive along the road you can see the rain curtain ahead of you. Beyond the curtain is the deep wild fog of torrential rain, where visibility is almost nil, where the world consists of nothing but hammering, bucketing water. The road itself becomes invisible, since it is hidden in a three-foot-deep layer of rebounding spray. The wipers on the windscreen will not work quickly enough to remove the coating of water. Cars loom up out of this chaos of water and wind and wildly waving branches, their lights glimmering like bulbs in an aquarium, and as they pass they send a fountain of water rattling against your windows. Because the water cannot escape as quickly as it falls, the road becomes—technically—flooded, and the car skids and jumps round the corners because the wheels are running in an inch of water. The next thing that happens is that the brake drums fill with water and pressure on the brake pedal produces no discernible effect at all.

I think today I must have been moving with the storm, for I was enveloped in the rain for fifty miles. Within five minutes I was soaked to the skin and needing every ounce of concentration to keep the car on the road and moving at twenty-five miles per hour. I passed Rawang and then Serendah, both notorious bandit areas. At Serendah there is a boys' home, and a few years ago a number of bandits walked in and shot the principal at his desk. I forget the supposed reason for this act—beyond a Malayan Communist's love of killing for killing's sake.

I also passed the fantastic limestone hills which rear themselves in sheer cliffs from the level plain in which they stand. They are always a majestic sight, more so when they are lashed with rain, when the sparse bushes that cling to their barren and eroded sides flap in the short-lived gale that tries to tear them from their lofty perch. They tower, perhaps, to a thousand feet, their sides pitted with cracks and the black holes of caves that only the birds can reach. They are the dank and brooding castles of nature, timeless sentinels of an ancient Malaya. Ten thousand years ago the Stone Age men of Malaya lived in the caves in the lower reaches of these fantastic cliffs. Today, further north, near Ipoh, there are whole collections of temples set in the self-same caves.

The rain continued unchecked as I entered the Slim River area where the road for thirty miles or more is not straight for more than a few yards. It twists like a thin serpent through endless miles of rubber. There was a lot of fighting round there in the war and, if a search were made today, a few bleached bones and a number of spent and rusty bullets would doubtless be discovered.

It was in the middle of the Slim River area that the shock absorber broke. In addition to the rain and the road, I now had the disability of a useless shock absorber making a noise like a tank. I passed no garage on the road whose appearance sug-

gested it could mend anything more complicated than a plough-
share until I arrived in Tapah.

Tapah lies at the foot of the Highlands, the Cameron Highlands. The road for the Highlands turns off the main road at
Tapah and toils its laborious way up on to the very summit of
the Malayan backbone to Ringlet and Tanah Rata. The rain
had stopped when I reached Tapah but the world was still
saturated with water. Over the hills, behind Tapah, bloated
clouds sat like black puddings above the tree-tops, and if you
listened carefully you could hear the muffled, wet sound of water
seeping through the soft earth of the jungle. The buildings, the
houses and the shops of Tapah were still dripping as a diver
drips when he leaves the water.

The garage was run by a young Indian who clearly knew his
trade, and within two minutes three Chinese boys, under his
direction, were crawling under the car with spanners, wrenches
and—ominously—hammers. Ten minutes later they emerged
with the words "OK now," the garage proprietor said "dollar-
fifty, please" and I was away again.

It was not far from Tapah to Ipoh, and within half an hour
I was refuelling there and, as the sky looked brighter, putting
down the hood. I was served at the petrol station by a pretty
Chinese girl dressed in bright red Chinese pyjamas—samfoo, as
they are called—and I was not sure whether she was simply a
relative of the proprietor, lending a hand in the evening, or
whether she was employed in the hope that her charms would
increase the sale of petrol.

Only one hundred miles were now left to Penang. These are
perhaps the easiest hundred miles of the whole journey. I was
soon in Kuala Kangsar, where I stopped for tea and toast at
the Rest House. It was soon produced—an enormous pot of tea,
and toast cut sensibly so that there was plenty of body to each
slice.

As I ate my tea and read Whiteaways' Mail Order Bulletin a
man came in whose face seemed to be familiar. I looked at him
and said "Atkinson?" and he said, "Yes—Moore?—I thought
so." I knew him years ago in Singapore and had not seen him
since he left to go to England. Malaya is like that—the Euro-

pean community is small and when travelling one more often than not runs into an acquaintance. We chatted about nothing in particular, and then his wife came to collect him and I paid my bill and left.

There is something infinitely exciting about that last seventy miles through Perak to Penang. When I left Kuala Kangsar it was just beginning to get dark, and that is the best time of all to make the journey. For the last fifty miles the road is an almost continuously straight line with a narrow canal on either side. Beyond the canals are the houses of the Malays and beyond their houses their rubber trees, coconut trees and ricefields. At twilight they have finished their work and the older people sit on the steps of their houses while the younger ones ride up and down on their smart and gleaming bicycles. You pass little groups of naked children playing in the streams and Malay women walking with the perfection of goddesses, carrying baskets on their heads. Every few miles there is a village, with shops, bright with lights and crowded with people for whom the work of the day is done. In the villages there are often small mosques with zinc minarets and as you flash by you can often see the rows of upturned bottoms, as the faithful at evening prayer touch their foreheads to the ground. At night, too, the insects fly in clouds, and as the car ploughs through them a layer of spattered insect bodies grows on the windscreen until, if you go on long enough, you have to stop and scrape them off.

The Bintang Hills on the right faded away and I was travelling in the tunnel of the headlights through the darkness. Now was the time to watch for the lights of Penang Hill on the left, which, when you first see them, look like stars. As I passed the road leading to the chain ferry at Prai I saw them, high in the night, as though someone had hung them there and then gone away and left them to burn until morning. I turned left into Butterworth, over the Bailey bridge, and then brought the car to a halt in the queue at Mitchell Pier. I bought some chocolate while I waited for the ferry alongside to disgorge its load of cars, and then drove down the ramp on to the low deck of the ferry and in a matter of minutes we were at sea.

It was quiet in the Straits. Apart from the gentle noise of the engine and the lapping of the bow wave there was no sound at all. The silence was strange after the racket of the wind and the rain and a hard-working engine. Every few seconds the southern sky was bathed in the sudden white flash of lightning, and the clouds standing motionless in the sky were revealed in solid outline. Then, with masterly precision, the ferry came alongside and I drove the car ashore. It was pleasant to be in Penang again, and as I went to bed I thought of the view I would see in the morning from my window, over the Straits to Malaya with its green and cloud-wreathed hills.

October 15th, 1954

Holland Village is very much the same as most other villages in Malaya. The Malays live separately in their little attap houses hidden among the trees, and the Chinese and the Indians occupy the main street and sell to the villagers the necessities of life. If you do not look closely at the squalor of the Malay houses they are attractive and so, too, are many of those who live in them. The shops, on the other hand, cannot under any circumstances be anything but ugly : tall, thin boxes of concrete and brick. On the higher ground, looking down on the village, is the police-station, bright with military whitewash. All the policemen are Malays, and it is they who keep the shopkeepers in order. Someone wrote that once the Chinese go to live and trade in a Malay village, the Malays become self-conscious, troubled by a feeling of inferiority. Perhaps the smart police-station, with its Malay policemen, makes them feel better.

Holland Village is as busy by night as by day, perhaps busier. Behind the shops is an open-air cinema where are shown an endless succession of Wild West films and interminable Chinese and Indian dramas. People in long straggling groups, pulling and carrying their children, come to this cinema every night from miles around and business becomes even better for the shopkeepers. All over Holland Village can be heard each night the subdued chattering murmur of the cinema. I sometimes wonder what the primitive Chinese peasant makes of Lana Turner.

The shops of Holland Village occupy only one side of the

main street. Opposite is an open triangular green, bisected by the 'bus company's parking area. Each Wednesday morning the grass is turned into a quagmire by an itinerant market which travels about the district. By eight o'clock in the morning it is in full swing and all the shabbier and cheaper products of the West are laid out on the surviving grass. Once more the people from miles around come to Holland Village, as much for the pleasure of gathering together as to buy the pots, pans, sarongs, saris, beads, necklaces, fineries and household utensils which confront them like the miscellany of a jumble sale. Again, business is good for the shopkeepers.

On the edge of the green, facing the shops, is a great wooden box full of brown sawdust. Within the sawdust are enormous blocks of ice which remain intact throughout the heat of the tropical day for the use of the coffee-shops and soft-drink sellers, who place the ice in brightly painted grinders or, more accurately, shavers. The flakes of ice are then placed in tumblers, where they resemble snow, until the highly coloured water of the soft drink is added. I do not know why these blocks of ice do not melt except that the sawdust appears to act, after it is first saturated, as a refrigerator.

There is a craze sweeping Singapore at the moment for a form of miniature billiards. Holland Village seems to have more miniature billiard tables than any other village in Singapore Island. They are brought out at night and set in a long row on the opposite side of the road from the shops, and the constant click of small billiard balls is added to the murmur of the open-air cinema. They say that a certain amount of betting goes on over the billiard tables, but if so it is accomplished far too surreptitiously for the Malay constables to detect the passage of money between the players or the onlookers.

I went to Holland Village last night to buy a packet of cigarettes. All the shops were closed except the modern filling station and the several coffee-shops. A few customers were sitting at the marble-topped tables: weather-beaten lorry-drivers, gardeners, knarled old squatters and pimply-faced youths. The proprietor, an incredibly thin, mournful-looking Chinese, sat on a high stool behind his rickety counter, his whole being concentrated on the tune he was playing on his home-made, one-string violin.

At the end of the counter sat an old, old man, with a thin, lined hatchet face, his pale lips stretched over the opening of an enormous bamboo flute. Between them sat a young boy, plucking at a roughly-made instrument resembling a mandolin. As they played their soft, strident music, he sang a long, sad song of ancient China. I do not know what the song was about. All I know is that it was not a happy one.

In all the villages of Malaya are found these trios and quartets which come together three, perhaps four, times a week to practise their limited repertoires. And no quartet of Mozart or Beethoven was ever played with more concentration or with more solemn abandonment to the meaning of the music.

October 16th, 1954

A delightful story of Siam: it happened in Cheng Mei, an ancient city of Siam, far north of Bangkok. Many, many years ago the British Consul in Cheng Mei decided that he would like to have a sedan-chair, in order that his passage about the town might be the more comfortable. By an oversight, however, the Siamese authorities had not informed him that the only person in Cheng Mei who was allowed to ride in a sedan-chair was the locally resident Prince—and there has always been a surplus of Princes in Siam. When the British Consul appeared in his new and shining conveyance a meeting was held in the royal residence to decide on the action to be taken. One thing was clear: it would be most inadvisable to arrest the British Consul. So they arrested, instead, the man who had made the sedan-chair. He was thrown into the darkness of the local prison and eventually brought before the court. The trial was not a lengthy one, since the prisoner was unable to deny that he had made the chair. And the judge said to the prisoner:

"I take it that the accused is satisfied that the case against him has been adequately proved, so nothing remains except for me to pronounce sentence, which in this particular case is death. Before I do so, however, has the accused anything to say?"

The prisoner answered that he did have something to say. And the judge asked him what it was.

"I am satisfied that my guilt has been proved, but I do feel that the penalty is perhaps a little severe."

And the judge said :

"I agree with you entirely—fined ten ticals."

October 17th, 1954

Someone must write a book of one of the most fascinating murders ever committed. The other day three men were sentenced in Bangkok for the murder, several years ago, of the King of Siam. No one for a moment believes them to be guilty, but scapegoats had to be found and these three were unfortunate enough to be chosen.

The king was found in a room—which no one, apparently, could have entered—dead. He held in his hand a revolver with which, it seemed, he had shot himself. But the experts said that, due to the direction in which the bullet entered the body, or to some other similar fact better understood by criminologists, the king could not possibly have killed himself and that he was, in fact, murdered. Perhaps the truth of the matter will never be known, but it puts one in mind of the story of the European resident in Bangkok who grew tired of the naïve questions of a visiting journalist. The resident said that not only was it quite impossible for anyone to say what was going to happen in Siam in the future: it was also equally impossible for anyone to say what *was* happening or what, at any time in the past, had happened.

October 20th, 1954

Deepavali and the Mariamar Indian Temple. The yellow, bizarre figures of soldiers and cows that decorate the exterior walls of the Temple gleam dully in the morning sun. An endless stream of Indians enter the main gate of the Temple, and others at the same time pour from it, so that the Temple, with this perpetual coming and going, resembles an anthill. Within the walls that surround the Temple a pit, perhaps three feet deep and from fifteen to twenty feet long, has been carved from the stone-hard earth. Black, shining figures, stripped to the waist, are throwing great bundles of firewood into the pit until they almost reach the surface of the ground. Then they set fire to it, and because of the heat and the light of the sun the leaping flames can scarcely be seen; but they are hot in the airless courtyard of the Temple, suffocatingly hot, and the people fall back with a murmur that is a mixture of surprise and appreciation.

It seems that all the Indians in the world are coming together in this small Temple, moving in every direction, through the restricted, wall-enclosed grounds, purposefully and yet without purpose, clambering over the corrugated grandstand which has been built at one end of the pit. From the grandstand a cat-walk has been built to the roof of the Temple, and already the children are racing up and down, clattering over everything within reach.

The flames from the pit leap high and then slowly die away, leaving a red, flat bed of heat. Then more men come with what appear to be granite chips—the kind of chips they lay on roads— and scatter them thickly over the embers of the fire so that the heat and the fire is contained under a layer of burning stone. Soon if a man goes near the pit, the heat rises and hits him in the face as if he had opened the door of a furnace. And still the people come, flooding and pressing into the Temple so that those who are standing in a circle round the pit are pushed, inexorably, inch by inch nearer the fire. Yet they do not seem to mind the heat, neither the heat from the pit nor that from the overhead sun which pours down into the Temple; there appears to be no limit to the amount of heat their dark bodies can absorb. The noise is deafening: the constant, high-pitched, excited babble of Indian voices.

It is a day of great rejoicing and every woman is dressed in her best sari, the colours of each sari being different from those of any other. There are big women, women with great buns of black hair, women towing children dressed in ill-fitting suits, pregnant women, women with diamonds in their noses, women from the dusty villages of the whole breadth of India.

The noise and the colour and the heat become almost unendurable, so that people are forced upwards on to the walls, on to the grandstand and up the flimsy cat-walk until even the sides of the Temple are covered with bodies, clinging to every available foot- and hand-hold. Up on the roof, those Europeans who have come early enough, festooned with cameras and cinematographic equipment, squat in the blinding sun for the moment for which they have waited a year to put on to celluloid.

The noise level suddenly increases, as though an unseen god has turned a switch, and the swelling sound is of anticipation as men come forward with long-handled rakes to turn over the granite chips, releasing waves of heat. Those in the front ranks put their hands before their faces, and yet they would rather faint and fall into the fire than move and have their places taken by others.

The sun has passed its zenith and the shadows of the Temple walls grow imperceptibly longer as the baking hours pass. Then the continuous high murmur becomes a sudden roar and the almost naked devotees appear at one end. They are dressed in white *dhotis* and for a week they have lived a spartan existence. They have slept alone on hard floors and eaten little during this week of preparation. They stand for a moment, looking as if they do not belong to this world. The roar dies down to its background babble, but at a more fevered pitch than before. The Temple trustee comes forward and scatters flower petals on to the chips, and the petals immediately wither and disappear as they would disappear if placed on the bars of a fireplace.

The time approaches, and the noise dies to a subdued murmur of intense expectancy. The sun falls lower in the sky and hundreds of cameras, high up in the walls and on the roof, are held ready. A thousand dark faces watch the devotees at the end of the pit.

One of them steps forward bearing flowers on his head, and a ripple of fervour runs through the crowd. The devotee steps on to the fire-bed and, half walking and half staggering, like a man in the depths of a terrible trance, his face contorted with a secret ecstasy, stumbles along the length of the inferno. For a moment he pauses and it seems that he will fall, and the voice of the people reacts; then it is clear they are with him and that while they are with him he cannot fail, and he recovers and reels to the end of the pit where he plunges his feet into the milk-white liquid which awaits him beyond the fire. Then he collapses into the arms of the waiting Temple attendants. They take him to the back of the Temple where he washes and puts on clean clothes. Meanwhile the next devotee makes his agonised passage through the pit. They follow in rapid succession, perhaps forty of them altogether. None of them burn their feet and tomorrow they will go back to their jobs as bus conductors, clerks, labourers or whatever it is they do when their simple minds are not defeating matter. When it is all over the fire brigade arrives and directs a fire hose on to the pit so that the imprisoned heat turns to billowing clouds of steam, and now the smell, as well as the heat and the noise, becomes unendurable. As the pit cools under the shower of water, the great crowd surges forward to the dead fire, each hand grasping for a charred fragment of the holy embers.

October 23rd, 1954

He is a little Chinese shopkeeper with a round, benign face and, as is the custom of the Straits Chinese, his sons call him Daddy, although they have long been men. Of late his business has not been good and the reason for this, he says, is the force of the competition he faces from nearby Indian shopkeepers who deal in the same commodities.

"They have no interest in building anything here," he says. "They want a small quick profit and what they make goes back to India and, although this profit is not much here, it represents far more in India. And if their business fails, what will they do then? They will go back to India! But we, if they ruin our business, we who have been here for four generations—my sons, me, my daddy and his daddy before him—where do we go? We have nowhere to go. We must stay."

This little conversation illustrates very clearly the difference, the vast difference, between the newcomers to Malaya and old Straits-born Chinese, to whom Malaya is a home and China something they have only read about in books. How strangely their outlook assorts with that of the Chinese High School students in Singapore—these young men who, as the *Straits Times* said today, "have a supreme contempt for everyone else's intelligence"—and with the song they sang for their hired man, Mr. Pritt, when they gave him a tea-party before he left Singapore the other day:

"Unity is strength; Unity is strength; This strength is iron; This strength is steel; Harder than iron; Stronger than steel; March forward towards the glorious ideal; Eliminate all unreasonable systems; On sun, on freedom, and on New China, the brilliant light shines."

Another song they sang is this:

"Fellow-students, listen carefully to what I say. When the Japanese Government was driven out, there came the self-claimed democratic Government. Under the signboard of democracy, it tries to enslave us. Since democracy has changed its pattern it tries to wipe out our Chinese culture by enforcing the New Schools Registration (Amendment) Bill. Fellow-students, the May 13 incident tells us that unity is strength. We can dispose of this New Bill by opposing it, with our united force."

I can no longer understand these young men, and it is difficult, any longer, to have any patience with them. No one will deny that Chinese education has been neglected in the past. But not only Chinese education has been neglected: so has every other form of education—English, Malay and Indian, primary and secondary. Perhaps it is true to say that Chinese education was neglected more than any other, but this was precisely because education provided by government in the past was English, and if certain sections of the people required their education in Chinese they could have it only if they provided it themselves. The Malays, as the people principally to be found in Malaya when the British began to govern it, were provided with a Malay education; Indian education has never been very much more than an attempt to keep the children of Indian tappers on rubber estates out of mischief. In the context of the times—pre-second world war—this system was acceptable to the vast majority of the people of this country. The children in English schools were

for the most part Chinese, so the Chinese were not *entirely* neglected. But after the war it was clear that a new policy was
necessary. And, rightly or wrongly, the Government put most of
its expansionist effort into the English schools.

Then, provided Chinese schools would yield to inspection by
the Department of Education, and provided they would be
guided in the matter of text-books by a committee composed
largely of their own more intelligent teachers, they were offered
grants-in-aid by the Government so that they could become
better Chinese schools than they were before.

Now it is suggested by the Government that the annual
grants-in-aid to Chinese schools in Singapore should be increased
from $3½ million to $12 million. Immediately, the rowdier elements in the Chinese secondary schools have said that this increase is an attempt to kill Chinese education and Chinese
culture. This ridiculous statement cannot stand examination for
one moment—except in the light of what their students really
mean : that Chinese culture is synonymous with Communism.
They say, too, that the proposed board that is to control the
Chinese schools under the new dispensation will be under the
thumb of the Government. So is every Board of Education in
every civilised country. Under who else's control can it be? And
is not Singapore to be self-governing next year?

These young men are not stupid. They are simply Communist.
No one watching their tactics can doubt for one moment that
they are being led by ruthless and determined men, prepared to
wreck the progress of one of the most wonderful cities in the
world for the sake of their own loathsome religion and their own
climb to power.

The menace in the Chinese schools cannot be eliminated at
once. There are, for one thing, too many real grievances. For too
long the Chinese schools have been neglected. The students have
claimed in the past that there was no University to which they
could go in Malaya, since their proficiency in English was insufficient to equip them for study at the University of Malaya.
Now their own people have established their own University,
the Nanyang University, with Dr. Lin Yu-Tang as its Chan-
cellor, because the University of Malaya either would not or

could not provide what they wanted. The students claim that an education in a Chinese school does not qualify them, for instance, for government posts and for innumerable other posts, both public and private, where the Cambridge School Certificate is regarded as being the beginning and end of all education. These are all solid grievances, and the wonder is that they have not been aired before. Now that they are being aired the situation is almost irretrievable, since the Communists have espoused the students' cause—as they will ally themselves with grievances the world over, not so much to eliminate the grievances as to gain more adherents to their own particular cause. The criminal idiocy of previous administrations which could allow this situation to develop to its present point is almost as alarming as the evidence we now have of Communist tactics of infiltration; of the way in which they can discipline these young men, organise and direct them towards their own vicious ends. And through and through the student propaganda is the ever-recurring theme: the total identification of Communism with New China, Red China, Chinese culture and patriotism—which makes the search for a solution ever more difficult.

But of one thing I am convinced: our situation will not improve until we begin to take Communism seriously. In Britain and in the Commonwealth scarcely anyone is prepared to believe that Communism is bent on the deliberate and urgent ideal of world domination. Mr. Attlee, after he visited China, stated in Australia that he thought China was going to be far too busy putting her own house in order to engage in expansionist policies overseas. There is not one shred of evidence to support this startling view. Such evidence as there is—and there is plenty—points to the precise contrary: China could call off the Malayan Emergency tomorrow if she wished. She was not too bound up in her own affairs to refrain from challenging the world in Korea; she was not too busy with her own problems to bother about Tibet; she seemed to have ample resources with which to hurl the might of the West out of half of Indo-China; she has no intention of allowing Formosa to remain neutral or Nationalist; she is quite prepared to take her part in the grand Communist strategy that sooner or later is going to creep across the entire globe, unless the free world acknowledges its danger and fights Communism as it has fought no war or disease before.

Here in Singapore and Malaya we are in the midst of the advanced Asian battle-line of Communism. We have been in it for years, and yet we are still so far behind the situation as only *now* to suggest giving Chinese schools a reasonable grant towards their legitimate activities. Even now we have done nothing about giving the Chinese students an entry into the commercial and administrative avenues which they desire. Did we not know the feelings of the Chinese students before the Communists fanned the flames of their discontent? Of course we did. It was simply that we did not give the Communists the credit for the astuteness, cleverness and power that they have shown. In the past there may have been some excuse for this attitude of mind. But there can be no excuse ever again. We are at *war—total war—* with an enemy that slips through our lines and into every corner of our lives. This enemy gives no quarter, and sooner or later we must resolve to give him no quarter either.

The situation in the Chinese schools is almost irretrievable. But at least we can talk, argue and persuade with deeds as well as with words. We must use every possible endeavour to persuade all the people who live in Singapore and Malaya that this country in which they live now must be the object of their primary loyalty. I very much doubt, for instance, whether any point of view whatever has ever been presented to the Chinese students with a tenth of the force with which the Communists have presented theirs. Why? Are we ashamed of our standpoint? Are we ashamed of the things we stand for? Why do we hear only of Communist cells? If the building up of support can be achieved by the operation of cells—as it obviously can—why do we not have democratic cells? Or do we spend so much time pointing out the errors of Communism that we have no time to declare, explain, propound, demonstrate, teach, impart and inculcate our own ideas? We have not even joined the battle for men's minds. The minds of the Chinese schoolchildren have been lost by default. And this I am convinced is because we have not at any time fully appreciated the extent of the danger in which we stand. We underrate both the abilities and the aims of the Communists.

The only course to follow in the world today is one of implacable opposition to Communism. We must oppose it inflexibly wherever it appears and with whatever means we can bring to bear. We must engage in a titanic struggle for the minds of the people who are not yet within the Soviet bloc. We must put our ideas across to them *at all costs,* for failure will mean that the dark Orwellian curtain of Communism will be drawn across yet another country until it covers the entire world.

I want the people of England to understand this. They do not as yet understand it, and each day brings closer the hour when it will be too late for them to understand it. Nothing now stands between them and destruction except an atom bomb. Unless they can find an alternative to the atom bomb, either the bombs or Communism will destroy them. The battle they must wage is world-wide, and perhaps its most important theatre of operations today is Malaya. In Malaya, if we are not actually losing the battle for the minds and hearts of the people, no one, possibly, can say that we are winning it.

October 24th, 1954

Drove to the top of Fort Canning this evening to the Muslim Shrine which is said to be the grave of the founder of Singapore who died nearly 600 years ago. No one is very sure who this man was, where he came from, or whether this ancient shrine, which for hundreds of years has been venerated by the Malays, is, in fact, his grave. But I do not think this matters, for neither the beauty nor the sanctity of the place would be different if we knew.

It is no scene of splendour, nor even of mere impressiveness. The low, corrugated-iron roof almost conceals the wall that surrounds the grave, and to reach it the visitor must either walk up the path from below or clamber from above down the rough eroded side of Fort Canning. Upon entering the shrine the visitor must remove his shoes and the Malay who tends it will hand him a framed and faded copy of an editorial which appeared only a few years ago in the *Straits Times*, but which, in its measured phrases, is already redolent of a more spacious and leisurely age, and which tells the reader something of the chronology of the early kings of Singapore. Possibly, as he holds the old newsprint to the twilight, under the ancient trees whose roots pass through the more recent concrete on which he stands, a Muslim, perhaps Indian or perhaps Malay, will bring an offering of a bottle of oil which the attendant will take and place in the lamps which are never extinguished. After the oil has been distributed, the Muslim will stand before the whitewashed tomb, over which is laid a green canopy and on which are scattered a few petals of flowers, and silently ask the spirit of the saint which resides within for his heart's desire—whatever that may be. Then he will take his empty bottle and return to the city below.

The light fades and the sprouting parasites of the trees, hanging like great chandeliers from the creepers which drop like tears from the old moss-covered branches above, revolve slightly in the evening breeze. There is time then on Fort Canning, all the time in the world. The men from Java and from Sumatra, from Siam and England and from Japan may come and plant their flags upon its summit. The great Empires—the ancient Hindu Empires of Majapahit and Srivijaya, the shifting Empire of the Thais, the proud Empire of the British and the frightened, confused Empire of the Japanese—all may come to Fort Canning and from the point where they have planted their flag look down upon one of the most ancient and important waterways in the world, the Straits of Malacca, which they control simply because they control Singapore. They may order the people to do this or that; they may build their fortifications and levy their duties and their taxes; they may ornament their kings with false grandeur, and decorate their officials with empty honours; they may either care for the people or oppress them. But all, all of them, drift sometime into the inevitable twilight of their fading day, leaving behind them only the impermanence of their creations—and Fort Canning, which rises above the island, and its shrine, and the spirit within it, these know that all who come must also later go.

October 27th, 1954

It is so easy to be dogmatic about Malaya and there are many traps into which the unwary may fall. One becomes so accustomed to regarding all Malaya's ills as either stemming from or leading to racial conflict that for a moment one is inclined to blink with incredulity when a person states that it is not so.

Today I talked with a charming, highly educated Malay. When one meets such a person, the first question is asked almost automatically: How is it possible for the Malays to hold their own against the overwhelming force of the Chinese, once self-government arrives? His answer was unexpected:

"The primary problem of Malaya is not racial. Its problem is largely an Asian problem, and the problem all over Asia is a land problem. It is a man's relationship to the land that must first be put right, and beside this problem all others fade into relative insignificance.

"The Malay and Chinese populations of Malaya are almost equal. Four-fifths of the Malay population are peasants and half of the Chinese population are peasants. The peasants in Malaya and all over Asia are exploited by the commercial classes which, in Malaya, are European, Chinese or Indian. Thus the Chinese exploit not only the Malays but also the Chinese, and if a Malay capitalist class is created, Malay will exploit Malay. I venture to suggest, therefore, that on the one hand the solidarity of the capitalists and on the other the solidarity of peasants, both the result of common vested interests or common injustices, will prove stronger than racial links.

"Again, it is fashionable to suppose that there are in Malaya today 'racial' leaders. This prominent Chinese or that Malay or Indian will be singled out as representative of the Chinese, the Malays or Indians. Possibly the Government honestly thinks these men represent their people in this country. Possibly they think so themselves. But in no case is it so. They are all of them leaders of economic groups. What, for instance, does the Government of Singapore imagine the Singapore Chinese Chamber of Commerce represents? It certainly does not represent the Chinese. It represents merchants and business men only and

cannot speak for the trishaw drivers or the fishermen or the
market gardeners. When Sir John Hay speaks on behalf of the
rubber industry I am inclined to take notice of what he says
since he is then representing an economic group, but I question
very much whether he can speak for Europeans, generally, in
Malaya.

"When Malay, Indian and Chinese leaders come together and
slap each other on the back and demonstrate with elaborate
showmanship the unity of the races in Malaya, supported the
while by an anxious government in the background, and make
speeches about communalism and how they are defeating this
spectre that stands within our midst, and arrange their alliances
as earnests of their good faith in their rejection of all racial
thinking, they are attempting to solve a problem which is non-
existent. They represent no one but their relatively small economic groups, and they do not realise that peasants think of
themselves as peasants and demand justice as peasants, and that
it does not matter whether they are Chinese or Malay or whether
those who offer them justice are Chinese or Malay, as long as
justice is given.

"And justice in the first place consists of land reform; a reform of the land code to prevent the fragmentation of holdings,
the provision of security of tenancy and rent control. In addition,
controls must be introduced to prevent their being exploited by
those who buy their produce.

"Once self-government arrives, those elected to power will be
those who have ridden there on the platform of freedom. They
will be the Nationalists; possibly the professional people—
doctors and lawyers—people who have made independence their
cause and won the support of the people by dangling the prospect
before them. Perhaps the second election after self-government
may not bring people to power who materially differ in this
respect. But the third time round—then things will begin to
change and you will find that the political parties will become
more concerned with economic problems and the people will
tend to vote into power those men who hold out the best hope of
doing something for them. And you cannot help the Malay padi-
farmer without also helping the Chinese padi-farmer. The eco-

nomically under-privileged are found in every race.

"So you see the problem of race is not so important as many seem to think. It is often the Government which creates the belief in racialism by working on false premises.

"I do not think that even the Emergency can bring about virulent communalism in this country, even though for years largely Malay Security Forces have been fighting Chinese bandits. People forget, you know. Europe has again embraced Germany, and America, who fought the Japanese in the Pacific with more venom than anyone else, is now their staunch ally. Economic and social factors will prove the stronger in the long run and racialism will fall by the wayside. It is only, in fact, while we have a Colonial government that communalism thrives. Only self-government can release the forces that can kill it.

"One of the means by which the people of this country can be unified is by a unified system of education. We live today in the era of the false premium of the English language. All manner of good men and true are precluded from public life because their knowledge of English is either nil or most imperfect. Instead, we have all manner of fools in public office for no better reason than that they are able to speak English. An Indian who is given office in this country would not stand a chance in India. The same applies to the Chinese. In the Philippines they have had English education since 1908. But here—we have scarcely begun. Even today a great many children are not given any education at all, and those that are provided with it are for the most part taught in almost anything but English. The English language has missed the bus by about fifty years. Self-government cannot wait until we all know English. In Trengganu, for example, scarcely *anyone* speaks it.

"But we must have a common unified system of education with a language common to that system and to the whole of the public life of the country. Possibly I suggest that it should be Malay because I am a Malay, but it is difficult to see what else it can be. When an Indian bus conductor quarrels with a Chinese hawker, he quarrels in Malay. When a Malay farmer barters with the Chinese wholesaler he barters in Malay. Malay is the lingua franca of this country. Apart from English, the only other possible languages are Tamil or Chinese, and since the first, to the majority of people, is unpronounceable and the second unlearnable, there would not appear to be much hope for either.

"Then, again, people ask how we are to defend ourselves when we have self-government. As far as external defence is concerned we must join one of the three main groups, since as a small country we are unable to defend ourselves. We must either join the Communist bloc or the American bloc (or the Western Powers, call it what you will) or the neutralist bloc, the third force, composed notably of India, Indonesia and Burma. For my own part I would prefer the Western Powers, since to join them is the most sensible thing to do in the circumstances. As far as internal defence is concerned we may well be better off under self-government than under Colonial rule, for if we still have the Emergency—and it looks as though we shall, although self-rule will do much to remove many of the reasons for the Emergency—we shall be able to call on the full resources of the West, including America, to fight it. Britain is now too poor to fight it adequately, but as an old, proud country she can scarcely ask America to fight it for her. If universal education is a requisite of survival we cannot at the present hold out any hope of survival, since neither we nor Britain can provide it. If the defeat of Communism means sweeping social reforms, intensified agriculture and industry, a marked and immediate improvement in the standard of living, then neither we nor Britain can defeat Communism in this country. But with the total resources of the West behind us, which we cannot obtain until we are a free and independent country, then, perhaps, we could defeat the Communists. Perhaps we could."

October 28th, 1954

J. has been to the village of Yong Peng in Johore. Yong Peng at one time was a bad area but it is much improved—or, at least, a good deal of the shooting has died down. She went with the Bishop, who had a number of Chinese Christians to confirm.

Out of the five thousand people who live in and around Yong Peng perhaps two to three hundred are Christians. At one time they had a little church some way outside the town, but it had to be pulled down when the bandits began to use it as a rice store. With the materials salvaged from the old church they built a new one, a very humble, perhaps unimaginative, little church.

The service was held while J. was there and she found something terribly incongruous—as who wouldn't—in the robes of a Bishop in a place like Yong Peng, deep in the rubber of Johore. He changed in a tiny bedroom which he shared with a Siamese cat and four kittens. In all, four people were confirmed— a man and three women.

The service was held entirely in Chinese and was conducted by a Chinese vicar, and one of the missionaries translated the Bishop's simple and effective address. He compared the laying-on of hands to the chopping of a manufacturer's mark on a tin of Malayan pineapples or a bale of rubber. He said that by Confirmation one became a friend of Christ and it was through the Communion that that friendship was celebrated. For a moment J. was almost convinced, and then she looked at those who listened so intently—the few old men, the children and the thirty-odd women—and saw the dull, hard, lined, impassive faces of peasants, poor peasants, Chinese, Eastern, Oriental peasants, and she wondered what they could possibly make of the Communion service however simply it was explained to them. They have to work hard, these people, labouring, small-scale farming, rubber-tapping, and at the end of their toil earn a pittance to which is attached no security. By day and by night the Communists whisper to them, both inside and out of the village, like the voices that surrounded Caliban:

"You can have more than this."

"You can have security."

"You can have your own land and a co-operative that will give you twice as much for your products as you get now."

"What does the Church do for you? Come on—tell us—tell us how it helps you."

"Your son is in the jungle, you would not like anything to happen to him, would you?"

"Look, look at the keen, keen edge of this knife!"

"You can have a better house, your children can go to school, you may even have a motor-car."

"Give us rice."

"Give us rice."

"Give us rice," say the Communists.

"We are winning and we shall remember you when the war is over if you do not give us rice."

"Give us money."

"Give us money."

"Give us money," say the Communists.

"For with money we can kill the traitors and their running dogs and rid your backs of the weight of the world."

"Collect scrap rubber."

"Collect scrap rubber."

"Collect scrap rubber," say the Communists.

"We can sell the rubber for money, and with the money we can buy rice, and with rice we can survive, and only if we survive can you survive as men instead of beasts."

"Come with us into the jungle."

"Come and fight for the glorious ideal."

"Come, comrades, do not be afraid. Your chains! Cast off your chains. Be men! Fight! Fight for freedom and the future."

"Fight for your rights."

"Fight for your children."

"Fight for your wives and your homes."

"You are good people. We are good people. All we want is justice."

"Look at the size of your garden!"

"Look at the size of the rubber estate on which you toil for other people."

"Look at your house!"

"Look at the houses of the rich who oppress you."

"How much do they pay you for your rice, comrade?"

"How much do they sell it for, comrade?"

"Where does the difference go, comrade?"

"Answer me, where does the difference go?"

"Do you get it?"

"Do I get it?"

"Do any of us get it?"

"Do you understand now, comrade?"

"Look at your wife. She is old and worn, comrade."

"Look at your children. They are thin and they do not get enough to eat, and when they are ill there is no doctor within miles."

"Is there, comrade?"

"Is there, comrade?"

"Is THERE, COMRADE?"

"What are you waiting for, comrade?"

"Is it your debts you are worrying about?"

"Is it your crops?"

"Is it that pain you have in your guts that gets no better but only worse?"

"Is it, comrade?"

"You are the dupes of capitalist swine!"

"You are the slaves of Fascist beasts!"

"You are the tools of reactionary Imperialism!"

"Are you content to live in your hovels and crawl on your bellies for the crumbs that fall from the tables of rich men?"

"Are you men?"

"We are in the North."

"We are in the South."

"We are in the East."

"We are in the West."

"We are in the cities and the villages, in the towns and in open spaces."

"We are in the estates and the mines, in the unions and in the offices."

"We are in the committees and in the councils, in the churches and in the schools, in the government and in the armed forces."

"We are in the jungle, on the plains and in the mountains, on the banks of the rivers, in the ricefields and on the roads."

"We are everywhere, comrade."

"Everywhere!"

"Soon we shall strike! Strike, comrade. Do you understand? And when we strike, where will you be, comrade? What will you be doing? What right will you have earned to share in the New Life?"

"Do you see what we mean, comrade?"

"Give us money."

"Give us food."

"Give us shelter."

"Do not refuse, for you know what may happen."

"Do not hesitate, for we may grow impatient."

"Do not speak."

"Do not lay information."

"Do not answer questions."

"For if you do any of these things we shall kill you. We may kill your wife. We may even kill your children."

"Remember, comrade, what we have said," say the Communists.

"Spare us, good Lord," say the villagers.

"Good Lord, deliver us."

"We beseech thee to hear us, good Lord."

"Lord, have mercy on our souls."

October 29th, 1954

A Malayan student is being expelled from Australia. From the accounts which have appeared in the Press it is clear that he has wasted his time there. He has attempted three University courses and has failed at all of them, and now he is doing odd jobs to keep himself. Just lately he has married an Australian girl who, as all Australian girls do when told that their newly acquired and coloured husbands are to leave Australia, has announced that she will stand by him come what may.

The Australian Government has gone to some pains to expose the waywardness of this particular student and has described the process by which he was given ample opportunity to reform himself before finally being told to leave the country. In the course of its announcement the Australian Government gave itself a pat on the back for the exemplary way in which it had helped Asia by allowing thousands of Asian students to study there.

Kuching, Sarawak.

The Fortune Teller.

Kuching River—

"*. . . . broad, brown, swiftly-flowing rivers which are real roads of Sarawak.*"

None of this is denied by Asians, and many of them are grateful for what they have learned in Australia.

But the point, surely, is this: this Ceylonese who is a Malayan student is being expelled simply because he is not white, and the significance of this is very apparent to Asians even if it is not apparent to Australians or to other members of the Commonwealth.

Australians will, I fancy, deny this. They will say that Australia cannot allow Asians to settle in Australia because their standard of living is lower than that of Australians, and they will therefore depress the general standard of living, which will lead to all manner of complications. But can any standard of living be very much lower than that of many of the central European displaced peasantry and industrial workers who have been allowed to settle in Australia in large numbers? And is the standard of living of an Asian who comes from a family with both the intelligence and the means to send its son to an overseas University necessarily all that low? And since, if Asians were able to go to Australia to settle, the reason for their going would be to improve their standard of living, would the resultant standard be as Australians seem to fear? If Australians want to know what a *really* high standard of living is, in economic terms, they could do no better than come to Singapore and observe the princely scale on which some of the Asian parents of Asian students in Australia are able to live.

Australians will also say that once Asians are allowed into Australia they will swamp the country. Perhaps a doubtful case could be made out for this contention, on the grounds that once in Australia they will reproduce at an alarming rate. But this would not, I think, happen once they had been there for a few years. Australians could, on the other hand, quite properly control Asian immigration into their country. A quota could be fixed for Asian immigration which would be perfectly just as long as it did not unfairly discriminate against Asians.

Our Malayan student is not prevented from staying in Australia on either economic or racial grounds, but purely and simply on the grounds of his unfortunate colour. Whether he is a good or bad student is beside the point; he is not allowed to stay however he turns out. If he were white, his conduct as a student would not be considered. And this seems to many Asians a most extraordinary thing.

So long as Australia allows immigrants into her country, so long as she desperately requires immigrants, an Asian cannot see why he should not be included. After all, Australians come to Malaya. No one says, "Oh dear me! You're white! You cannot possibly stay here!" And unless countries like Australia change their ideas they will find, when Malaya has attained her independence, that her new government will say precisely that. And quite right, too.

If a person wishes to understand why Asian countries do not strain themselves to attend conferences like SEATO they have to look no further than present *colour*—not *racial*—discrimination within the Commonwealth and in America. Asian countries see a number of white nations anxious to bind them to what they term mutual security pacts, when the only security they are really interested in is their own. What, after all, *does* Australia care, for example, about Malaya when she is not sufficiently friendly to be able to contemplate for one moment the thought of Malayans permanently in her midst? "I am your friend. I shall protect you! I shall not let these horrible Communists harm you! But, for God's sake, don't touch me!" What kind of friendship is this?

Nothing is more certain than the fact that the East will continue to distrust the West, will continue to remain sceptical of the West's every advance, until the West has shown that the colour of a man's skin is a matter of total indifference to it. There is nothing the West can do of greater importance, and which will contribute more to the peace of this world, than reject its current practices of colour discrimination.

The extraordinary thing about the problem is that in Singapore, this citadel, in the eyes of many, of a decadent Imperialism, where, it is fondly imagined, a white man has only to clap his hands to produce a string of abject and coloured slaves, Europeans have a greater difficulty in understanding the motives of the colour bar than anywhere else on earth.

October 30th, 1954

Smith tells me of an example of the uselessness of the Chinese written language in the twentieth century:

"An enterprising company in Kuala Lumpur began, some time ago, to compile a Chinese telephone directory. It sent out canvassers, and all firms were invited to contribute five dollars towards the project, in return for which their names were to be included in the new directory.

"We duly paid five dollars, and heard nothing more until yesterday when we were brought a copy of the completed directory. It was placed on my desk with elaborate ceremony by the Chinese who had in the first place collected our five dollars, rather as a jeweller will place before his most important customer his most prized exhibit. Then he sat down to await my approbation.

"I asked him where our entry was. He smiled, and taking up the directory opened it apparently at random and went down the column of the page with his finger. His finger travelled down all four columns before he turned the page and repeated the process on the other side. Perhaps three or four minutes elapsed, during which time he examined a great number of pages. Finally, almost with a shout of triumph, he found the elusive entry and, since the numbers were given in Arabic figures, I suspect that he spotted the entry by running his eye down the numbers until he came to the one written on our telephone.

"How can one set about classifying a long list of names in Chinese characters? How can a semblance of alphabetical, or any, order be produced? It seems that it cannot. And the Chinese typewriter resembles the complications of an electronic brain. If it is true that Chinese culture is rooted in its system of writing, is it not time that the Chinese conceptions of both were revised? Until they do revise their ancient form of writing, and restrict it to display in their museums, then the prospect of the East understanding the West must indeed remain remote."

I am reminded of a story told to me by a European lawyer in Singapore. Two Chinese clients had made an agreement on a matter of business and the agreement had been broken. Once they discovered this they repaired to their respective lawyers, hungry for action. And one of the Chinese, in describing the circumstances in which the agreement had been broken, told his lawyer that he had at one time set out in writing for his erstwhile partner certain inescapable facts of the matter. "I told him," he said, "I told him in plain Chinese . . ."

October 31st, 1954

The dockers in England are to go back to work. Although I do not see how the principle, however watered down, of compulsory overtime can ever be maintained, my judgment of any matter affecting waterside workers in England is still coloured by my experience of them during the war.

In 1943, when we were still losing the war, I was sent to join an aircraft carrier that was still in the course of construction on the Tyne. When I joined, it was within four or five weeks of completion. Perhaps it was the fault simply of a weak and ineffectual management—although it is difficult to see how this could be in a company large enough to contemplate the building of an aircraft carrier—but I never knew an occasion when the men working on the ship spent their overtime doing anything more constructive than playing cards.

Among the men who served on the ship, even among the most recalcitrant characters, there was always at least a dim awareness that a war was on, that we could not properly be said to be winning it, and that it would be disastrous for us if we lost it. But among the Tyneside men who worked on naval ships there was clearly no such awareness. The fact that their slacking took place before men whose occupations were going to be considerably more hazardous than knocking rivets into sheets of metal, men who sooner or later would probably be killed, had no effect upon them. Instead, they littered the ship, from the keel to the bridge, from the forecastle to the quarter-deck, absorbed in their criminal games of cards, for which they *demanded* and received double wages, while the world fell about their ears.

Ever since those days I have been inclined to doubt the utility of appealing to any sense of patriotism among waterside workers of any kind. Perhaps this generalisation is, in some cases, unfair. But the Port of London can lie idle for weeks, the economy of the country can founder, perhaps never to revive, and I fancy that not very many dockers will be very greatly disturbed, until the resultant confusion begins to affect their own livelihood.

November 1st, 1954

A week-end on St. John's Island. St. John's Island belongs to the Singapore Medical Department and is used as a quarantine station where hapless travellers from China are left to get the Kwantung bugs out of their systems.

The bungalow on the hill where we stayed faces south-west, and it is only when you look out from this hill that you realise just how land-locked Singapore's harbour is. Islands stretch round it in an almost unbroken chain, so that, whatever happens to the sea outside, the repercussions can scarcely be felt within the island barrier.

Almost due west lies Bukom, a Shell island-kingdom where the tankers come and go in an unending stream, slowly making their way through the channel which leads through the hazardous coral reefs lying in submerged mountains and plateaux below the surface of the sea.

The garden of the bungalow ends in a cliff, and along the base of the cliff passes a stately procession of merchantmen using the harbour's southern entrance. There is hardly a moment of the day that a ship does not pass, and as they pass you can hear above the swish of the bow wave the thumping of their engines, and see men standing urgently on their bridges. Entering the harbour of Singapore is not a matter to be taken lightly, for four times a day the tides swirl round the islands like great rivers in flood. A great sheet of water slides perpetually past the base of our cliff and whips itself into whirlpools which become encrusted with dead foam and reach down like roots to the irresistible movement below.

Perhaps the best thing about this bungalow is the view it allows of the sunset, for there can scarcely be anywhere in this world where sunsets are more compellingly beautiful than here in Malaya.

As the sun sinks, and reddens through infinite shades of gold, it casts its burning light along the water so that a path of light leads over the water to the purple mountains of Indonesia lying just below the sun. As it sinks still farther you see that it is behind them, so that the purple mountains become jet black in a golden sea. They seem almost to be on fire, for surrounding them is a corona of flame which burns in their blackness as coals burn in a fire.

When the sun falls beyond the horizon and when, in the city which lies behind us, it is already dark, the dying but still theatrical searchlights shoot upwards to throw shadows upon the clouds, and the darkened, light-shot clouds throw shadows on the midnight-blue and turquoise of the sky above them. Then the sky is a fading fan of golden, reddening, dying light, until over the Indonesian hills there is only the faintest trace of light still bearing witness to the day that has gone. And out of the black darkness comes the austere white flash, flash, flash of Raffles Light.

November 2nd, 1954

No one ever looked twice at Emerald Hartley, but had one done so he would have seen a face that in the arrangement of its features was not entirely displeasing. Yet it was a face that had somehow lost its savour, without, at the same time, losing all those precious traces which reveal the fact that it was once attractive. Emerald Hartley could never have been considered pretty, but it is possible that when she was very much younger than she was when she first came to Singapore, she may have been thought at least potentially handsome. If so, the early promise had never been fulfilled. Yet there lingered still, about the sad, square face, an element of beauty. Perhaps it lay in the occasional flash of her deeply blue eyes; perhaps in the occasionally almost provocative set of her lips; perhaps, simply, in the patient acceptance of her expression. Only one thing was certain; a trace of beauty remained and no one knew where the beauty had gone. Emerald Hartley was, in fact, something of a mystery.

Her name, for instance—Emerald. It was altogether preposterous that such a person should be called Emerald. Emerald was the name of a film star, or of a barmaid, or of an Irish girl so beautiful that she could rise above it. But not Emerald Hartley. And yet it was her name and she was perfectly satisfied with it.

Emerald was the illegitimate daughter of a Church of England clergyman and his housekeeper. At the time of her conception her father held a living in a remote village of the Midlands, where the news of his misadventure would have been received by his parishioners both with a gravity greater than that reserved for those occasions when men receive news of the outbreak of world wars, and with a glee, albeit guarded, more appropriate to the occasions when men learn that they have won them. It was therefore unthinkable that knowledge of his predicament should be allowed to spread farther than the two souls who had been a party to it. On reflection, he discovered that there were only two avenues that offered any hope of escape from the terrible censure of both his flock and his ecclesiastical superiors. Either he must make an end of his life, or he must send his Mrs. Barnaby to the opposite end of the land where she could deliver herself of his offspring in complete anonymity. Then, having made, under his direction and by means of his financial support, provision for its adequate care, she could, if she wished, return to his vicarage, little the worse, and probably the wiser, for the experience. Or, if she preferred, she could stay where she was until the child was old enough to look after itself.

The Reverend Roger Hartley felt that his downfall had come about partly through his own excess of zeal for the good life. Although he had never succeeded in emulating for any length of time the physical denial of the Trappist Monk, he had led a life that had for many years been one of but rarely relieved virtue. He was, therefore, on finding himself in an otherwise empty vicarage with a person of the character and proportions of Mrs. Barnaby, the less able to resist her captivating advances. He also felt (but perhaps not very clearly) that God had scarcely played fair in planting Mrs. Barnaby within such distressingly easy reach of his own vulnerable body.

With the aid of these arguments he was able to rule out the unpleasant prospect of suicide which, it may as well be admitted, he hardly considered seriously at all. The problem amounted simply to this : Mrs. Barnaby had to be sent away, and urgently, at that. The problem was not insoluble. It was therefore unfortunate that it was at this point, his mind made up and with a firm plan of action clearly forming in his head, that he discovered that he loved the woman.

Mrs. Barnaby had lived in the district all her life, and as a young girl had married the proprietor of the only shop of which her village could boast. It was one of those peculiarly English institutions, a village shop, which sold practically everything which the average person could require during a simple, country lifetime. It was primarily for groceries, and yet sold iron-mongery, stationery, ready-made clothes and toys. The term groceries was interpreted in the widest possible sense, and so included vegetables, confectionery and patent medicines. Under the direction of Mr. Barnaby the business grew and expanded, so that when he was suddenly carried off in an epidemic of influenza, his widow, having sold the business, was left a person of considerable substance.

She retired to live the sort of life that became a widowed gentlewoman of thirty-five in a cottage in Roger Hartley's village which had previously been occupied by a retired stockbroker, one of that group of relatively affluent outsiders to be found in every English village, whose highest ambition in peacetime is to sit on the local bench and hob-nob with the gentry and in times of war to become the local Home Guard Commander.

By moving into this particular house, Evelyn Barnaby entered a limbo of lost souls. Had she moved into one of the new council houses, no word would have been uttered against her. But now, to her erstwhile acquaintances she was stuck up, or had big ideas, or had fleeced the public when she had been a grocer's wife, or was simply silly or proud or snobbish. On the other hand, the farmers, the few professional men, and people who, for one reason or another, possessed either more money or more intelligence than the average farm labourer, were aloof and distant. Evelyn Barnaby no longer fitted into an institution which traditionally was split irrevocably between money or a modicum of education on the one hand and relative poverty or ignorance on the other. And no one was more sensitive of this position than Evelyn Barnaby herself and possibly, later, the vicar.

That was how the whole trouble started : a disconsolate and not unattractive widow in a highly polished, brightly linoleumed cottage, almost next door to a lonely vicar in a cheerless and empty vicarage.

Calls on each other increased until they became a habit, and habit became surreptitious lest it should be noticed. When Evelyn Barnaby became his housekeeper it was largely a device for their seeing more of one another without arousing the suspicions of those who might observe them. Evelyn would repair to the vicarage at seven-thirty in the morning and would remain there, more or less continuously, until, perhaps, nine or ten in the evening. She cooked, cleaned, dusted, swept, washed and mended, and for her services received a reasonable wage. When she first accepted the post a number of evil tongues wagged speculatively but, since they were unable to prove any of their numerous theories, their interpretation of events was not generally accepted.

Then, suddenly, Evelyn Barnaby announced that she was going to spend a holiday with a cousin in the Lake District, and her departure was sufficiently elaborate to cause her to board a train bound approximately in that direction. She was never seen or heard of again by anyone in the village.

Two months later the Reverend Roger Hartley, after two painful interviews with his Bishop, also left suddenly and was replaced by a cherubic young man whose wife had already delivered herself of four children. Roger Hartley, too, went out of the lives of the villagers for ever and, although much malicious gossip followed his departure, it brought less enjoyment than might otherwise have been the case since the subject was no longer easily available for public inspection. The cottage was put up for sale by an agent, and in the course of time the village ceased to talk of the Reverend Roger Hartley and Evelyn Barnaby.

Not long afterwards, a Mr. and Mrs. Hartley took up residence in a very ordinary terrace of houses in the city of Exeter. Those who saw them arrive saw that Mrs. Hartley was pregnant but, since such a condition was not unusual among married women, they thought no more about it. Five months later, Emerald Hartley was born.

Roger Hartley had found himself a post teaching classical languages to repellent little boys who had fallen behind in their studies in more acceptable educational institutions. They made Roger's life miserable, a misery which he was obliged to endure in return for an inadequate salary. In the beginning he was prepared to put up with life as he found it, to lie in the bed he had made for himself. After all, he loved the woman who had become his wife and she, without doubt, was devoted to him. But Roger was dogged by his conscience, and his disappointment in himself increased as the years passed. He began to regard himself, or at least his conscience did, with disillusionment, even with dislike. He slowly developed, and at first imperceptibly, into a bitter, middle-aged man. At the same time Evelyn Barnaby grew fatter and less and less pleasing to behold, so that in the end his love for her faded and became, like his clerical profession, a thing of the past, remembered only to be regretted.

In this atmosphere of disillusionment, dissatisfaction and atrophy, Emerald spent her early life. She knew at that time nothing of the early history of her parents, who had lived previously, so they had told her, in Scotland, where her father had held a teaching appointment in a similar school near Aberdeen. She grew up knowing a father who had nothing in common intellectually with her mother. She watched him retire ever more closely into himself, while her mother, deprived of affection, began slowly to lose the self-respect which before had kept her house in order. She grew lazy, and when she grew fat took no steps to reverse the process, and she lost all interest in her person and in its appearance to other people.

Occasionally there would be terrible quarrels in this loveless, friendless house and Emerald would stand horrified as her parents, driven almost to blows by their intense, mutual irritation, revealed the ultimate detestation they felt for each other.

Emerald was an ungainly child. At school she distinguished herself neither athletically nor academically. Her school reports spoke of a dull, introspective child who, in all things, seemed to lack enthusiasm. She had inherited neither her father's intelligence nor her mother's looks, but only an amalgam of them both in which the two qualities were halved. She made few friends at school and took part in none of the extra-curricular activities provided. She was a lonely, uncommunicative child who, finding herself unable to compete with other children, sought comfort within herself, hiding, as it were, within her shell, as a tortoise avoids its enemies.

When Emerald left school she took a job as a typist in the office of a local company. She had managed to pass her School Certificate examination and in her last year at school had learned to type, so that there was no reason why she should not be able to make a career for herself as a secretary. And after she had worked for six months a hidden strength and initiative began to make itself apparent, both to herself and to those with whom she worked. She was then nearly seventeen.

Her appearance improved. The straight lines of her body softened into the suggestion of curves. She took more trouble with her hair and she began to use a modicum of make-up. Although she was still heavily built and would never be able to rid herself of her physical stolidity, the idea that a man could be attracted towards her, particularly an older man, became conceivable. It was her face which compelled attention: a square, regular face, a face full of an expressed sadness which made it sometimes beautiful. The angular line of her jaw, the high cheek-bones, the broad expanse of her forehead and the uncompromising line of her yet perfectly shaped lips gave her an appearance both of austerity and of gentleness—a sad, calm, appealing gentleness.

At this period in her life she was still lost and without prospect of finding herself. She knew that she hated her home and yet that she should not hate that which had sheltered her for so long. She felt a distant affection for her father and none at

all for her mother whom she had grown to despise. She hated
the daily drudgery of typing, hammering away at black and
white keys that floated before her eyes. She could see no sense
in her work nor in the letters she typed. She knew only that
there was a better life if only she could find it—not simply a
good life, a life where she could marry and raise children in a
contented and secure home, the sort of life that millions of
others made for themselves unconsciously, by accident rather
than by any deliberate design; but more than the merely good
life, a life which could be dedicated to some ideal, guided only
by something which she could see, perhaps only dimly, at the
end of her life, like a beacon, which would light her way as she
struggled devotedly towards it.

These ideas formed themselves slowly in her mind as she
toiled in the dusty, decrepit offices of Sowerby & Sons Ltd., ex-
porters. She was at this time terribly unhappy. Her ideas were
vague and disorganised, and the girls who worked with her
could not understand this pale, gentle lump of a girl, who showed
no interest in the things that interested them—men, clothes and
cinemas. Had she spoken to them about her thoughts they
would not have understood her, partly because she would have
expressed herself so badly. Nor could she speak to her parents,
since she could scarcely bring herself to speak to her mother at
all and her relations with her father were neither sufficiently
close nor sufficiently distant to make confidences easy.

She began to read. It was a thing she had never done before
with any degree of enjoyment, and the books she borrowed from
the public library covered an immensely wide field of interest.
They had, however, one thing in common: they were solid,
valuable books which had something tangible to contribute to
her ideas of man's purpose in the world. As she read, she began
to perceive more clearly her own place in life and what it was
that she had to do. And with this knowledge came a happiness
she had never known before.

Two years later a young girl of twenty boarded a ship at
Southampton. She was dressed in a white linen suit belted about
her waist. Her legs were still thick, and she wore flat, brown
brogues. Her fair hair was pulled back into a bun at the back

of her head. She watched England slip away from her without
any visible show of emotion except that, if anything, her face
was sadder and more melancholy than usual.

That was the last anyone in England saw or heard of Emerald
for fourteen years. She corresponded with no one, and the only
indication of her continued existence that those who had known
her received were two wreaths which turned up mysteriously
when first her father and then her mother died. Apart from
this, Emerald might as well have been dead. When, fourteen
years later, she did return to Exeter, no one remembered her.
Those who had been her school friends or who later had worked
with her had either gone away or died or simply forgotten her.
Emerald spent several days in Exeter, staying in a small and
unpretentious hotel, and not one of the town's inhabitants recognised her.

Emerald herself did not know why she went back to Exeter,
wandering like a ghost among the ruins of her childhood. Perhaps in the inelegant but still familiar streets she found something which for a time sustained her when the life she had led
abroad had ceased to do so. She visited the graves of her parents
and stood for a long time staring dry-eyed at the sad little
mounds of soil. She walked slowly up and down the street in
which she had lived, and on one occasion invented a pretext for
knocking at the door of her old house, so that when it was
opened she could catch a glimpse of the cramped interior which
seemed familiar but which was now so different.

Then, as suddenly, she left Exeter and came to Singapore. No
one ever knew what happened to Emerald in Africa, and even
today it is a secret which she alone holds. Perhaps she was terribly hurt, mentally, physically or even spiritually. Perhaps she
had a love affair which in some way ended in disaster. Whatever
the agony had been, and it was clear that what she had suffered
had been a form of agony, it had shocked her out of the life to
which she had unreservedly devoted herself for fourteen years.
The terrible blow, when it had fallen, had injured her in such
a way that her previous work became impossible and the only
comfort she had been able to seek had been a fleeting return to
the unhappy haunts of her childhood. Either her faith in her

work or her belief in herself had been so damaged that she could no longer endure life as she had known it. It seemed that somewhere a man had been involved—but no one knew how—except that Emerald's experience had been a terrible one.

When Emerald arrived in Singapore she had recovered her equilibrium to a slight extent or, if it is not true to say that she had recovered it, she had, at least, acquired a new one. In appearance she was not noticeably different from the girl who had sailed from Southampton so many years before. She was neither fatter nor thinner, and her austere clothing was still much the same. Her face, however, was older and wiser, and burnt to an almost leathery toughness. Myriads of little lines were already gathering at the corners of her eyes, and her lips betrayed a pallor that the tan of her face made more pronounced. But some of the sad serenity was returning, replacing the distant hopelessness with which she had paced the streets of Exeter.

She had come out to Singapore to take charge of two small European girls whose parents had decided to keep them in the East for a further three years before sending them to school in Europe. Since no schools in Singapore were thought to be good enough, Emerald was engaged for the interim. Although she had no academic or professional qualifications, the missionary body for whom she had worked had spoken most highly of her aptitude for teaching small children.

The children were Mary and Jennifer Matthews, aged eight and six respectively. The Matthews lived in one of those ancient Singapore residences which were clearly better designed to hold regiments of troops than small families. It stood on an eminence in Tanglin behind a velvet lawn which swept unbroken to the road below. But many advantages attended its size: for example, Emerald was able to occupy what amounted to a flat, and so was able to pursue an existence reasonably separate from that of the remainder of the household.

She came to Singapore in the P. & O. liner *Carthage*, and was met at the quay by Fred Matthews, the father of the children she was to manage. He brought with him Suwarno, his Malay, or, more precisely, Indonesian driver, to carry her bags to the waiting Chevrolet. Fred Matthews was an Insurance man and

was what is known in Singapore as a "Number One." This odd
title means that the person so called is the head as far as Singapore is concerned, of the company for which he works, and carries with it the dubious distinction of causing him to be invited automatically to a number of dinner-parties to which
nothing so lowly as a "Number Two" is ever admitted, except
when his "Number One" is on long leave. Fred Matthews enjoyed, or appeared to enjoy, every minute of his life. He enjoyed
his work, his home, his family, and the wonderful feeling of
being a "Number One" among dozens and dozens of other
"Number Ones." He loved the dinner-parties and the pleasant
somnolent feeling of a dinner too well eaten, the Sunday morning
rounds of golf and the noisy lunch-time conversation in the club.

"I'm Fred Matthews," he announced, holding out his hand.
"Miss Hartley?"

"Yes."

"Good trip?" He picked up her meagre luggage and handed
it to Suwarno. "This, by the way, is Suwarno," he added.

Suwarno flashed his white-toothed smile.

"*Tabek*, Missee."

"How do you do?" answered Emerald, pushing back a wisp of
her fair hair.

Suwarno marched off and even Emerald could scarcely fail
to notice his beautiful proportions, the incredibly thin hips and
the swelling shoulders bulging beneath the white uniform bush
shirt. He was handsome too, with wide brown eyes and a firm
mouth. His straight black hair was impeccably combed and
signs of the barber's singe showed at the nape of his neck. He
walked with the controlled agility of an athlete, as though he
too, like his womenfolk, could carry a burden on his head without in any way modifying his gait.

"You've been in the tropics before," Matthews was saying, "so
you know what it's like, eh?"

Matthews had been long enough in the East to have formed
the habit of pronouncing all question marks. It was an easily
acquired habit where the answer of "yes" did not always give
any indication of comprehension, more often the contrary.

"Yes," replied Emerald, "I was in West Africa for fourteen years."

"Well, you will know what heat is, then. Here we are! Should I lead the way?"

He pushed his way through the congealed crowd of people that encumber the gangways of all passenger liners just arrived in harbour and made his way down to the baking quay, followed by Emerald. The heat danced off the white concrete and the corrugated iron roofs of the godowns shimmered in the sun, their outlines hazy and indistinct.

They walked over to the car and climbed into the back, while Suwarno stowed the luggage in the boot.

"*Piggi rumah*," said Matthews.

"What does that mean?" asked Emerald.

"*Piggi rumah*?—go home. I don't speak much Malay—you can do without it in Singapore. Up country it is useful, but English is as much as you need here."

They drove along Anson Road into Robinson Road and then out on to Collyer Quay where the little ships mass within the protection of the breakwater. From the side of the road to the horizon the sea was full of ships, ships from almost every country of the world.

"Wonderful sight, isn't it?" Matthews remarked. "This is the hub of the Orient, whatever Peking thinks."

"Yes, it is wonderful," agreed Emerald.

She leaned forward from the deep upholstery and watched as they passed the ships until the car turned on to Cavanagh Bridge and over into St. Andrew's Road. Emerald leaned back and for a moment found herself watching Suwarno's neck, a straight brown neck, and she experienced the slightest of inclinations to touch it with the point of her finger; it looked so hard, and yet she knew that it would yield to her finger and that a tiny lightened spot would remain for a second where she had touched it.

"This is the City Hall," announced Matthews. "Pretty, isn't it?"

Emerald looked and saw the long white building, resplendent with its Grecian columns, facing the Padang.

Malacca River.

Tea and Jungle, Malaya—

"Everything in Malaya has been wrested from the enveloping power of the jungle and to the jungle it will all return if man ever loses interest in the fight."

Soon they were in Orchard Road and the car turned into the Cold Storage car park and came to rest.

"I won't be a second. I arranged to pick my wife up here—I'll just go across and get her."

Emerald watched him pick his way through the traffic and then disappear inside Cold Storage, which she assumed from its appearance to be a grocer's shop. The heat was unbearable and she opened one door to take the greatest advantage of the slight breeze. Suwarno sat quietly at his wheel staring vacantly through the windscreen. Then he took a comb from his pocket and carefully combed his heavy black hair and, so that he should not disturb the perfection of his parting, he glanced into the driving-mirror and there saw Emerald's intensely blue eyes, and for a moment the eyes held one another and then darted away.

"This is Miss Hartley, darling."

A tall, angular woman bent to look through the car door and put forward a thin and bony hand.

"I'm so pleased you're here, Miss Hartley—how do you do?"

She climbed into the car as Emerald moved over, and Matthews squashed in beside them. Suwarno put the car in gear and moved slowly out of the car park.

"Did you have a good trip?" asked Sheila Matthews.

She used a heavy, pallid make-up and the perspiration that oozed from below gave it a waterlogged appearance like half-dried mud. She dabbed at it frequently with a tiny handkerchief which achieved no more than a superficial drying of the wetter areas.

"Lovely, thank you," answered Emerald.

"Good food?"

"Yes, very good!"

And so the conversation continued along Orchard Road and into Tanglin. It was a difficult conversation in which Fred and Sheila Matthews strove to extract from Emerald some thought, some comment which they did not themselves have to put first into her mouth. Emerald simply answered their questions, politely and directly but no more, so that by the time the car arrived at St. Peter's Drive the Matthews were beginning to wonder what manner of woman they had hired, this infinitely neat, stocky woman with the large breasts, who sat upright and looked to the front with large blue eyes and spoke only when addressed.

I think that Emerald, at that time, was nervous more than anything else. Before she had gone to Africa she had been a young girl who knew only a relatively unhappy childhood. She had been endowed with neither physical grace nor great mental ability and her personality had not been one which attracted friends. During those early years she had been compelled to turn inwards on herself and, until she had found her missionary work, had found there only an emptiness. Then came Africa and a single-minded life in lonely places, where she had devoted herself to an interest and a cause that precluded all else. Then the culminating pain of which she would not speak, the crucifixion that had failed in so far as it had failed to kill her, followed by the restless pacing of Exeter streets. Emerald had scarcely met the people of this world, and the world that she saw and yet did not understand was coloured entirely by her own peculiar experience of the little she had known. She was like a person who has spent years of isolation in the Malayan jungle. Men who did so during the war found, when they emerged, that the sentimental situation of the most trivial film would cause tears to stream down their faces. Emerald was unsure of her emotions, unsure almost of everything except the consciousness of pain. Perhaps these were the reasons for her reserve.

"This is it," said Matthews.

They climbed from the car and crossed the gravel to the steps that led up to the front door. A Chinese boy hurried to meet them, a wide grin on his moon-like face.

"Hello, Ah Han," said Sheila Matthews. "Will you take the bags?"

Ah Han took the bags from Suwarno and followed the little procession into the hall.

"I'll take you to your room," said Sheila. "We've put you at the back of the house where it's quiet and you will be near the children."

Emerald followed Sheila up the stairs and on to the polished wooden landing. The noise of her employer's high heels rang through the house as they marched down the long corridor which led to the rear of the house.

"Well, I'll leave you for a bit. I expect you'll want to change and bath. You'll eat with us, of course. Tea will be in about half an hour. The children are out with their *amah* at the moment but you'll meet them at tea—they've gone to the Botanical Gardens to feed the monkeys."

She closed the door and Emerald heard her heels clack-clacking down the wooden corridor and then down the stairs. Emerald sat heavily and erectly on the bed and stared in front of her. She felt suddenly lost. A feeling of helplessness and futility enveloped her and a feeling, too, of fear. She feared these two, no doubt obstreperous children, feared not only the inroads they would make on her life but also her own ability to control them. But this was not all, for she knew also a secret, nameless fear that had been with her since Africa but which now was suddenly intensified. She sat, quite still, apparently composed, her big hands clasped together on the taut material stretched across her broad thighs. She put one hand to her forehead and brushed back a wisp of straight hair and tried to force it into the tight little bun that sat on the nape of her neck. She felt suddenly that she would like to cry—but Emerald had never cried.

She heard the slam of a door in the garden and she rose and crossed to the window. It was Suwarno closing the garage door. He had taken off his white uniform jacket and was holding it over his arm. He wore a tight T-shirt which clung to the contours of his arms and shoulders, and as he sauntered towards the servants' quarters he glanced over his shoulder to the house and Emerald moved quickly away from the window; but she did not know whether or not he had seen her.

After the first fortnight she found that she was not going to be as unhappy as she had thought. The children she taught were not altogether unattractive and both were possessed of a measure of intelligence. The task of instilling knowledge into their minds was not as arduous as it might have been. Her afternoons were her own entirely and most of her evenings were free.

She spent much of her spare time reading and walking, and could often be seen striding purposefully along Holland Road, always dressed in her uncompromising linen suit, the single mound of her bosom giving her an almost military air. Within a few weeks she had explored on foot almost the whole of Singapore island. When she had a free Sunday she would take herself off in the early morning with a bag of sandwiches, returning in the evening, burnt and exhausted, having walked goodness knows how many miles in the blazing sun.

Then the Matthews decided that Emerald—they all called her Emerald, even the children—must have a clearer interest in life.

"Emerald," said Mrs. Matthews one lunch-time, "we need a new secretary for our Association. Would you like to take it on?"

The Association was one that had been formed by a number of European and Chinese ladies who found time lying heavily upon their hands. They devoted themselves to good works, which helped not only to fill their time but also to ease their conscience. They were not wedded to one particular charity, but simply helped where they felt themselves to be useful. Much of the organising work fell upon the secretary, and Sheila Matthews's suggestion was made in such a way as to be fairly certain of ensuring that it would fall in future upon Emerald. But Emerald was happy to agree. Some of her reserve was falling away and she no longer looked upon contact with other people with quite the same degree of diffidence as when she had first arrived in Singapore.

"We have a meeting this evening which you may like to attend," added Sheila.

Emerald went to the meeting and was duly installed as secretary, to the general satisfaction of the other ladies present, all of whom had seen themselves being saddled with the arduous, unspectacular duties of organising the Association's activities. Emerald and Sheila drove home from the meeting together.

"It will get you out," said Sheila. "You will meet people and all that. Good thing."

Emerald said that she was sure Sheila was right, and the next day threw herself into her new task with the fierce determination with which she tackled everything. Her walks, her reading, her acceptance of the post of secretary, even her original decision to come to Singapore, all were ventures undertaken to alleviate the empty aching that went on without cease within her. And all of them were unsuccessful, since they were simply substitutes for something more fundamental. It is true that during the short time she had been in Singapore a certain change for the better had taken place. She was busy with work that interested her, and to the extent that it took her mind off the problem of her own individual existence, it helped to lessen her moods of introspection. But the moment there was a break in her activity the dull misery would return, so that she would lie in bed in the darkness staring at the faintly-lit ceiling, listening to the sweet, sad sounds of the tropical night, the insects, the frogs and the distant beat of a drum.

The drum became for her a symbol of her plight. It was situated somewhere down in the Malay *kampong* beyond the garden and she only heard it at night when she was alone and when the house was still. She would listen for the drum, and sometimes its sound would not come, and at others it would play softly and in varying rhythms for perhaps half an hour or more. She would lie rigidly below the single sheet, and the drum would awaken something within her that she did not understand but which she did not want to lose.

Meanwhile, she was busy with the children and the work of the Association. Often, in the evenings, she would have to call at the houses of members, and the Matthews would always lend her the car when they themselves were not using it. Suwarno would drive her and talk to her when she talked to him. He knew a little English and he offered to teach her Malay, and the lessons took place in the car as they drove from one house to another. Once he suggested that she should sit in the front with him, but she did not accept the invitation, although she did not forget that it had been made. Suwarno was perhaps thirty years old and in his outlook essentially boyish and irresponsible. His greatest joy was to do nothing, and if it were necessary for him to work he cherished no ambition to work at anything more exacting than driving a motor-car. He was, too, a ladies' man, a bit of the Malay dandy, to whom dark glasses are an indispensable item of equipment. Emerald was thirty-six, but her outlook was older than her age warranted, and her attitude to Suwarno became, unconsciously, protective. The protective instinct was highly developed in Emerald, and she quickly adopted an informality with Suwarno which she would have found impossible with others and which her employers would have found most improper. Suwarno enjoyed the sense of intimacy which grew up between him and this strange ungainly *mem* and, being fundamentally an opportunist, resolved, if he could, to make use of it. But there was something deeper than this which troubled Suwarno, as it also troubled Emerald. It found expression in sidelong glances when Suwarno could see the fine, fair hair, swept tightly back from the clear forehead, glinting faintly in the dashboard lights, and the soft, firm outline of her profile.

One evening, after Emerald had called on the treasurer of the Association, a Chinese lady whose husband had amassed a fortune by finding himself in possession of an immense stock of pepper at a time when the price rose daily to undreamed-of heights, Suwarno opened the front door of the car as Emerald walked down the front steps of the house. On a quite unpremeditated impulse Emerald climbed into the car and sat in the front seat, while Suwarno climbed in at the other side. As they drove home she could see his proud face, intent, for the moment, on his driving, but revealing, she thought, the slightest suggestion of triumph.

"Don't you think you should be more careful?" she said to him. Suwarno did not reply but drove the car home rather faster than usual and nothing further passed between them until he had turned into the drive. He drove the car beyond the front door and round to the side of the house where there was a side entrance which Emerald often used to avoid going through the main house. Before she could move, he leaned over and unlatched the door, and as his fingers came away she felt them brush lightly over her thighs. It was over in a second, and then Suwarno was sitting at his wheel with the utmost propriety. Emerald got out and slammed the door and went up to her room. She was furious and ashamed. She paced about the room in a kind of torment, and then sat on the bed and looked at her skirt where the strong fingers had brushed. She heard the slam of the garage door and the crunch of footsteps on the gravel, and she went to the window and looked out into the white and moonlit garden. Among the bushes, where the garden began to slope down to the *kampong*, she thought she saw a figure. Then it was gone and she was alone, a wide, black silhouette, motionless as the trees.

She undressed and got into bed, and when she had lain there for perhaps five minutes she heard the drum, very softly and nearer than usual, almost as though it were at the bottom of the garden. It was so soft as to be inaudible, except to those who waited for its sound, a tiny, regular throb, like the beat of a pulse, like the beat of the pulse of the night, the white night, the night absorbed in the recovery of power and the silent, rustling processes of reproduction.

Emerald lay tense on the hard mattress. She heard the Matthews come to bed, the flick of switches and the anguished whistle of emptying cisterns. Then again there was silence, silence except for the tiny tap of the drum. She flung herself on to her side and covered her head with the already damp sheet, and then she could not be sure whether she heard the drum or whether it was her imagination retaining a vision of the sound. So she sat up. It had not gone, and she thought perhaps it was closer than before. She lay down again, and as the minutes ticked by a terrible calmness enveloped her. She no longer thought, but simply allowed herself to float on a cloud that came out of the night to bear her away. When she rose from her bed the harsh lines of determination were swept away, replaced by a soft malleability enclosed in a frame of fair hair that fell from the top of her head and curled in wisps below her chin. She put a housecoat over her nightdress and silently opened her door. She walked down the steps like a sleep-walker, and as she stepped into the garden there was a muted, fervent crescendo from the drum, which then fell silent. She walked in the shadow of the wall that ran along the edge of the garden and came at last to the shelter of bushes at the end of the slope. She walked on down through the bushes until she came to an empty space in the midst of them. There she stopped, staring before her like a saint on her way to her death. She felt the hard fingers tugging at the fastenings and pulling the coat from her shoulders. She allowed the strong arms to bear her to the ground and gave herself to the flexing fingers that freed the great breasts from the constriction of the material that had always hidden them.

"Do you know that Suwarno has bought himself a new radio?" asked Fred Matthews a few weeks later of his wife. "It must have cost two hundred-odd dollars. Where is it coming from, all this money? First a flashy bicycle, then new clothes, now a radio."

"And he's getting too cocky," said Sheila. "Have *you* noticed anything, Emerald?"

"No," said Emerald quietly, "not in his manner. But he did tell me he had a new radio."

The following week Emerald gave her notice. She gave no reason, beyond the fact that she wished to return to England. The Matthews expressed both regret and annoyance, although the latter sentiment was mollified by Emerald's returning the greater part of her passage-money and buying her own return ticket.

On the day of her departure the Matthews travelled with her in the car, driven by Suwarno, to the ship. When they arrived, Suwarno carried the luggage and Emerald walked behind him watching the thick, strong neck, its muscles taut with the weight of the suitcases he held in either hand.

They arrived at Emerald's cabin and Suwarno pushed the luggage under her bunk. The Matthews stood outside. She held out her hand.

"Good-bye, Suwarno."

He took the hand and held it and looked deep into the kind, blue eyes. Then he turned and walked away.

Emerald and the Matthews talked for half an hour before the bell rang announcing that all visitors should leave the ship. The three of them walked up on deck and stood by the gangway. Emerald said:

"I have much to thank you for. I have not told you before, but I am going back to Africa to my old job. When I came to Singapore I was lost, and now, although not in the approved manner I am afraid, I have found myself again. That is why I must go. I hope you will understand. Give my love to the children."

She saw the Matthews through a mist of tears as she took from her pocket a little package.

"I want you to give this to Suwarno. I . . . I have no further use for it. Good-bye. Good-bye . . . and God bless you."

The Matthews stood on the quay as the great ship moved away, and Suwarno, standing by his car, raised his arm in salute.

No one heard very much of Emerald Hartley again. She had given all her money to the man who had saved her and whom she had loved. She had no other worldly possessions. She returned to Africa and, although her soul was perhaps not as white as it had been before, she became to all who met her an example of devotion and piety and a person of boundless and enduring happiness, with a charity extending to all men.

November 3rd, 1954

Robertson told me a story about the Chinese domination of trade in Malaya: A group of Malay fishermen on the sea-coast of Malaya, so he said, were provided with outboard motors for their fishing boats by one of the several benevolent agencies which operate in this part of the world. It had been the habit of these fishermen to put out to sea each day and on return to sell their catch to a Chinese merchant who would normally be waiting for them. He would offer them a price for their catch which, he would tell them, was related to the current market price, the fluctuations of which the fishermen themselves were unable to follow.

When the fishermen had fitted their outboard motors, they found that their work was speeded up to such an extent that they could obtain two catches in one day. After they had left their first catch on shore, they went out again and obtained a second catch of equal proportions. But that evening the merchant did not come.

They went to sea twice again the following day and yet again the merchant did not come to buy their catch.

By this time they had so much fish that they did not know what to do with it. Some of it went bad. On the third evening the merchant at last put in an appearance and they said to him, "Where were you the last two days? We have had great catches but you were not here to buy them."

The merchant said that he had been very busy and that there was a great slump in the market for fish.

And the fishermen said: "What, then, are we to do with all this fish? Can you not buy any of it?"

The merchant again described the calamitous slump that prevailed and said that he was very sorry but he could not buy a single fish.

So the fishermen said: "What, then, shall we do for a living? We have no money, and unless you buy our fish we shall be unable to buy petrol for our motors."

The merchant thought for a long time and made it clear to them that he was doing his best to help them. They stood round him in a little group waiting for his solution of their problem. Suddenly his face lit up and he said:

"I will give you $200 for each outboard motor and then you will not have to buy petrol in order to take your boats to sea."

The fishermen thought that this was a very good idea and agreed at once. The merchant sent a lorry to take away the outboard motors and the fishermen put to sea the next day under sail. They were at sea the whole day and they did not catch many fish, but when they returned to shore they found the merchant waiting for them and he gave them a good price for their fish.

November 4th, 1954

I called to see a Chinese today who is prominent in the new Nanyang University. He said: "I believe in ancestor worship. I do not believe that ordinary people can grasp the idea of a non-anthropomorphic God. Now, take the Christian religion. First of all, they have their God who is not fashioned in the shape of man. It is soon found, however, that what the people want is a God that they can recognise, and so you have in the Christian religion the Son of God in human form. But even this is not enough, for the people require something even more tangible to worship. Then a great many Saints are created and statues of these Saints are made and placed in the churches. The Son of God is also given a Mother and a statue is made of her, too. The people can then see what it is they are worshipping and can recognise their Gods. Is this not idolatry? And is it in any way different in principle from worshipping one's ancestors?"

November 5th, 1954

The extraordinary things that can happen in the tropics, especially when people are fond of animals. The telephone rang one morning in the General Hospital at Singapore. A voice enquired whether it would be possible for her to borrow an invalid's wheel-chair. The hospital replied that this might well be possible since they did lend such appliances, but before they could do so it would be necessary for them to have some further particulars. They asked the nature of the complaint and the reply given was that the invalid had polio. The hospital then asked the enquirer the sex of the patient, and again the answer was readily given.

"Male."

"And has the patient been ill for very long?"

"Oh yes, for a long time."

"And what is the name of the patient?"

"Keats."

"Mr. Keats?"

"That is correct."

"How long has the patient been ill?"

"For about three years."

"And it has not been necessary for the patient to be provided with a wheel-chair before?"

"No."

"Has, then, the condition of the patient recently worsened?"

"Yes."

"Has the patient seen a doctor?"

" . . . er . . . yes."

"What is the name of the doctor?"

There was a long silence from the other end of the telephone and then the voice asked testily:

"Is it really necessary to ask all these questions?"

"I am afraid it is."

"Well, as a matter of fact I look after the patient myself."

"Oh! How old is the patient?"

"He will be seven years in June."

"Oh, I see. You need a wheel-chair for a child?"

"Er . . . yes . . . I mean, no."

"But if he is only seven years old he must be a child."

"But he is a very big child."

"But a child of that age cannot be so big that a child's wheel-chair will be of no use."

The voice at the other end was by now very angry and said:

"I do not want a wheel-chair for a child. I want a strong wheel-chair for an adult."

"But why do you want a wheel-chair big enough for an adult for a child only seven years old, even though he is, as I understand, a very big child for his age?"

"Well, I am telling you he is very big and very heavy, and a child's wheel-chair will not do."

"Can you bring the patient to the hospital?"

"No, I cannot bring the patient to the hospital."

"Why can you not bring the patient to the hospital?"

"Because it would look rather silly."

"Silly?"

"Yes, very silly."

By this time the hospital could think of no more questions to ask, and yet was far from satisfied with the information that had been given. Finally they asked:

"How much does the patient weigh?"

There was a long silence from the other end and then the voice said:

"About twenty-five stone."

"Twenty-five stone?"

"Yes, twenty-five stone. You will see that a child's wheel-chair will be no use for the purpose."

"You want a wheel-chair for a child aged seven, male, who has not seen a doctor, has infantile paralysis and weighs twenty-five stone? We are sorry, madam, but we do not believe you."

"Well, if you must know," said the voice furiously, "the chair I require is for my pet Orang Utang!"

November 6th, 1954

Buddhism is one of the religions of Malaya. Buddhism often seems to me to be superior to many other religions, in that it appears to have a higher regard for animals and a greater concern for their welfare. Indeed, animals are to be found in many Buddhist temples, some being devoted almost entirely to one kind of animal. There is in Malaya a temple known as the Snake Temple.

When one enters the Snake Temple, one does not at first see the many snakes which festoon the Buddhist trappings of worship. They tend to lurk behind doors and in the shadows of the ancient walls, but the incredible thing is that as far as is known they have never so much as blinked an eye at the sight of a human being, let alone attacked one.

There is a story told of this temple which is possibly not true, but the truth of the matter is unimportant: it is sufficient that it be credible. In a courtyard adjoining the temple, captive in a cage let into the floor, is a quite enormous python, the kind of snake that can swallow a whole goat and afterwards experience no particular digestive troubles. It is said that any man who puts his hand into this cage, and then into the mouth of the python, will become a millionaire, if the python does not bite him. Pythons do not usually, I believe, bite their enemies, but rather crush them to death, but this particular python must, I fancy, be of a special variety which does bite when presented with the correct type of stimulus. I have never, myself, seen it open its mouth, but judging from the size of its head, gigantic by any standard, its mouth, in the extended position, must be capable of dealing with several hands simultaneously.

Ng Koong Yong was a very poor man. He had come from China in a junk in great discomfort, discomfort so acute that it was only rivalled by his poverty. But he had been sustained on his voyage by the vision of the fortune he was going to make in the promised land of Malaya. He had no doubt of this and believed without any reservation at all that he would be returning to China within twenty years possessed of a considerable fortune. When he first arrived in Malaya he obtained work as a coolie in the harbour and received for his hard labour the merest pittance. But before embarking on his chosen career of becoming a millionaire he had first to amass capital, and since he reckoned that $50 would be sufficient to set him up in a fair way of business, working in the docks was as good a way as any to obtain it. By living frugally and by rigorously abstaining from the more common vices of gambling, women and opium, he was able to save this sum within four months.

At the end of this period, with five crisp ten-dollar notes in his belt, he set out to conquer the world, and bought a half-share in a tiny food-stall belonging to a local Chinese hawker. The business appeared to be a flourishing one and within two weeks his investment of $50 had increased to $75. Ng, however, had failed to take the precaution of ascertaining whether the stall of which he had become part-owner was sited in an area where hawking was permitted. As it turned out it manifestly was not, and early one morning it was destroyed by the police who had, it subsequently transpired, several times warned Ng's partner of the consequences of such an infringement of the law. They were both brought up in court and fined $10 each, so that Ng had lost not only the $50 he had invested in the business but also $10 of his profit of $25.

But he was undaunted and thought little of this purely temporary (he considered) setback. With the remaining $15 he bought a number of wooden stools, which had been mass-produced by one of the local workshops, strung them from either end of a long pole and carried them into the town, where he hoped to sell them at a price which would yield for him a profit of $5. Unfortunately, in his anxiety to reach the shopping area with the stools, he came into collision with a lorry, which considerably damaged him and completely destroyed the stools.

When he came out of hospital he had, once more, no money at all. He went back to work in the docks, and by virtue of the strictest economy managed to save another $50. This, again, he invested in a succession of curious enterprises, all of which turned out to be unsuccessful, so that within a month of his leaving the docks for the second time he was again penniless. Altogether he repeated the process five times, and each venture was as unsuccessful as the last until, after eighteen months in Malaya, he was on the verge of suicide.

He spoke to his friend of his great trouble and told him of the wonderful plans he had once had to become rich in Malaya and how they had all come to nothing. His friend then told him of the python in the Snake Temple, and said that if Ng was contemplating suicide, would it not be better if he first tried putting his hand into the mouth of the python? At first Ng was unconvinced. He did not in the least fancy putting his hand into the mouth of a twenty-foot snake which could swallow a goat whole without trouble. But as at the time the only alternative appeared to be suicide and since there was always the possibility that the snake would not bite him, he allowed himself to be persuaded and asked his friend to come with him to the temple.

They went early one Sunday morning, not long after dawn. Ng walked into the temple and through into the courtyard where he met face to face a snake bigger than any he had ever thought possible. As they walked up to the cage the thick gross body stirred within its endless coils and two beady eyes surveyed Ng with a calmness which Ng could not possibly share. He began to sweat and to tremble so violently that his friend had to hold him up. He experienced an overwhelmingly keen desire to run away as fast as his legs could carry him and to throw himself from the first high building he came to, a form of death which seemed infinitely preferable to one in any way connected with this dreadful snake. But his friend spoke gently to him and after a while his trembling to some extent subsided. Once more he opened his eyes and looked at the snake, while his friend took from his pocket a pair of small wire-cutters, specially stolen for the purpose. He watched him cut through one of the strands of the netting that covered the top of the cage, thus making a small hole big enough to allow the passage of Ng's hand but not big enough to permit the escape of the snake.

Ng became like a man in a trance. He muttered under his

breath incoherently a number of ancient Chinese prayers and prepared himself for the death which he felt was imminent. He no longer seemed to have any control over his limbs and, in fact, it was his friend who pushed his clammy, shaking hand through the hole in the netting. Ng was as incapable of looking into the cage as he was of removing his hand. He simply stood there helplessly, a small, frightened figure in the still, cold light of the early morning. His friend retired a few paces and watched with fascinated horror the movements of the snake and listened to the scaly, wet rustle of its ponderous body. He saw the great head rise up and uttered an involuntary whimper of horror as it opened its enormous mouth. Then he saw the mouth snapped shut about Ng's wrist. Ng remained motionless, his head averted, no cry of pain or of any other sensation escaping from his lips. For some time his friend did not know why this was so and rushed up to Ng and clasped him about the middle and pulled him so violently from the cage that they both fell in a heap on the floor. Then they saw that Ng's hand was unharmed. For a moment they stared at it without comprehension and then, in the great release of tension, laughed and cried together in their infinite relief. Although the jaws of the snake had snapped over the wrist, the teeth had stopped short a fraction of an inch before they reached the skin, thus allowing it to be withdrawn unharmed.

They walked back to town hand in hand, already planning how they would spend their million dollars. Ng offered his friend a partnership in his business, an offer that was immediately and gratefully accepted, since plans to amass a fortune could not possibly go wrong when they had been inaugurated in such auspicious circumstances, attended by the manifestation of an omen that was so obviously good.

Once more they went back to the docks and earned the necessary fund of capital. Once more the capital was invested, and immediately their business ventures developed according to plan. Everything they touched turned to gold. It did not matter what commodity they bought, its price would rise in world markets the following day. It did not matter where they bought land, since at once someone would want to build a railway over it or erect a factory or a block of flats. They were men possessed of a supernatural knowledge of what would sell and what would not; men who were able to obtain what would sell at a very much lower price than anyone else and sell it for very much more. Their $50 became $500 and their $500 became $5,000. But still they did not live extravagantly. They spent scarcely anything on themselves. They diligently ploughed all their profits back into their business and within five years they were both of them millionaires.

It had been Ng's plan, once he became a millionaire, to build the finest house in Malaya. He chose a large and expensive plot of land overlooking the sea, and employed the most respected architects to design his palace. As the great house rose, brick upon brick, Ng could be seen on the site each day consulting his architect and contractor. He spared nothing to make it the finest residence in the land, and took a personal interest in every aspect of its construction.

When it was finished, standing new and pristine high on its hill, looking out over the sea, he arranged a fabulous party. He invited all his business friends and their wives and mistresses and concubines, their sons and daughters and relations, to a banquet to be held on the magnificent lawn between his house and the sea. Altogether there were a thousand guests, and contracting caterers were at work for days before arranging the tables and the seats and the stage on which a most expensive entertainment was to be presented.

Ng was happier than he had ever thought possible on the day of the banquet. Fifteen of the rarest courses were served and alcohol flowed like water. Many of the guests became very drunk. The noise on the lawn became indescribable and the only words that could be distinguished were the perpetually reiterated "*Yam Seng*," the Chinese cry of "Bottoms up." At length the meal drew to a close and sufficient order was induced into the assembled guests to allow Ng to rise to his feet to deliver the little speech to which he had devoted much careful thought and attention.

He spoke to them in Chinese, and scarcely had he uttered his first few words when it was apparent to those who watched him that he had suddenly experienced a great pain in his leg. He bent down swiftly and clasped one hand to his ankle, where blood oozed through his silk trousers. Those sitting near to him saw the black tail of the cobra disappear like a flash of black lightning into the bushes and, as they shouted to others to run after it and kill it, Ng died in the arms of his friend.

November 7th, 1954

You can hear the roar two hundred yards away, the high, ragged yet regular roar of human voices raised in a common insistence to be heard. Beneath the roar can be heard the occasional and muffled clink of glass. You enter the lighted room and the sound and the smell of humanity wells out like a river in flood, and as people pass before you and are named, you lean against it until the current catches you and sweeps you into the centre of the stream, where you lie helpless and floating and become part of the driving current, driving onwards to extinction and death in the oozing marshes of boredom.

Backs! Backs rounded and blotched, and the flexing of blades under pimpled flesh. Backs rising up to wrinkled necks where the loose skin hangs like the skin of old apples. Bubbling from the chaotic laughter:

"No, he's not married. He simply lives with her."

"How *fascinating*!"

The fascination of the repressed! Twirling and whirling on the angry river lie the broken hopes of lasciviousness, and those that float with them reach out scrawny hands to grab, and then retreat empty, back into the laughter and the overwhelming camouflage of tears.

Pot-belly pressed against pot-belly. Bellies that meet and touch like twin footballs, others that fit, one above the other, like an upright and an inverted pear placed side by side. Tight material stretched taut above the yearning.

"Have you heard this one? About a man who attended a sales convention in the Middle West of America and who was asked by his wife to bring back a special kind of ironing-board?"

"No. Go on."

"Well ..."

A black face and a yellow face set among the white faces, white teeth shining in blackness, gold teeth gleaming in parchment, firm teeth, strong teeth, teeth set in rigid grins, the teeth of the elect grinning the agreement of those too contaminated with agreement to resist.

And sweat! Sweat running in rivulets into shaved armpits and sweat mingled with make-up, dripping sluggishly into poised glasses. Sweat icy cold in the draught of fans, the smell and the thunderous evocation of the smell blown in straight lines into hot nostrils.

> *"And there we two are,*
> *Promising never,*
> *Never to part. . . ."*

The sly pairing of sluts and drunks, waiting upon non-existent proprieties.

The quarrel in the corner:

"The trouble with you is that you're suffering from an over-inflated ego."

"Not in the least. You don't listen!"

"Have a drink, old boy."

The dense press of people wedged upright between four walls. The conversation which has risen to a peak flattens and begins the slow descent, and those who have other engagements and those still sober enough to realise that nothing more than a hangover is to be gained by staying, begin to drift away, and those who are left eat what is handed them and dance to the gramophone.

"I have never been able to understand why it is that people dance, and yet do not follow the motions of the dance through to their ancient and logical conclusion."

"Dancing is simply a means of inducing anticipatory pleasures usually without hope of fulfilment."

"Dancing has become a process whereby that which is better performed in the horizontal is more readily imagined in the vertical."

"But why?"

"Would you care to dance?"

The cold ride home through deserted streets where the exhaust ricochets from slumbering walls, echoing the coming misery of the morning, the concomitant of cocktails.

November 8th, 1954

Herbert Fresley is an American and the only American I know in Singapore who faithfully follows the MacCarthy line. Much of what Herbert Fresley says to me makes a good deal of sense. It is only in the ultimate extension of his arguments to their logical MacCarthyist conclusion that he seems, like so many Americans in America, to leave the realm of sanity. Only then does he become hysterical and begin to advocate unreasonable lines of action.

In Singapore we meet many Americans and it is likely that we obtain here a better idea of what Americans are thinking than, perhaps, do English people in England, where Americans tend to be important Americans. Here we meet ordinary Americans who are concerned mainly in going about their every-day occupations. That they often think differently and certainly live differently from us there is no doubt; but the difference between the Englishman here and the American, in so far as their approach to Communism is concerned, is largely a matter of degree. There is much common ground; as the diplomats now say, there are large areas of agreement, but the major difference between them lies in the fact that the American will take his arguments several steps farther than we will. Whether he is right in doing so, I do not know; all I know is that it is impossible to show that he is wrong. He is certain, and will bring forward numerous concrete instances to prove his point; we are uncertain, and lose ourselves in suggestions, on the one hand, that he is hysterical and, on the other, that the substance of what he is saying is unbelievable. We simply refuse to believe him, while admitting that what he says *is possible*. This, I think, is silly of us. But it perhaps explains why the Americans tolerate a witch-hunt and we do not.

I lunched with Herbert Fresley the other day on the verandah of the boarding-house in which he lives. He is a small, nervous man with thin grey hair, who thinks of little but the menace of

Communism. It has eaten into him as acid will eat into metal, so that he has become a walking, talking, anti-Communist machine. From his mouth flows a perpetual spate of arguments, and when he is not talking, which is not often, he is furiously pounding his portable typewriter, recording the break-up and defeat of the free world, a process already, according to him, under way and a process which, he believes, will continue at an ever-increasing pace unless we all take off our blinkers and recognise the enemy for what he is. As he talks he tends to swing his arms about, as though he were attempting to drive his point home to a mass meeting, and all that is required of his companion is gently to guide him back to the point at issue whenever he leaves it to rush up a blind alley of his own creation.

"There is some poison at work in our society. The Commies are everywhere"—he always calls them the Commies—"and no one will do anything about it. Now I have proof, incontrovertible proof, that kids—kids, mark you—turn up in the Chinese schools here and dump their Communist literature on their desks under the very noses of their teachers. Nothing is done about it. Nothing at all. No, sir! What is the use of all these Emergency regulations if they are not implemented? What happens is that someone in authority is protecting them.

"As soon as you try and say anything really anti-Communist here, there is a terrible outcry. You can be as Red as you like, but it is only when you start telling the truth about Communism that the muscle is put on you. Who is behind these things? The Commies!

"If you try to tell the people that their administration is riddled with Communism you are stopped, and presumably the people have to wait until the enemy is right on top of them before finding out the true state of affairs—as they did in Indo-China. Only when the battle there was lost did they discover that every French military plan went straight out to the Commies, so that in many cases the Communists knew French intentions before the French armies in the field knew them themselves.

"Are you not sickened by the articles in the newspapers that suggest that there is a change of heart in Russia or China? How can there ever be a change of heart among men who have as much blood on their hands as Hitler ever had?

"Who told the Communists that Sir Henry Gurney was going to the Cameron Highlands, so that they could shoot him down as he went?

"Tell me something. Have you ever heard of a democratic cell? No, sir! The Government is actually going to spend less on the information services. It does nothing whatever to counteract the Communist cells. Why? Who recommends that less money be spent on this aspect of anti-Commie work?

"Look at the bookshops. They're full of Commie literature! I have not yet found one book here that adequately describes the horrors of Communism. Yet there are Bevan and the boys. Their books are there!

"Look how the newspapers snapped up the Attlee drivel. Do you know they printed his remark that China was not interested in expansion without comment, when their country was at war with Communism, and therefore with China and Russia.

"Who inspires the false idea that the Commies have a better right to Formosa than Chiang Kai-shek?

"I went out to dinner the other night and a woman said—a woman who should have known better, 'But do you not think that the Chinese Communists are very different from the Russian Communists?' And another guy who was there said, 'Oh! they are nothing more than land redistributors.' Can they think, and yet think like this?

"Why wasn't *Brain Washing in Red China* published in England?

"Why was it suppressed in Japan?

"Who stopped the Allied armies from finishing off the Reds in Korea? Both MacArthur and Van Fleet have said that they could have taken the whole of Korea had they been allowed to do the job. But they were stopped! Why? And by whom?

"It is all brought about by Commie agents working within our midst. We have got to get them!"

Hysteria? Without a doubt. But it is not easy simply to dismiss *all* that he says. Is a witch-hunt the answer? God forbid!

But if what he says is correct, or even if just a little of what he says is correct, a witch-hunt, sooner or later, becomes inevitable.

November 9th, 1954

She sits in one of the pestiferous alleys off Trengganu Street in Singapore. She wears the black and shiny *samfoo* of the poor, and her feet, pushed into worn embroidered slippers, are cruelly deformed, nothing more than bent stumps, as though her feet had been amputated. She sits on a tiny, unpainted stool, no more than a few inches high, and before her stands a small wicker shopping-basket in which she keeps most of all that she possesses.

She has a fine face, this ancient Chinese lady of the streets. Her skin has taken on the quality of tree bark; weather-beaten like that of a sailor, care-lined in the fight for survival. Her forehead is high and broad, covered with a filigree of lines which run in confusion in every direction. She has not, like some of her contemporaries, gone blind in old age: her eyes are still clear and bright, and the smile that is never far from her face tends first to play among the converging lines at the corners of her eyes. Through the long years she has pulled her hair back to the bun she still wears, but she has pulled it so fiercely that the hair has receded from her brow and from her temples so that the front segment of her head is now bald and also lined, and the hair, in addition, has begun to grow grey. When she smiles, the cracked lips open on the brown stumps of what were once fine teeth : age, decay and neglect have run their course.

I do not know where the old lady comes from, nor how she comes to be sitting in an alley gutter. She cannot speak my language and I cannot speak hers. But it is possible to make a number of guesses: she came when she was a small girl from China, the plaything of a rich Chinese merchant who bought her and therefore considered her his property; or her father worked as a coolie in the docks of Singapore, contracted T.B., for which there was no cure, and died, leaving his wife and daughter to make the best of a hopeless job; or perhaps she had once been happily married and had simply outlived her husband and, possibly, most of her offspring. It makes no matter. That which matters is the present and to some extent the future; the past is past. And to the old lady sitting in the gutter the present is made up largely of the necessity to earn a living.

She tells fortunes. She will light a small joss-stick and wedge it smouldering into the top of her basket, and this signifies, I think, as much as anything, that her shop is open. Her customers are mostly of her own age and of comparable poverty, people who are prepared to pay for only a fleeting vision of security.

The customer squats beside the old lady, who produces a set of cardboard strips on which are printed sundry Chinese characters. These are placed in an old cigarette tin and the customer is invited to select the one of her choice. She hands it to the old lady, who then thumbs through a tattered, yellow-paged book, each page crammed with characters, and reads out to her customer what she finds there.

But it is not, apparently, so simple as this, for the prophecy is not always immediately accepted. There is much questioning, followed by ready, clearly explanatory, answers. The face of the old woman who wishes to know what the most propitious day of the following week will be, or on what day her daughter should marry, or on what day she herself should visit the grave of her long dead husband, alternately lights up and as quickly fades to receptive interest. Clouds of doubt, of noncomprehension, of scepticism and even of disgust pass momentarily across her face, to be followed by delight and pleasure. The Chinese race is not, I fancy, as impassive as some would like us to believe.

A little crowd gathers round the two women in the gutter and I wish that I could understand what it is they are saying instead of merely guessing. Dirty children with shaven scalps push ever more closely to the basket, until the old lady with a word and a gesture sweeps them away.

Then the ceremony is over. An old brown hand creeps within the black folds of the *samfoo* and brings out a piece of folded brown paper. The paper is undone and the fingers extract a twenty-cent piece, which is handed over, irrevocably, reluctantly. The old lady takes it, bobs her head in acknowledgment, and places it in another cigarette tin in her basket.

November 10th, 1954

He is a totally bald Chinese and this, in my experience, is a very rare thing. He is also very rich and this is not in the least rare.

Leow Teck Hin is essentially a simple man. He has lived in Malaya all his life and, like so many of his compatriots, began life as a very poor man. The way of life acquired in the early days of struggle has never left him, and to this day he finds an environment of comparative poverty more acceptable than one of luxury. He long ago, of course, bought himself an enormous American car, a car so big that when he sits on the back seat you can only see the shining top of his head bobbing up and down on the foam-rubber upholstery. But I do not think he likes his motor-car; he puts up with it simply because it impresses his business acquaintances and generally helps his credit. He would, if anything, rather walk to office.

Although no one enjoys a riotous Chinese banquet more than Leow Teck Hin, his tastes through the years have become strangely Westernised. His children have been educated in English schools and so have only a smattering of the language of China, and perhaps this more than anything else has contributed to his gradual rejection of things Chinese. He likes, for example, Bach. He may often be seen at the Victoria Hall, sitting quietly and inconspicuously in the cheaper seats, whenever a visiting celebrity gives a concert. For a rich Chinese merchant this is very strange. He is also a very keen photographer and spends hours in his dark-room producing tremendous enlargements of his pet subjects. This is less unusual, but he might instead be entertaining his concubines, or making merry in the opium-house, or whiling away his time with mahjong.

Leow Teck Hin is a gentle, upright person, generous to those in trouble and kind to those who seek his advice. And, although they say that a man can never make a million without stooping to dishonesty, I believe that Leow is the standing exception to the rule.

He has been a millionaire for a long time now, and many years ago, because his friends persuaded him that he needed it, he built himself a beautiful house by the sea. It was a very large house—a mansion, in fact—with an expensively laid-out garden. Along the whole of its front, which faced the sea, there was a great tiled terrace which led directly, through sliding doors, to an extensive lounge and dining-room beyond. Everything about the house was big and it could, without difficulty, accommodate a dozen guests and their servants and their motor-cars. It was furnished by a local company which shared the Singapore weakness for highly polished teak, teak polished so brightly that any item of furniture made from it could be used, alternatively, as a mirror. The dining-room contained one of those completely sensible Chinese tables which are both huge and circular. The centre of the table is removed by the maker so that there is a circular hole in the middle of the table with a diameter of some four feet. The circle of wood removed is then mounted on ball-bearings and replaced. The touch of a finger will then set it silently revolving. When the table is laid, the eating-bowls and utensils are placed on the outer rim and the various dishes containing the food on the revolving centre. When you have helped yourself to whatever is provided, you simply push the centre, which revolves and brings the food to your neighbour. Similarly, if in the middle of the meal you require, say, the salt, you give the table the lightest of pushes and round comes the salt, without any of the European nonsense of asking people to pass it. The system is admirable.

When the house was completed, Leow Teck Hin and his wife moved in. They held a house-warming party, to which hundreds of guests were invited. Pictures of the house appeared in the local paper and a particularly idiotic female was sent to write an article on the décor for the women's page in the Sunday issue. Many of their friends came out to see them at week-ends and for a while Leow enjoyed his wonderful house.

Then, one evening, sitting on one of his highly polished teak chairs, which was more impressive than comfortable, he began to wonder. There was no one in the house but his wife, a dumpy little woman who always wore the *kebaya* and sarong of those Chinese who have lived so long in Malaya or Singapore that their link with China has almost broken, and she, perched on her enormous glossy chair, did not look comfortable either. Leow wrinkled his fat, good-humoured face. He picked up a magazine and thumbed listlessly through it. Then he crossed to the ornate radiogram and tuned in to Radio Malaya, did not like what he heard and switched off again. He walked out on to the terrace and looked out to sea. He could not see the water, but he could hear the little waves lapping on his private beach. For a long time he paced up and down and his wife looked up from her needlework and watched him, but said nothing, partly because it was not her place to say anything and partly because she knew he would make his own decision. At last he came in and stood before her, his hands clasped behind his back, and quite suddenly burst into roars of laughter. She laughed with him, for she already knew that he had made his decision and what that decision was.

"When shall we go?" she asked.

"As soon as we can get the tenants out."

And three weeks later Leow Teck Hin's stately house went up for auction and was bought by a man who wished to carry out the minor conversion necessary to turn it into a hotel. Leow and his wife stood to the rear of the group of buyers which had assembled and watched without regret the disappearance of something they had never really wanted.

When it was all over they climbed into their Packard and drove to Peng Seah Street where their little two-bedroomed terrace house was situated. Peng Seah Street was very crowded; all of its houses were bursting with people, and children played on its pavements from dawn until midnight. Above the shouts of children could be heard the distant cry of the hawker, the chatter of the people in the streets, the clip-clop clatter of their clogs, the blare of the Rediffusion loudspeaker in the house over the road, the rumble of the coffee-stall wagon and the high-pitched rattle of mahjong tiles. Leow on his first evening at home brought his simple wooden chair to his front door and sat on it and listened to the noise of the street. And his face wrinkled with pleasure, for he knew that what he heard was good.

Ah Chow sells coffee in Albert Street. Every month he pays twenty dollars to the City Council for permission to hawk his coffee from the allotted space of roadway which he has held for thirty years. Ah Chow can remember when people visited his stall in their carriages.

Every evening at about six o'clock, for thirty long years, Ah Chow has trundled his little cart bearing the tools of his trade to his site: his copper coffee-pots, his little glass jars of biscuits, his wire basket of eggs which his customers like to take "coddled." He sets up and lights his charcoal stove, mixes his coffee and is ready for business. According to his licence he is allowed to remain open until two a.m., but on good days it may be three or four before he gets home to bed.

The bare boards of his trestled stall are black with age and coffee. The heavy tarpaulin which covers it, so that Ah Chow and his customers may remain dry during the torrential downpours which frequently sweep across Singapore without warning, is similarly black with age. But people do not go to Ah Chow for the appurtenances of the smart restaurant, but simply for good coffee.

They sit on a form in front of the stall while Ah Chow pours the coffee from the tall pots which have been simmering over the charcoal. He performs this function with a concentrated yet strangely effortless expertise. He fills each thick cup with exactly the same amount of black liquid and then, with a delicate gesture, takes up a china spoon, dips it into the tin of sweetened, condensed milk and places it in the first cup. Then he takes up another spoon, fills that with milk, and places it in the second cup. That is how coffee is drunk in Malaya and, if at first the Westerner does not like it, there will come a time when he will prefer Ah Chow's coffee to any other. It is essential to realise that the sweetened, condensed milk is as important and as unchangeable an ingredient as the coffee itself.

Ah Chow himself is one of the most benevolent-looking gentlemen it is possible to meet. His face is a mixture of that of a cherub and Charles Laughton. He has a perfect set of teeth which he has never defaced with gold, and the slightest word from a customer will bring forth, first of all, a broad and completely happy smile. He wears khaki shorts, a white vest, and on his head is an ancient brown trilby hat. He wears it with the brim pulled down all round and its crown stands up in a rounded summit of benevolence.

What has gone wrong in a world where a race can produce a man like Ah Chow on the one hand and a Communist killer on the other? It may be possible to say that Ah Chow has been badly treated by society; that he is compelled to earn a living by working in the road all night; that he is unable to make a sufficient profit; that he ought to join a coffee-seller's union; that everything about Ah Chow, politically, socially and economically, is wrong. Yet it is my firm impression that Ah Chow is a completely happy man. A man cannot be unhappy and have Ah Chow's expression. And if he is happy, happy working long hours for thirty years, maybe he has something to teach those who are unhappy—the rich, the pampered, the worried, the over-burdened and, most of all, perhaps, the Communists.

November 12th, 1954

A frail old Eurasian lady—quiet, unassuming and careworn. She has known a life of toil, disappointment and some blessings. Her husband, who is now dead, left her a little money, and her children, those who are still alive, are kind to her and occasionally take her for rides in their motor-cars. She lives now with her sister, who is also a widow, in a little house in Katong. She can tell you quite a lot about old Singapore and the way it has grown and become progressively more important and how, when she was a girl, nobody worried about politics. She can also tell you about the Japanese occupation and of the people the Japanese "took" who were never seen or heard of again, of the shortages of food and the brutality of the soldiery, of those who made up to the Japanese because that was the only way of improving their lot.

And I said to her:

"What did *you* do in the occupation?"

She answered and said:

"Me? I just kept quiet, just kept quiet."

I wonder if it is any accident that "Just kept quiet" has become a common saying in Malaya. Wherever you go you hear it. "I just kept quiet." A man is murdered, a woman jumps into the canal, a house is robbed, a child is knocked down in the street and killed: "We just kept quiet."

Possibly it is a saying which comes naturally in a colonial society where no form of government has been known by the people except control by the powerful of those who are less powerful; where the best form of government they have ever experienced has been a remote Colonial administration. The unwillingness to assert themselves becomes second nature after endless centuries of direction. Keeping quiet becomes a habit. The danger of the attitude lies not so much in the willingness to allow things to continue as they are as in the willingness to tolerate whatever conditions may arise in the future. Not only will they keep quiet, instead of helping to bring about a democratic form of government, but they will still keep quiet when democracy is destroyed by their very determination to do nothing about it. I do not know what kind of future can be in store for the people of a nation who, for the most part, are so disinclined to stick out their necks.

November 13th, 1954

Called on Francis Coupe today. He is a very successful business man, still comparatively young—perhaps thirty-seven or eight. He has been largely responsible for the growth of his business, which was only established after the war. He is a good employer and each one of his staff of a hundred know they will be well looked after.

Coupe has a most orderly mind, and is almost unique among business men in Singapore in that his political views are not coloured by his concern for his business. His opinions are those which he honestly believes to be right—whatever their consequences—and one can be certain that he has not arrived at them without a great deal of thought.

Francis Coupe is a Socialist. Yet he belongs to no political party and is, in fact, often horrified by Singapore Socialists who, more often than not, are noisy irresponsibles. He is continually pained by the persistent inability of local politicians to grasp the essentials of a matter, and their failure, if by accident they do grasp them, to argue logically from them. Coupe's Socialism is therefore a theoretical Socialism which holds itself aloof from the local battle for power. It is for this reason that his opinions are valuable: they are not coloured by irrelevant issues, old hates and new loves. They hold the key, I am convinced, to many of Malaya's problems. One of his favourite topics is the creation of a Malayan nation:

"I am distressed by the attitude of Socialists in this country, who invariably shout for freedom, demand it unconditionally, before they are prepared to formulate any kind of political platform beyond this simple primary demand. That they say that only freedom can release the energy that democracy needs if it is to function effectively does not alter what to me is the primary objective of Socialists: to bring about Socialism in the land in which they live. Socialism may exist equally in either an Independent or a Colonial country. If they bring about Socialism first and demand self-government afterwards, then independence will be given to a country in some measure equipped to deal with it. If they demand independence first, and then hope to rule the country, with either a Socialist or any other form of government, the country will probably founder in the morass of its own ineptitude.

"I am driven to believe that any man who shouts for freedom in Malaya without first formulating and attempting to implement a programme of economic and social reform is primarily interested in the power and the prestige he thinks that he himself can obtain under the new dispensation. This is, to a greater or a lesser extent, true of all politicians. The driving force behind any but the most idealistic must of necessity be partly, often largely, personal ambition. But with this ambition must go some responsibility towards the country, entirely divorced from hopes of political preferment. It is doubtful if any politician in Malaya can claim to acknowledge this responsibility when he unconditionally demands a political step which has led, almost without exception, in all other Asian countries to confusion, chaos and, often, bloodshed.

"They say that this is the old cry of the reactionaries : 'Look at Indonesia; look at Burma.' Very well, let us look at them. I have no doubt that all manner of energies were released in these countries when they gained their independence, but since they had no foundation, except that left behind by a capitalistic, Colonial economy, on which to build their free society, the net result was of benefit only to those who had brought about the change. Precisely the same will happen here. No party has an adequate programme of reform, and unless these reforms are first carried out, or at least set in motion, self-government will not necessarily be of benefit to anyone, except those very few who will come out on top.

"Some present-day political leaders will tell you that there is nothing like the slogan of 'Freedom' for catching votes. The tragedy is that this may very well be so among those people who are *going* to vote. But what of those who are not going to vote— in Singapore far more than half of the population—either because they are not entitled to do so, or because they are too ignorant or apathetic to care? Do these people really want to rule themselves? So we stand in danger of precipitate independence brought about by a few vociferous orators appealing to a mob instinct, when even the mob does not represent anything like a majority of the population.

"All right. We have to make the rest of the population take a proper interest in the country in which it lives. How? By preaching independence? By preaching the virtues of democracy? By telling them about the horrors of Communism? What can all these things mean to them? And if these things mean nothing to them, how can they make good citizens of a free democracy? Is independence going to make them understand the abstract conceptions of democracy? Is independence going to harden their hearts towards Communism? No! Any man who says so is either a fool or a knave. What, then, are we to do?

"The crux of the entire problem of Malaya and Singapore lies in giving every man a stake in the country—not an abstract stake or an imaginary stake, but a tangible economic stake. Until each person has an economic stake which is worth something to him, which is a better stake than he is likely to get by going elsewhere, progress towards a united and satisfied Malaya must remain at a standstill. This aspect of Malaya's progress is appreciated by some people; I think that it is appreciated to some extent by the Colonial Government. But time, unfortunately, is running out, and reforms lag ever farther behind the demands of the situation.

"This stake in the country *must come first*. If independence comes before it has been obtained for everyone, then most people may *never* get it, unless the Communists give it to them. Once the economic incentive is there, then a good deal of the apathy will disappear. Once the squatter has been given a reasonable plot of land to cultivate, he will be more inclined to regard himself as part of Malaya—which he certainly does not at the moment. Once a greater part of the profits of the rubber and tin industries go to the men who work on the estates and in the mines, they will automatically become less receptive to Communist doctrine. When the people of Singapore cease for the most part to live in rabbit hutches and cubicles, they will begin to think that perhaps there is something to be said for democracy after all. For God's sake let us deal with the essentials of life first and give everyone a decent living wage and make some provision for them when they are unemployed, and stop all this spineless pandering to would-be, ten-a-penny Presidents and Prime Ministers.

"My point is threefold: firstly, this task should be the primary objective of all politicians in the country, taking precedence over the call for independence; secondly, that if independence comes first, 'fair shares for all'—a cliché, but I can think of nothing better—may never come; and thirdly, if they do come after independence, they may well do so through the medium of Communism. In fact, unless we have 'fair shares,' democracy and a pride in the country are largely impossible.

"Malaya is a country consisting largely of comparatively poverty-stricken people who came originally from other lands. Most of them still owe their primary allegiance to the country of their origin. In talking of economic stakes we should not think simply in terms of allowing them to enjoy an economic position better than that which they enjoyed in India or China. This, after all, is saying very little. The yard-stick can only be their present prosperity and happiness in Malaya. Decent houses, a decent education for their children, decent provision for old age, unemployment and sickness benefits, good conditions of work, a reasonable wage that allows of a few luxuries, land for the farmers, and guaranteed and better prices for their products; when all these things have been provided, I shall be prepared to listen to the 'freedom' politicians.

"The question now is: How are these things to be provided? The answer is that within the present capitalist economy they cannot be provided. And even if the economy were immediately to become a Socialist one, it is still doubtful whether money, labour and materials could be found quickly enough to offset the encroachments of Communism. But Socialism—and the reforms I have just outlined, coupled with public ownership of the basic industries and steeply-graded taxation—can go a long way towards laying the foundations of a new and free Malaya.

"The problem, however, is bigger than the people of Malaya can tackle alone. The problem of Malaya is very much a problem of the West, if Communism is to be defeated here. There is, at the present time, remarkably little appreciation of this fact in the West. I will concede that Western aid would be more freely forthcoming if Singapore and Malaya were not part of the British Empire. But I can see no alternative to our remaining a part of it for some time to come. Meanwhile, we must go ahead with our reforms as fast as we can—much, much faster than we are going ahead with them now—and obtain what external aid we can. We can still make a success of it. And even if, in the end, we are shown to have been too late, at least we shall have spent our time and our energy on something worth while, instead of simply allowing ourselves to be overtaken by events."

November 14th, 1954

The first thing they say to you in Sarawak is: "This country is still living on a backlog of goodwill created by the Rajahs." It is doubtful if anything of a similar nature could be said anywhere else in the world today. When the rule of the Rajahs ended, many in Sarawak mourned. A feudalistic state died and scarcely anyone cheered. This being so, there must have been something about the white Rajahs of Sarawak which many today would be loath to credit to any feudal ruler.

Today, when you arrive in Kuching, as I did this morning, you step out of your aeroplane into a world of whose existence you had almost forgotten. Kuching, the old Brooke capital, is quiet and leisurely, almost, it seems, asleep in the sun. Because none of the roads out of Kuching are fit for modern transport after the first twenty-odd miles, there is a wondrous absence of traffic and therefore of noise and hurry and bustle. Such motor-cars as use the roads proceed at a less homicidal speed than in Singapore, and this, I fancy, is because their drivers, having become soaked in the very civilised atmosphere of Kuching, realise that there *is* no point whatever in hurrying

I was brought to the Rest House, one of those spacious tropical buildings that still defy architects to build anything cooler or, for that matter, more gracious. From my window I can look across the road to the Sarawak Museum on the hill, standing in its grounds like a great country house, built by the Brookes for no more ponderous a reason, I imagine, than that they felt it would be a good thing to have a museum. Just below the Museum a building that looks as though it is going to be a hotel or a block of flats is being erected, and I know that it is going to be hideous simply because it is being built of concrete. It will stand, upright and square, like a painfully geometrical exercise, among the trees and older buildings which surround it, a silent but sadly permanent reminder that many things we do today could, a hundred years ago, be done much better. Concrete does not mellow as brick and wood mellows. It does not grow old, but becomes only shabby and decrepit. It seems so silly to use it when it has to be made from cement brought all the way from Japan or England and when there is enough hardwood in the Eastern Isles to build a thousand cities; wood so hard that nails grow hot as they are driven, blow by blow, into its iron-hard sides; wood so heavy that when it is thrown into water it sinks like stone.

Down the road from the Rest House is the town itself, the centre taken up entirely by a hotchpotch of government offices. Those that are old were built with an entirely sensible view to excluding the sun. Roofs, tiled with wooden tiles, overhang the walls and are supported on round and simple pillars. Inside the rooms are shaded and cool, and air-conditioning machines, humming and blowing their cold hearts away, would be an encumbrance. The main Secretariat is modern, built since the war, and although it conforms precisely to accepted ideas of functional design and is not, in itself, unpleasant to behold, there is nothing about its external appearance to distinguish it from a Lancashire cotton-mill. It is air-conditioned throughout—possibly because, having built it they discovered that it was too hot—and once inside chill air blows into hot clothes and the visitor may as well be back in Singapore.

Why can we not leave things alone? Why do we complain that the people of the East do not have ideas of their own and simply import what we in the West manufacture? The old-style buildings of the Europeans in the tropics owed the greater part of their inspiration to the Malay house, and batteries of expensive, western-trained architects have not yet produced anything better than that simple edifice. I see no point in keeping up with the times if the times produce nothing better than cotton-mill constructions on the one hand and the æsthetic bankruptcy of the "shop-house" on the other.

Beyond the government offices is the river, and when you have seen the river you have seen most of Kuching. The stream flows swiftly with the tide, carrying with it its brown load of silt and the waste wood of the jungle which grows along every inch of its banks. It surges along the wharves of Kuching and scours the sides of the steamship *Rajah Brooke*, which plods unendingly between Kuching and Singapore. By the wharves are the godowns of the importers, and around them can be seen men from the interior: Dyaks, for instance, with great holes in their ears, dressed incongruously in the cast-off clothing of the West, who come to work in the town. It would have been so much better if they had stayed away, for there is nothing on the wharves of a seaport which can do anyone any good.

It was tea-time, and I walked slowly back to the Rest House. I passed the inglorious conglomeration of "shop-houses"—inhabited for the most part by Chinese, who, in Sarawak, as in most other Eastern countries, are the mechanics, the electricians, the metal-workers and wood-workers, the merchants, the shop-keepers and the bankers for most of the people who live there—and came to the little Cathedral of Sarawak. This is a totally unpretentious wooden building with a perfectly proportioned but diminutive spire. It stands on a hill by the road, and as I passed I heard the sentimental notes of Chopin. The music came from the church, so I walked up the steep pathway and stood in the darkened shade of the western door. A Chinese was playing the piano so intently that he did not notice me, and as I listened I had the impression that almost any music in that hallowed little church would have sounded sacred. It was so quiet and cool, and the blackened wooden pillars were still strong and unyielding, and the light was a shaded, gentle light, just sufficient to enable one to read the painted texts on the walls. The Chinese played well and the piano possessed a golden quality which would not have been evident in a newer, more spacious, building. As he played I was attracted to some framed drawings on the wall which were plans of the new Cathedral that the Church intends to build among the eternal green of Sarawak, under the hot, damp sun of the tropics, to the greater glory of God. It was not noticeably different from an ice-rink or a more up-to-date Olympia.

It may be that the existing Cathedral is no longer safe—but this I do not believe. It may be that the new Cathedral, when completed, will be tremendously impressive and dignified. But quite apart from the thought that it seems unlikely that God cares whether He is worshipped in a palace or a hovel as long as He is worshipped, this new Cathedral cannot possibly sit at rest in its Sarawak setting. It will look as incongruous as a block of flats in an empty desert, or as misplaced as a bowler hat on a tennis court. While there is nothing intrinsically unsatisfactory or unpleasant about either a block of flats or a bowler hat, their environment can make them so.

So I wish they would not build this Cathedral in Sarawak or, at least, if they insist on building it, that they would alter its design to something more serene and less aggressive.

November 18th, 1954

You can stand on the banks of the Sarawak river and look across to Government House, where there is now installed a British Colonial Governor instead of the old Rajah. And as you look you begin to wonder at the incredible audacity of the first white Rajah in coming to rule in Sarawak, a feat all the more audacious in retrospect, since it did not at the time seem audacious at all, least of all to James Brooke. It was not only audacious, but also incredible, since he was for a long time unwilling to saddle himself with the responsibility of ruling a country which for the most part was engaged in piracy, head-hunting and civil war. James Brooke did not want Sarawak. It really was *too* much of a responsibility. But then the possibilities were so enormous that he could scarcely refuse it. And so, when he was offered it, he took it.

James Brooke went to Sarawak over a hundred years ago, having inherited from his father a sum of money sufficient to buy himself a ship and to sail it to the East. Borneo in those days was almost unknown, and as much as anyone knew about it was an uneasy suspicion that it was inhabited by wild men. When James Brooke arrived, he found terrible misery among certain sections of the population who were preyed upon by other sections. The Malays, nominally in control of the country, were the major culprits and the sea-Dyaks, who made a hobby of piracy, were a secondary menace to the peace and well-being of Sarawak. Into this chaos sailed James Brooke in the *Royalist*. He entered, not without a certain disinclination, into the hot-bed of murderous intrigue which absorbed the royal courts, and almost before he knew where he was, so to speak, found himself Rajah. Sarawak, as a part of the British Empire, came into being as did many other British possessions overseas, almost when the British weren't looking.

Once in command, Brooke devoted his life to the country that was his. He sat for hours in his bungalow by the river dispensing justice, and even travelled about the country settling disputes wherever he found them. He entered, from time to time, into the local wars, when he and his English sailors would astonish the Malays with what appeared to them to be quite foolhardy bravery. To charge a strongpoint was, in Malay eyes, tantamount to suicide. After all, war was not so serious a thing as to necessitate any of the participants exposing themselves to danger. But Brooke went off with his friend Admiral Keppel to shoot up the local pirates, who were, in the end, entirely subdued. It was all utterly amazing when, in the whole of Sarawak, there were less than a dozen Europeans.

When Brooke returned from one of his infrequent visits to Singapore, the good people of Kuching would turn out in their best clothes and, with music, banging and dancing, welcome him home. They knew that their lot was better than it had ever been before and that at least there was a modicum of justice in the land.

The house that the Brookes built in Sarawak still stands proudly on its hill, flanked by the fort that protected it. Sarawak was a modern fairy-tale. The kingdom grew in size and importance until it covered practically the whole of the northern seaboard of Borneo. It grew to a great extent because the people wanted it that way.

Brooke, like most people who created a part of the British Empire, was criticised in England by ignorant people, who, as is often the case today, knew not the first thing about the subject on which they presumed to speak and hold opinions. Brooke went home to England a broken man, but his successors ruled wisely in one of the most beautiful little countries in the world. It was a pity that the dynasty had to peter out, as some might think, ignominiously.

November 16th, 1954

Robert Lim is one of those Chinese who are so charming, so reasonable and so generous that it becomes difficult to believe that the history of the Chinese in South-east Asia, in territories ruled by the British, has been largely one of their neglect.

James Brooke in Sarawak, like the British in Malaya, favoured the Malays, and left the Chinese to their own not inconsiderable devices. Perhaps, as a race, we prefer the Malays because they are not, like ourselves and the Chinese, consumed with a passion for work. Because of this entirely sensible Malay attitude the Chinese tend to overwhelm them, so that they have become, economically at least, the underdogs, and the Englishmen can always be counted upon to favour the underdog, especially when he is possessed of a fighting spirit. When the Chinese in Sarawak in the middle of the last century revolted, laid a good deal of the town of Kuching to waste, butchered a large number of its inhabitants and sent James Brooke scurrying into the jungle in his nightshirt, leaving his blazing house behind him, it was the Malays who supported and succoured him and eventually set off in pursuit of the marauding Chinese with murder and revenge in their hearts. When, after the last war, it was proposed to make the country of Sarawak a British Colony under the Colonial Office, instead of its white Rajah, it was the Malays who were most emphatically opposed to anything so silly. They received all manner of benefits from the Rajah—such as free land, for example—and they knew that once the country was controlled by the Colonial Office, set upon welding all the races in the country into an integrated whole, even though Malay privileges were not, in fact, removed, it would be difficult for the new authority to resist extending them to other sections of the population.

The Chinese, both in Sarawak and Malaya, quite naturally take a somewhat jaundiced view of Malay privilege. Even Robert Lim feels that it is not really fair, for he has lived in Sarawak for as long as he can remember and has long ago lost all contact with his family overseas.

Sometimes, when one meets Chinese, one can suddenly become

entirely sympathetic to all movements in the past that have tended to favour the Malay and in effect to protect him from the encroachments of the energy of the Chinese. Then one meets a man like Robert Lim—and there are many like him—and one's mood is reversed. What a pity, one feels, that all people—not simply all Chinese—are not like him. What a much better place the world would be if there were less aggression and assertiveness, if there were, in effect, fewer dominating personalities and more who asserted themselves by gentleness and integrity.

Robert Lim is also one of those Chinese who, to the European, does not seem Chinese. I have come to the conclusion, after a number of years in the East, that the Chinese in outlook and character is often very much nearer to the Englishman than, say, a Frenchman or an Italian. He shares many of our virtues and possibly all our faults. He is not usually, as novelists would have us believe, any more impassive or inscrutable than we; he is, for the most part, neither more nor less aggressive; he entertains a profound regard for his country and a certain permissible contempt for foreigners, an attitude wholly shared by the English; he is hard-working, industrious and honest, which qualities have also gone to give England a territorial and commercial Empire; his home is his castle; he is an inveterate gambler and would gladly fill in Chinese football coupons if he had them; and he enjoys nothing more than a first-class meal, which the Englishman would enjoy equally if he had ever succeeded in learning the art of cooking it.

The differences between the Chinese and the English are largely those of custom and usage. Some will point to his sense of humour and say that it lacks pity; but if a Chinese were to feel pity for every one of his countrymen in some measure of distress, his life would quickly become unendurable. Others will point to his cruelty, rather forgetting, on the one hand, that the rigours of existence in China for thousands of years have placed a fairly low value on human and other life and, on the other, that we ourselves have not always been the acme of charity.

And so, when you talk to Robert Lim, you are not conscious in the slightest degree that he is foreign and of another race; you talk simply to another person whom you trust, respect and like.

I cannot help thinking that the solution to some of the ills of the world lies largely in inter-racial marriage. When the people of Malacca stood behind their stockades and Portuguese ships stood in the harbour ready to attack, it was a Javanese woman who swam out to warn the Portuguese of Malay duplicity. She did this because, it is said, she loved one of the Portuguese sailors. This incident has been repeated innumerable times in innumerable wars, and almost always for the same reason: the love of a man for a woman. It is difficult to imagine a better reason for betraying one's side. And if all the men on one side loved all the women on the other and *vice versa* there would not, I think, be any war—or, at least, any bloodshed. Therefore it is conceivable that if each country introduced a law making it illegal for a man to love, marry or indulge in sexual relations with any woman of his own race, nothing but good could come from such an apparent imposition. If in some cases such inter-marriage should prove difficult, it would be least of all difficult in the case of Chinese and English.

All day Robert Lim drove me along the few roads radiating out of Kuching. Eventually they all petered out in jungle tracks or on the banks of rivers—broad, brown, swiftly-flowing rivers which are the real roads of Sarawak. The day was glorious, with great banks of white clouds mounting in the blueness of the sky from the peaks of the distant mountains. And there lay the acute shortcomings of Kuching to the temporary visitor: he cannot move away from the place without protracted and advance arrangement. Sarawak is still a country not vastly different in appearance from the land the first European visitors saw when they approached its shores in their sailing vessels, edging cautiously through the coastal waters that had never been sounded or charted. Most of the people still live much the same lives except, perhaps, that they have given up their head-hunting and now shoot the dwindling animals of Borneo with shotguns instead of with blow-pipes and poisoned darts. I wanted, while in Sarawak, to visit a Dyak long-house, where perhaps a hundred families live together communally. But to do even this is an expedition of some magnitude, not to be accomplished simply by catching a bus, and I was left with the untried conviction that a people so equable as to be able to live in the same house with dozens of other families must be of quite remarkable virtue.

We visited pepper gardens, now no longer producing the exceptional profits that they did during the Korean war boom, when pepper-garden owners were able to invest huge sums in town property. We drove along the newly-built road until we reached the river, where they were building the landing-stages of a ferry which will link up with the road still to be built on the other side of the river and which will lead, eventually, to the goldfields. We ate heartily of a Chinese lunch, and visited a Chinese bookseller to read him a lecture on the dangers of imported pirated school-books. Then we crossed the river and peeped far enough into the grounds of Government House, the Astana, to be able to take a photograph, and clambered round the old white Fort Margherita and took photographs through the niches originally intended for rifles. Finally, we adjourned to Robert Lim's house for tea and oranges and biscuits, and I wished that I, too, could live in Sarawak and eat oranges and biscuits for tea every day instead of, as in Singapore, never having time for tea at all.

November 17th, 1954

Back to Singapore, flying low through the rain clouds massed over the southern tip of Malaya, over the shipping, dripping in the rain that falls in sheets on the inner harbour, down on to a soaked Kallang airfield. Home again. Sarawak may well be ten thousand miles away. In many ways, other than in terms of miles, it is. An extraordinary number of people there seem to be more or less happy or contented. The Communists, apart from their favourite field of Chinese schools, have scarcely touched them. A man can own a gun there without having also to sleep with it. Perhaps Sarawak's travail is yet to come. Perhaps, being a country of such tiny importance, it may never come.

One thing remains uppermost in my mind after so short a visit and that is a remark by a Sarawak Government official:

"It is difficult to see what the future can be, just so long as we remain unable to provide the young Chinese with an emotional appeal comparable to that provided by Red China."

November 18th, 1954

Tom Harrison, Curator of the Sarawak Museum, one of the characters of Kuching, whose acquaintance must be made before any visit to Kuching can be said to have been properly accomplished, when recently in London found with a publisher several hundred copies of a book, published by Henry Sotheran & Co. in 1909, called *A History of Sarawak under its Two White Rajahs 1839–1908*, by S. Baring-Gould and C. A. Bampfylde. This is a source book for those who would know about Sarawak, and it is extraordinary that the publishers who held these stocks should not have known what to do with them. Anyway, Tom Harrison appeared, bought them all at a cheap rate, and brought them out to Sarawak. Now it is almost as scarce a book at it was before.

The British Empire came into being largely through the exertions of a few brilliant men. They were rarely motivated by thoughts of personal advantage or pecuniary gain, and more often than not they received more help from those whom they sought to bring within the Empire than from those at home in England. It was their lot—and it sometimes seems that, in this respect, times have changed but little—to do battle with stupidity, apathy, alarming ignorance and prejudice in England. Raffles, for example, was a man who did such battle. But for him, Singapore would never have been founded by the British. But for him, the brilliant men who came after him could scarcely have created British Malaya. But for him, there would probably have been no British Empire in South-east Asia. In the process he lost his wife, most of his children, his health, most of his worldly possessions and was sent, unhonoured and unsung, to a debtor's grave. Clive of India was driven by the inexplicable venom of the British to suicide. And Brooke, just about the only man who knew what he was talking about when he talked about Borneo, was villified, ridiculed and slandered from one end of the country to the other by professional humanitarians, by the towering conceit and ignorance of British Members of Parliament and by every third-rate journalist who saw profit in the exploitation of a popular prejudice, until they broke the man, broke his health and his spirit, but in the process proved, unwittingly, that Brooke, like many of his ilk, was indeed a great man; for Sarawak survived in spite of them.

In this history by Baring-Gould and Bampfylde there is still much food for thought.

In 1839, James Brooke, the first Rajah, arrived off Borneo in his schooner *Royalist.* He wrote:

"The bay that lies between Capes Datu and Sipang is indeed a lovely one. To the right lies the splendid range of Poe, overtopping the lower, but equally beautiful, Gading hills; then the fantastic-shaped mountains of the interior; while to the left the range of Santubong end-on towards you looks like a solitary peak, rising as an island from the sea, as Teneriffe once appeared to me sailing by the Meander. From these hills flow many streams which add to the beauty of the view. But the gems of the scene are the little emerald isles that are scattered over the surface of the bay, presenting their pretty beaches of glittering sand, or their lovely foliage drooping to kiss the rippling waves. There is no prettier spot [than the mouth of the Sarawak river]; on the right bank rises the splendid peak of Santubong, over 2,000 feet in height, clothed from its summit to its base with noble vegetation, its magnificent buttresses covered with lofty trees, showing over a hundred feet of stem without a branch, and at its base a broad beach of white sand fringed by graceful casuarinas, waving and trembling under the influence of the faintest breeze, and at that time thronged by wild hogs."

But of the people he had a slightly different story to tell:

"It is of the hill-Dyak, however, I would particularly write, for a more wretched, oppressed race is not to be found, or one more deserving the commiseration of the humane. Though industrious, they never reap what they sow; though their country is rich in produce, they are obliged to yield it all to their oppressors; though yielding all beyond their bare sustenance, they rarely can preserve half their children, and often— too often— are robbed of them all, with their wives. All that rapacity and oppression can effect is exhausted, and the only happiness that

ever falls to the lot of these unhappy tribes is getting one tyrant
instead of five thousand. Indeed, it is quite useless to try to explain the miserable condition of this country, where for the last
ten years there has been no government; where intrigue and
plunder form the occupation of all the higher classes; where
lying is a virtue, religion dead, and where cheating is so common; and last, where the ruler, Muda Hassim, is so weak that
he has lost all authority except in name and observance."

And further:

"All those who frequent the sea-shore lead a life of constant
peril from roving Dyaks and treacherous Malays, and Illanuns
and Balaninis the regular pirates. It is a life of watchfulness,
hide-and-seek, and fight or flight, and in the course of each year
many lose their lives or their liberty.

"This is the country I have taken upon myself to govern with
small means, few men, and, in short, without any of the requi-
sites which could insure success; I have distraction within and
intrigue abroad, and I have the weakest of the weak, a rotten
staff, to depend upon for my authority."

James Brooke derived his authority from the Sultan of Brunei
who, at least nominally, had ruled Sarawak before the arrival
of the *Royalist*. The following entry concerning the Sultan appears in James's diary:

"His right hand is garnished with an extra diminutive thumb,
the natural member being crooked and distorted. His mind, in-
dexed by his face, seems to be a chaos of confusion, without dignity and without good sense. He can neither read nor write, is
guided by the last speaker; and his advisers, as might be expected, are of the lower order, and mischievous from their ignorance and their greediness. He is always talking, and generally
joking; and the most serious subjects never meet with five minutes' consecutive attention. His rapacity is carried to such an
excess as to astonish a European, and is evinced in a thousand
mean ways. The presents I made him were unquestionably handsome, but he was not content without begging from me the
share I had reserved for the other *pangirans*; and afterwards
solicited mere trifles such as sugar, pen-knives, and the like. To
crown all, he was incessantly asking what was left in the vessel,

and when told the truth—that I was stripped bare as a tree in winter—he frequently returned to the charge."

Baring-Gould and Bampfylde, writing about the Rajah's tasks in Sarawak, said:

"The revenue of Sarawak was in utter confusion. Over large tracts of country no tax could be enforced, and the Rajah, as he had undertaken, was determined to lighten the load that had weighed so crushingly, and was inflicted so arbitrarily on the loyal land-Dyaks—loyal hitherto, not in heart, but because powerless to resist. To carry on the government without funds was impossible, and the want of these was now, and for many years to come, the Rajah's greatest trouble. Consequently, the antimony ore was made a monopoly of the government, which was a fair and just measure, and to the general advantage of the community, though it was subsequently seized upon as a pretext for accusing the Rajah of having debased his position by engaging in trade. But it was years before the revenue was sufficient to meet the expenditure, and gradually the Rajah sacrificed his entire fortune to pay the expenses of the administration.

"In undertaking the government he had three objects in view:

1. The relief of the unfortunate land-Dyaks from oppression.
2. The suppression of piracy, and the restoration to a peaceable and orderly life of those tribes of Dyaks who had been converted into marauders by their Malay masters.
3. The suppression of head-hunting.

"But these ends could not be attained all at once. The first was the easiest arrived at, and the news spread through the length and breadth of the island that there was one spot on its surface where the native was not ground to powder, and where justice reigned. The result was that the land-Dyaks flocked to it. Whole families came over from the Dutch Protectorate, where there was no protection; and others who fled to the mountains and the jungle returned to the sites of their burnt villages.

"How this has worked, on the same undeviating lines of a sound policy, under the rule of the two Rajahs, the following may show. Writing in 1867, on revisiting Sarawak, Admiral the Hon. Sir Henry Keppel said:

" 'In 1842, piracy, slavery, and head-hunting were the order of the day. The sail of a peaceful trader was nowhere to be seen, not even a fisherman, but along the length of this beautiful coast, far into the interior, the Malays and Dyaks warred on one another. Now how different! Huts and fishing-stakes are to be seen all along the coast; the town of Kuching, which on the visit of the *Dido* had scarcely 800 inhabitants, now has a population of 20,000. The aborigines, who called themselves warriors, are now peaceful traders and cultivators of rice. The jungle is fast being cleared to make way for farms.' "

From time to time, Brooke, pressed financially, would offer Sarawak to the British Crown. He may as well have offered them a desert island.

" 'It is easy,' wrote the Rajah at the close of the previous year, 'for men to perform fine feats with the pen; it is easy for the rich man to give yearly thousands in charity; it is easy to preach against the slave trade or to roar against piracy; it is easy to bustle about London, and get up associations for all kinds of objects—all this is easy, but it is not easy to stand alone—to be exiled—to lay out a small fortune—to expend life and health and money—to risk life itself, when the loss would be without glory and without gain. . . . I am enabled to dispense happiness and peace to many thousand persons. I stand alone; I appeal for assistance and gain none; I have struggled for four years bearing my life in my hand. I hold a commanding position and influence over the natives; I feel it my paramount duty to gain protection and some power. I state it in so many plain words, and if, after all, I am left to my own resources the fault of failure is not with me. This negotiation with government is nearly at an end, or if protracted, if I perceive any intention of delay, or any coolness I will myself break it off and trust to God and my own wits. . . . If they act cordially they will either give me a plain negative or some power to act, in order that I may carry out my views. If they haggle and bargain any further I will none of them, or if they bother me with their suspicions, or send any more gentlemen for the purpose of espionage, I will assert the independence I feel, and send them all to the devil!' "

There had been much bloodshed in Sarawak, and it was James Brooke's ruthless extirpation of the pirates that led to the virulent criticism that was made against him in England. There was no doubt that Brooke's ships had steamed headlong into pirate craft and riddled the occupants with shot. But they were, after all, pirates, utterly inimical to Borneo's economy, such as it was; bloodthirsty, cut-throat brigands who gave no quarter to those who fell within their power. The Rajah had shown complete determination, too, to stamp out in his country the savage customs that prevailed among certain sections of his people. If the way in which he accomplished his aims was wrong, then it is impossible for anyone to say which would have been the right way in the absence of help and support from England. And when the piracy and the head-hunting and the cruelty were eliminated, there remained no doubt that the majority of Sarawak's inhabitants were thankful.

The second Rajah brought to Sarawak a Ranee. She came with her husband after their marriage in England in 1870.

"When the Ranee arrived in the country which was to be her home for many years, and where by the exercise of a kindly and tactful influence she was soon to gain the enduring affection and esteem of all her people, Kuching presented a very different appearance from what it does now. It was a small place then, with but few roads, with no places of recreation or amusement, and with a very limited society. But it possessed the charm of romance, of beautiful, though sometimes to the English exile, wearying scenery, and above all an interesting and lovable people, proud and courteous, yet simple and childlike in many ways. Kuching is more than double the size now, and all the recreations and amusements in which Britons delight can now be indulged in there.

"As the *Royalist*, on board which were the Rajah and Ranee, rounded a tree-covered point, the lower suburbs of the town opened up. On the right hand, Malay Kampongs, set in groves of dark-foliaged fruit trees, enlivened by groups of welcoming Malays on the verandahs and on the banks, dressed in their best garments of bright colours, and by little brown children sporting in the wash of the steamer. Opposite, the Chinese sago factories, gay with strips of Turkey-red cloth embossed with words of welcome, and enveloped in the smoke of an incessant salute of crackers and bombs. At the head of the long and broad reach the river-banks on both sides rise to small hills, as if guarding the entrance to the main town. At the foot of the hill on the left are the Borneo Company's office and godowns; above, their bungalows set in deep verdure. On the hill opposite, where now Fort Margherita domineers over the town like a castle with its square tower and flanking turrets, were the Residency (now the Commandant's house) and the barracks. Rounding the bend between these hills, the main town, seated on the banks of a broad stretch of river, broke into view, the Chinese bazaars, or town, and the public buildings on the left, with the old white fort (now the jail) on the point above. On the right, the Astana, or palace, standing in park-like gardens amid tall palms and other trees. On both banks above are the upper Malay Kampongs, and in the distant background the jungle-clad range of Matang in sapphire blue, rising to the noble peak of Serapi.

"The bazaars were gaily decorated in the showy and profuse fashion affected by the Chinese, and the native shipping—brigs, schooners, junks, and prahus of all descriptions—were gay with bunting, the ensign of Sarawak predominating, and here and there the red, white and blue flag of the Netherlands, the Natuna flag, black with a white canton; and the triangular mercantile flag of China, a green three-clawed dragon on a yellow ground. From the British Consulate only, flapped in the light wind the Union Jack.

"As the *Royalist*, with the Rajah's flag flying at the main, steamed slowly up to her anchorage, the booming of cannon announced to the people far and wide the return of their Ruler with his bride, and simultaneously with the first gun, down the whole length of the town burst forth a deafening crash of crackers and bombs—the Chinese time-honoured method of saluting.

"From the parade-ground, led by the Commandant, defiled a line of white uniformed Rangers, with black facings and belts, the guard of honour marching to the Astana. The Siamese state-barge manned by Rangers, and with the Resident on board, shot alongside to convey their Highnesses ashore, and, as they landed, an orderly unfurled the symbol of sovereignty—the large yellow umbrella.

"At the Astana landing-place were all the English residents, Malay chiefs, the leading Chinese, and a few Indian merchants. A bright picture this assembly presented, with the handsome uniforms of the officials, the rich-coloured robes and turbans of the hajis, and the loose silk costumes of the Chinese. Above was seen a knot of brown Dyaks, the men wearing long decorated waistcloths of gay colours, black leglets and ivory armlets; the women in short petticoats fringed with silver coins, and in all the splendour of their brass and copper corselets, armlets, anklets, and coronets, burnished and sparkling in the sun.

"With a tear on his bronzed cheek, a tear of joy, the old Datu Bandar, the worthy son of a gallant father, steps forward to welcome his beloved Chief with his beautiful bride, and his was not the least valued of the many fervent greetings they received that day."

What price exploitation now? Today, the idea of benevolent paternalism is an anachronism. In Malaya we strive instead to produce a democracy, a happy, contented, durable, self-governing democracy out of a population consisting of almost all the Eastern races. It may yet come to pass, and yet again it well may not. It is, I suppose, a gamble. If it fails, then the misery of Malaya will be greater, almost, than it has ever known before. And with the prospect of the misery before us perhaps it is as well to consider again whether or not paternalistic concepts in Malaya are as silly as they at first sight appear. Baring-Gould and Bampfylde, completing their book on Sarawak, almost fifty years ago, wrote:

"In this country like Sarawak, peopled by Easterns of so great a diversity of races, customs and ideas, a union of people for their common weal is an impossibility. For them the best and only practical form of government is that which they now enjoy, a mild and benevolent despotism, under a Ruler of a superior and exotic race, standing firm and isolated amidst racial jealousies, as no native Ruler could do, and unsuspected of racial partiality; a Ruler who has devoted his life to their common welfare.

"Strength of character and intregrity of purpose, tact and courage, firmness and compassion, combined with a thorough knowledge, not only of their languages and customs, but of the innermost thoughts of his people, to be gained only by a long experience, are qualities without which a despotic Ruler must fall into the hands of the strongest faction and, eventually, bring disaster on himself and his country; but are those which have enabled the Rajah to tide over many political troubles, to consolidate the many and diverse interests of his people, and to guide the State to its present position of prosperity and content."

I wonder if we are so justified as we think in our blind faith in democracy?

November 26th, 1954

Those who live in Singapore will occasionally take a long week-end and go to Malacca. Malacca is something like a hundred and sixty miles away and the proposal to drive such a distance for the pleasure of a quiet week-end must appear to people in England as a special kind of madness. It may well be true that on the Monday morning the net result is shown to be an increase, if anything, in fatigue, but on looking back on the sweet heaven of the two clear days' holiday, the only possible conclusion must be that it was worth every drop of the sweat. And driving to Malacca *is* a sweat.

We left after lunch with a loaded car today, Friday. Things began inauspiciously enough, for when I reached home from the office at twenty-past one I was met by J. who asked where the children were; had I not remembered the arrangement that I should collect them from school? Since school finished at half-past twelve they would either have been drooping disconsolately round the school gate for an hour or would have been taken to the house of one of the teachers. The question was, which teacher? We have two children, both at different schools, and I found one of them running about in the school grounds and the other, tearful and resentful, at the house of the nearest teacher. At the age of three, desertion is not well received.

So, by the time we had reached home again and had eaten a

quick lunch, the intended two o'clock start was no longer possible. We eventually left at two-thirty in company with D. in his Mayflower. In the car we had four adults and two children and no very great guarantee that the ancient machine would stand the racket of three hundred and twenty miles all told. It was not so much the people that the car carried as the miscellaneous mountain of equipment that human beings seem to need when they go away for even two days: bedding, folding chairs, suitcases, grips, boxes, toys, books, spare tyres, everything except a stout length of rope which, in the last resort, is the only thing that is going to get you out of mechanical trouble in Malaya today.

Not far north of Johore Bahru we turned left along the pleasant winding road that weaves its way through countless acres of rubber trees to the West Coast at Pontian Kechil. From there we followed the coastal road all the way to Malacca. It is a long, flat, almost wholly straight road and it rained practically the whole way. Along its entire length live Malays in their often delightful wooden houses. Some can afford only what are little better than attap shacks, others are able to build for themselves veritable bungalows—bungalows in the tropical and not the Western suburban sense. They are made of wood and often brightly painted. Since they stand on stilts, steps are a necessary part of the front entrance and their railings are often finely carved—probably by Chinese who, in South-east Asia, have made a profession of copying native arts until the natives lose their ability and the Chinese gain a monopoly. Sometimes, in especially ornate Malay houses, the steps of the front door are gaudily tiled, but this, I think, is a retrogressive tendency. The wooden walls of the houses are fitted with numerous windows, all of which can be tightly closed with wooden shutters against the rain. Here another indication of the financial status of the owner can be evident; no curtains, ordinary curtains or highly-coloured, vivid curtains. But whether they have curtains or not, these houses, shaded by the surrounding trees, always look delightfully cool inside.

It is a pity that there is now a very much increasing tendency among the Malays to roof their houses with corrugated iron, which can always be depended upon to go rusty in patches, thus destroying the prospect of rural beauty. But I believe there are advantages: it is said to be cooler than attap since it reflects the sun's rays; it does not harbour livestock; it is waterproof and, perhaps most important of all, a fourteen-pound coconut in its husk, falling perhaps eighty feet from its swaying tree-top, will usually, albeit with a noise like the sounding of the last trump, bounce off, when it would pass straight through flimsy attap like a bomb through light cloud. Coconuts are a hazard of Malay life; they are, as it were, an occupational risk. They are picked, of course, before it is time for them to fall of their own accord, but one left by accident is a potential murderer and many deaths have been known. One can speak of coconuts in much the same way as one can speak of atom bombs: if you get in the way of one—and if it is of any consolation—you will never know what hit you.

On the way to Malacca by the coast road it is necessary to cross two wide rivers at Batu Pahat and Muar. It is said that Malaya is too poor a country to build the expensive bridges that would be needed to span these two rivers near to their mouths. I do not believe this. What is in fact the case is that no one has ever demanded them with sufficient conviction. Sooner or later they will have to be built and the only people who will suffer will be the present ferry monopolists.

The rain has cleared when we drive into Batu Pahat, a pleasant, well-laid-out little town on the banks of the river, spoilt only by its large areas of "shop-houses." Why is it that Malaya cannot get the poverty of the "shop-house" out of its system? Who was the malefactor who first produced this concrete, hutchlike conception of living? Is it simply that a "shop-house" is cheap? that it needs no imagination? that after the first one was built no further would-be builders would need architects but only contractors with a sufficient knowledge of building to lay one brick upon another? The "shop-house"—three walls and an open front, with an overhanging second story so that passers-by on the pavement are sheltered from the rain—is a hideous and æsthetically decadent monstrosity. Today private enterprise and Town Boards and Municipalities and the Government are building them faster than ever. They are a symptom of that utter paucity of imagination that has led numerable towns in Malaya, in this country of rich and often fabulous history, to label their streets, since their inhabitants could think of nothing better, Cross Street One, Cross Street Two, Cross Street Three and so on. There are several laws that could be made with great benefit to Malaya tomorrow, and one of them is that any man building a "shop-house" should be confined in it for the rest of his natural life.

The ferry at Batu Pahat, as at Muar, consists of what is not very much more than a raft. It slopes upwards at either end to prevent vehicles running on into the river and has railings at either side in a half-hearted attempt to deter the children from falling in. When it is well laden with cars, lorries, buses and bicycles, a small launch, protected with old motor-car tyres, secures itself alongside the raft and goes full speed ahead into the rushing current, taking the raft along with it. The two contraptions, locked like doomed swimmers in a hopeless embrace, then proceed crab-wise to the opposite side.

A long time ago the Sultan of Johore wondered how he could reward a particularly good cook who was retiring after long and faithful service. He decided that perhaps a monopoly of the Batu Pahat and Muar ferries would be a splendid thing, and so he gave them to him and his descendants for a hundred years. This is why we still cross the river in this archaic fashion without a cent of the fee being put by for an eventual bridge.

But as you lean on the rail, looking up-river or down to the sea, you begin to wonder whether a bridge would be such a good thing after all. It would speed things up too much and we should no longer have time to look at the brown, surging river under the flat and rain-washed sky. Besides, a bridge would be unsightly. Along the banks of the river stretch the mangroves and the palms, and here and there are Malays in little boats paddling along on leisurely errands. Here, when you visit your friends, you time your arrival and departure by the tide. Twice a day the water surges in from the sea and twice a day sluices out again, carrying with it the eternal load of silt and the refuse of the jungle. If you fly above these rivers where they enter the sea, the sea for miles around is stained brown by the river water, saturated with suspended silt and vegetation. A bridge would simply be progress; but progress is not always a good thing. There is no fundamental reason why progress should always be forwards. Even the "shop-house," when it was first built, was fondly imagined, I have no doubt, to be a singular mark of progress.

We approach the landing-stage at an angle of forty-five degrees and the Malay in charge of the launch finely balances momentum, thrust and tide in an exquisite triangle of forces. He needs no trigonometry to help him; he accomplishes a balancing act of great complexity simply by instinct. There is a gentle shudder as we scrape the stout bamboo poles driven into the mud at the side of the landing-stage, and the raft comes gently to rest, precisely in the right position. There is a whir of starters—and woe betide the man in front whose engine will not start at a time like this—and we are off on the long straight road to the next ferry at Muar which is practically a replica of this one.

As we enter the great rice bowl which extends round ancient Malacca, it is growing dark. The road is no longer straight but weaves from side to side, over little hillocks and down into gentle valleys. On either side stretches the unbelievably vivid green of the young rice, a green so very green that it seems alive, possessed of some mystic, powerful spirit of its own, a breathing, living, limitless expanse of life. Among the rice an occasional conical-hatted figure can be seen standing statuesquely in the encroaching gloom, fishing—fishing in the fields of rice, fishing in what appears to be dry land but is, in fact, almost wholly water. Along the road we pass the first bullock carts that are seen in this particular form only in and around Malacca. They have roofs of fine attap running from front to back, and the spine of the roof is bowed in the middle so that either end sticks up like the corner of a Chinese roof. They move slowly, these wondrously proportioned vehicles, the somnolent driver switching occasionally at the bullock's rump.

Then the rain begins. The most difficult time of all to see properly when driving is at twilight, when it is no longer light but yet not entirely dark, when headlights are ineffectual. Add

to this the thick, driving mist of tropical rain and it is like driving in a smothering blanket of darkness which nothing can
penetrate. The loaded car buckets round unforeseen corners, and
we enter Malacca at a speed not very much in excess of ten
miles per hour. We pick our way through the sodden, dripping
town and out at the other end, for we are bound for Tanjong
Kling, a promontory which lies on the coast a few miles to the
north of the town of Malacca. Here there is a government bungalow which may be taken for holidays. Its position, I am told, is
perfect, but I shall not be able to verify this until morning.

The third car, containing the remainder of our party, arrived
at nine o'clock and, after a cold dinner at the immense dining-
table, swallowed with a good deal of restorative alcohol, we
argued until midnight about self-government, independence,
socialism, women and Ava Gardner, who is at present on the
way to Singapore. I rather fancy that the greater part of the
male inhabitants of Malaya, if offered the alternative of independence for life or Ava Gardner for a month, would be more
than tempted to take the latter.

November 27th, 1954

In the fresh light of not very early morning, Tanjong Kling
lives up to its reputation. The enormous bungalow, as it is called,
although it is not a bungalow at all, stands right up to the sea,
yet high off the sand. The trees that surround it run right down
the steep bank to the beach and some of them seem able to grow
in the sand, their old, exposed roots standing like rock strata
ossified by the water.

Tanjong Kling stands at the northerly end of a great and
peaceful bay. At the southerly end lies Malacca, and from this
distance all that we can make out clearly is the radar defence
aerial. All along this curving gentle coast stand the tall palms,
some straight and others bent grotesquely by the wind to grow
at different angles to the ground. Behind our bungalow is a
cluster of Malay houses, one of them exceptionally smart, painted
a bright yellow and black, the colours of a Malay Teacher's
College of which the occupant was principal before he retired

to the quiet of Tanjong Kling. Opposite, across the mirror-smooth, seldom-ruffled Straits of Malacca, lies Sumatra, pinioned below a majestic pyramid of clouds. On really clear days Sumatra can be seen as France can sometimes be seen from the southern coast of England. More often than not the visitor to Malacca only thinks he can see Sumatra, for it is difficult to distinguish the land from the continents of cloud that stand above it.

This stretch of water is one of the most important in the world. From time immemorial it has carried the trade route that runs between East and West. Malacca is situated at the cross-roads of the monsoons and, because of this, at the cross-roads of trade. Malacca lies, as the ancient traders knew, where one monsoon ends and the other begins. The roaring North-east Monsoon would bring the Chinese junks scudding down from China, across the choppy China Sea, bringing the silks and porcelains, ivory and jade. These goods would be unloaded at Malacca. Spices from the Moluccas, gold from Sumatra, pepper from Java, nutmeg and cinnamon from the Celebes, tropical produce from all the thousands of islands of the Malayan Archipelago—all these goods came to Malacca. Some came direct by ship. Some were landed on the eastern shore of Malaya, it is said, and brought right across the peninsula, up the Pahang river and thence by a short journey overland to the headwaters of the Muar river and down to the sea again to Malacca. At Malacca there was an abundance of fresh water. Its harbour was eternally sheltered. It was sufficiently far down the coast to be south of the mountain backbone of Malaya so that the two-way traffic of goods across the peninsula was possible without a wide detour to the south of the mountains where they fade into the plain of Johore.

Before the South-west Monsoon ran the ships from India to fetch the riches of the East. They came to the harbour of Malacca in their hundreds so that mediæval travellers who had known the great seaports of Europe were astonished at its size, and went away declaring that Malacca was the greatest seaport in the world. The precious cargoes flowed out of Malacca in a steady, mounting stream, across the Indian Ocean to India and then on to the Middle East and into the Mediterranean to Venice, where those who could afford to pay for them bought them. Along the same trade route flowed the wisdom of the Prophet, so that the merchants from the western coast of India, from Cambay and the Coromandel Coast, became missionaries also. This new religion swept all before it in the Archipelago, and the Malay peoples of Malaya, Sumatra, Java and of all the myriads of islands that surround them discarded the ancient faith that the Hindu, also from India, had brought them, and kneeled towards the West, where there was but one God Allah and where Mahomet was his Prophet. The impetus of the Muslim faith stopped short at Bali, and so that heaven on earth was left unconverted and art could flourish as it might have flourished in the remainder of the Archipelago if the Muslims had not converted the people who lived there.

Malacca was the centre of trade, the centre of communications and, in a more local sense, the centre of Malaya. The Sultans of the States of Malaya paid tribute to the Sultan of Malacca, and when emissaries from abroad came to Malaya it was to the Sultan of Malacca that they handed their credentials. It was said that in the town of Malacca no less than eighty-two languages were spoken, since merchants from every quarter of the Eastern world assembled there for the purpose of profit. The Sultan of Malacca sent embassies to China, to the Emperor who nominally protected him from the Siamese. And the Emperor, in turn, sent embassies to Malacca with precious gifts and, it is said, beautiful women.

And then, bursting into this haven of Eastern commerce, came the thunder of the West. The Portuguese discovered that "he who held Malacca had his hand on the throat of Venice." The Portuguese were aware of this before they knew precisely where Malacca was. They knew that it existed, but they did not know how to get there.

In the sixteenth century the Portuguese sent their ships pushing south down the western seaboard of Africa. Old maps and some sixth sense that is only known to seafaring nations told them that by so sailing they would eventually reach the East. Year by year the strong-rigged ships sailed farther south. Putting out from Lisbon they would be away for years until, one day, Bartholomew Diaz found himself, after months of holding a southerly course, battling eastwards round the Cape. He was the first Portuguese to sail into the Indian Ocean, but his sailors were frightened to go farther and he turned back to bring the good news to Lisbon. It was left to the great Vasco da Gama to penetrate the Indian Ocean, and once this was accomplished the way to Malacca was open. From then on, the Portuguese Empire spread across the East through a system of forts from Goa in India to Macao in China.

An Admiral de Sequeira was the first Portuguese to anchor in the harbour of Malacca in the early sixteenth century. The Muslim merchants of Malacca urged the Sultan to attack him, for news of the Portuguese had travelled ahead of them and the merchants knew that they wanted not only trade but converts. The will of Malacca to resist was twofold: their religion as well as their trade was in danger. So the Malays planned to attack the Portuguese on shore, but the Portuguese discovered the plot in time and escaped, though not without leaving behind a number of their men as prisoners of the Malays. The people of Malacca heaved a great sigh of relief and went about their business. Years passed and there were no repercussions attendant upon their daring. Then, all at once, it happened. The great Alfonso D'Albuquerque arrived. Clifford has told the story:

"But this evening the beach was thronged more densely than was common, there was withal a subtle restlessness, a tenseness of expectancy in the air. Word had reached Malacca of the approach of the mysterious strangers from afar, the men with the bearded faces and the corpse-like complexions, the rumour of whose evil doings on the Coromandel coast had carried into the remotest corners of the East. The besetting peril was at hand, even at the gates of the city, but how it might be averted, stayed or met were problems surpassing the wisdom of the wisest.

"And then, before the last of the daylight died, as the mobs of gaily-clad natives stood upon the shores, oppressed by fear, restless with suspense, their dark faces darker in the gathering gloom, suddenly the West was upon them ere they well knew it. The fleet of D'Albuquerque, 'all decked with flags, and the men sounding their trumpets,' swept into sight from behind the sheltering islands to the north, the great bellying squares of strangely rigged canvas catching the faint breeze. On and on it came, inevitable as Fate, the Power of the West sailing into the heart of Malaya unresisted and irresistible, and with panic in its heart the East stood in impotence watching it from the shore. One by one the vessels came to anchor, and then from all there roared a salvo of artillery, the salute of the white men to their victims, an explosion that broke upon the peace of the quiet scene and sounded the knell of the brown man's free enjoyment of the lands which God had given to him."

It is from Albuquerque that the present old buildings of Malacca date. Parts of the fortress he built, *A Famosa*, still stand and will doubtless go on standing for many years yet. Because Malacca possesses these old buildings, the town is unique in Malaya. Almost everything in Malaya is of far more recent vintage, and for this reason it is said that Malacca is the only town in Malaya with an atmosphere. Whether other towns in Malaya are devoid of atmosphere is debatable; that Malacca has one peculiarly its own is undeniable.

The Portuguese attack was made on St. James's Day and the cry of the soldiers as they stormed the town was "St. James." The Malays fought bravely, but gunpowder and shot were too much for their more primitive weapons. The Sultan fled and the Portuguese were left in control, and to this day Malacca is a centre of Catholicism in Malaya, even as it was when Francis Xavier went there, and many of the Portuguese Eurasians there still speak a Portuguese patois. In those days Portugal was mighty; how sadly the mighty now are fallen. As has been the case in almost every Empire that ever existed, the men who came afterwards were not of the calibre of the men who made it. The Portuguese, secure in their tropical and wealthy town, grew lazy and avaricious. They paid scant regard to the welfare of the local people; that they should work for them, adopt the Catholic faith and fornicate with them when necessary, was as much as the Portuguese required of them. Otherwise they treated their subjects in a callous and brutal fashion, an attitude that carried within it the seeds of its own destruction.

But there was another factor. The Dutch were also trying to reach the East, and they too eventually discovered the passage round the Cape of Good Hope. They made their headquarters at Batavia in Java, but they were not slow to see the advantage of owning Malacca too. They made war on the Portuguese from time to time and eventually "slammed their sea gates," and blockaded the town for eleven years. When the Portuguese were sufficiently weakened the Dutch attacked, also in the name of God, crying "Help us, God," and the great Fort of Albuquerque fell to the armies of the Netherlands.

It is to the Dutch that Malacca owes much of its present character. The government offices today are still known as the *Stadthaus* and are still very much as the Dutch built them. The Church of England church nearby was built by the Dutch and some of the streets of the town centre are completely Dutch in character, some of the houses still faced with Dutch tiles. Here sleeps a little, forgotten corner of the Netherlands, the only other reminder being the names of many of the people of Malacca.

After the Dutch, Malacca passed into English hands, and then back again to the Dutch and, finally, back into English hands, as it remains today. But throughout all these trials and tribulations the importance of Malacca was declining. First Penang to the north, established by Francis Light, began to take away its trade. Then Raffles' foundation of Singapore in the south dealt the death-blow to what had been the greatest seaport in the world. Today the harbour is silted up and ships of any size cannot possibly enter it. The streets are quiet, giving the impression of being asleep in the sun, and the ruins of the Portuguese buildings, and the Dutch buildings that are still in use, give it a quaint and peaceful aspect. Life flows gently in Malacca, where the vulgar and feverish scrabble for riches no longer upsets the even tenor of existence.

There is nowhere more conducive to a quiet week-end.

November 28th, 1954

We left in convoy after lunch today. We turned inland at

Batu Pahat instead of continuing to Pontian Kechil and this was the mistake that started all the trouble. The TR2 led the way, our car followed, with the Mayflower bringing up the rear. We reached Ayer Hitam and we turned south on to the main Johore Road to Johore Bahru. Gradually the TR2 pulled ahead and the Mayflower fell behind. In a very short time we were scattered over several miles. The road undulates through rubber and secondary jungle and for mile after mile there are no outstanding landmarks except the prominant milestones which give the mileage to Johore Bahru. At the forty-second milestone our car's engine began to give trouble and we did not have to travel far, at a very much reduced speed, to know that the expensive engine noises were caused by burnt-out bearings. We clanked on for another mile until the car came to an irrevocable halt with a blocked fuel pipe. Not only was the engine almost in pieces, but no petrol was reaching it. We were at the thirty-ninth mile.

We got out and looked helplessly at the engine. Then a car travelling in the opposite direction stopped and offered help. But there was nothing the driver could do except to tell us that "we couldn't have chosen a worse spot to break down." We rather gathered the area was alive with bandits. A lorry came chuntering along the road and the Chinese driver was good enough to give us a length of rope. Then we waited in the terrifying silence of Malaya with nothing more hospitable surrounding us than miles of scrub. It is on occasions like this that the flesh begins to creep a little and you wish that you did not have young children with you, strutting gay and oblivious up and down the road, children who, if bandits appeared, would probably run up to them before being cut down.

It was not long before the Mayflower turned up and we made ready to tow. As we were fixing the tow-rope another car from the opposite direction drew up and the driver said that our friends in the TR2 were getting anxious about us since they had just been shot at from the right at the thirty-eighth mile. They had carried on to telephone the police, and when we failed to show up shortly afterwards wondered whether the Communists' aim had been more effective in our case.

On receiving this item of intelligence we abandoned our car and piled the luggage into the Mayflower, which was somehow made to accommodate six adults, two children and all of their baggage. It was a feat that under normal circumstances would have been considered impossible. The Mayflower was flogged unmercifully, and as we swayed past the thirty-eighth mile there was a distinct feeling of strain in the car. The bright conversation flagged. But nothing happened, and a few miles farther on we encountered the TR2 gallantly coming back to look for us. We stopped at the first police-station and reported the circumstances and this evening, back in Singapore, the police telephoned to say that they had towed our car into their compound.

As we travelled down the centre of Malaya to Johore Bahru we passed, at one point on the left, what must have been a battle of considerable magnitude. Rifles barked repeatedly and there was the sinister chatter of automatic arms. This was Malaya on a Sunday evening and it has been this way for years. After you have been stranded helpless on a road in Malaya with a child aged three and another aged six, neither of them old enough to have the slightest conception of brutality, and after your friends have been shot at a mile away, and when you know that if you are seen, you and your family will also be shot, then, I think, you begin to take a slightly different view of coexistence. It may be that this is an emotional view. It may be that the view is simply a local one, whereas the main problem is infinitely larger and more complex. I have no doubt that it is. But Malayan Communists—and for the moment what made them Communists is irrelevant—are part of the bloc with whom we would seek to coexist. Coexistence, as at present conceived, holds out the prospect of trade and intercourse and every kind of relationship that may prove to be possible within the limits of the coexistence of two rival and opposed camps. But the plain fact of the matter is that I do not wish to have the slightest contact—cultural, commercial or political—with any man, group of men, country or group of countries who set out deliberately to kill my children or anyone else's children. In fact, I shall only be happy when

they have been deprived of their arms and rendered helpless and harmless. And this satisfactory state of affairs is not compatible with coexistence.

December 12th, 1954

Flew to Ipoh this morning, and thence by taxi to the Cameron Highlands. It is to the Highlands that we come to cool down when the year's work is over. From Tapah the road winds upwards until at Tanah Rata, some forty-odd miles distant, it is nearly five thousand feet high. Here the air is fresh and at night it is necessary to use blankets, and this is perhaps the greatest pleasure of all. It is possible, as the road winds and climbs through the surrounding and overhanging jungle trees, to feel the air changing, to sense the slow evaporation of its humid closeness, replaced by a cleaner and brighter atmosphere with the slightest suggestion of a nip that puts a new vigour into the matter of living.

Our hotel stands in front of the golf-course, a smooth, nine-hole depression in the midst of Malaya's majestic hills. The hotel is pseudo "olde worlde" from top to bottom, yet pleasingly and successfully so. Its rooms are bright with red fires, and to sit before them in Malay is a special kind of bliss. The Smoke House Inn is one of the few remaining hotels in the world where a visitor is made to feel as though he is a guest in a private house, with none of the attendant disadvantages. How many hotels are there today where the proprietor will offer you the use of his motor-car and ask you, a complete stranger, to dine with him? And how many proprietors of hotels ask their guests each morning what it is that they would like cooked specially for their dinner? I suppose that in some ways the Smoke House Inn is an anachronism. If so, it is a pity there are not more of them.

December 19th, 1954

Our holiday is almost over, and we wish we could stay longer in this paradise of laziness. We have read nothing more

exacting than Simenon and the numerous illustrated magazines
provided; done nothing more energetic than play gentle rounds
of golf with an incredible lack of expertise; engaged in no
pastime more serious than darts. We have slept too much, eaten
too much and drunk too many glasses of Anchor beer. We have
spent, in short, a perfect holiday.

Our only expedition has been to the top of Bukit Brinchang,
a hill a few miles from Tanah Rata, surmounted by a wireless
station. The wireless station stands at 6,666 feet above sea-level,
and so the road leading to it is the highest in Malaya and the
view from it the finest to be obtained by the simple use of a
taxi. On every side stand the cloud-wreathed hills, swooping upwards to their serried pinnacles, plunging down again to their
steep-sided valleys. And over them all, over every square inch of
the thousands of square miles that can be seen at a glance, stands
the awesome Malayan forest. It is not the hills and the mountains that the visitor sees, but the tops of millions upon millions
of trees which follow the contours of the hills they totally obscure. This is the real Malaya, a land impenetrable except at the
cost of an immense outpouring of energy. This is not the Malaya
of the coasts; of the fishing villages; the broad brown rivers;
the orderly rubber plantations and the busy tin mines. These
hills are the inviolable heart of Malaya. The trees are the flesh
and the hills the bones, and if the trees were removed only a
skeleton would remain.

On the way down, the brakes of the taxi grew so hot that
we had to stop and pour cold water on them. The brake drums
sizzled. This operation was carried out in the midst of a tea
plantation where the bared hillsides are dotted with diminutive
tea bushes. They do not look so spectacular as the jungle but
they are safer; bandits cannot hide in them so successfully. The
manager's bungalow, a little way up the road, is surrounded by
barbed wire and floodlights illuminate every inch of ground
round it. That bungalow, too, as well as the forest, is the real
Malaya, the Malaya we have come to know in the last few
years.

Farther down the road we come to the Chinese vegetable gardens, terraced along the hillsides, the precious earth kept in place

by logs, placed at right angles to the slope. Here the Chinese in their conical hats labour under the sun until they die and produce Malaya's finest vegetables, that are sent down to the plains by lorry. There is something infinitely pleasing about the cultivated patchwork of Chinese vegetable gardens, reaching out in every direction. The patiently intensive use of the soil is like an English patchwork of fields in miniature.

Among the vegetable plots stand the stark ruins of the burnt-out Green Cow Hotel. The bandits burnt it long ago in the curious conviction that they were aiding the advance of Communism. They also tried at one time to kill the proprietor of the Smoke House Inn. They ambushed him in his armoured Ford V8. First of all they shot away the tyres so that it ran into the ditch by the side of the road. They poured rifle and machine-gun fire at the car. Finally, they lobbed hand grenades at it. Then they fled. Unaccountably the occupants of the car lived and the car to this day is pock-marked with the little depressions the bullets left in the armour. Some of those marks are in random places and others run in wavy lines where the machine-gun raked, searching for the join in the armour between the top of the doors and the roof.

Farther down the hill we came across an aboriginal carrying his blow-pipe. All the way up from Tapah, along the edge of the road, stand little aboriginal settlements where the inhabitants engage in a little sedentary farming and live in tiny houses made of bamboo and attap. We stopped to photograph the man we met and before he would allow us to do so he asked for money. In such a way does civilisation contaminate those who have no need of it. They say that the aboriginal peoples of Malaya—the Negritos, the Senoi and the Jakun—are dying out; that they suffer from malnutrition and skin diseases and every kind of ailment that could be cured by medicine. They say that they derive no benefit from the government of the country and that the only tangible gain they have made from British rule has been a release from Malay bondage. They say that there is no place for these shy jungle people in a modern society and that the only time we really bother about them is when they fall into the clutches of the bandits. And yet to use another phrase current in Malaya—"What to do?" Is it better to herd them into protected reservations? God forbid! Is it better to search them all out and bring Western medicine to them on a grand scale? If so, they will pick up other things from such an increased contact with the West which will be at least as deleterious as the diseases they suffer from at present. Are we just to let them be? Perhaps this is the kindest solution, since they have existed for thousands of years in the face of privation and oppression and there is no really valid reason to suppose that they will suddenly begin to die out—even though some people think they will.

Then back to the Smoke House, and the friendly fire and the beginning of Christmas decorations. It was impossible to imagine a greater contrast.

December 31st, 1954

It is difficult to perceive an essential difference between the course of events we remember from the late 'thirties and that which we are experiencing now. In those days we were faced with a ruthless and expanding dictatorship. Now we are faced with a dictatorship no less ruthless and no less expansionist. Sooner or later we must stand up to it. It may be that sooner or later we must fight it.

I never read Mein Kampf, but it is said that in this book Hitler foretold to a remarkable degree the course of his European aggression. Similarly, in the Communist bibles the pattern of Communist aggression is equally clearly foretold: a pattern devised to lead to the eventual domination of the world through the fermenting of revolution in first one country and then another. Is half the world so blind it cannot see that this is so?

The case for coexistence fell to the ground the day the Communists murdered the High Commissioner of the Federation of Malaya, Sir Henry Gurney. The hail of fire that shattered his body was a crime that in some of its aspects escaped the people of Britain. The crime would not have been in any way different if it had been Queen Elizabeth of England whose body they had shot to pieces. The High Commissioner was the representative of the Queen: the Queen was murdered by proxy.

Are these the people with whom we are to coexist? Are these the people with whom we are to parley? Do you invite the man who has murdered your wife to dinner? Do you play football with the men who have hacked off the head of your daughter? Can a reasonable man contemplate any form of contact with these Communist butchers? Communism is an international organisation, and the Malayan Emergency could be called off tomorrow if Peking or Moscow wished. Why, then, do so many people refuse to understand the depth of the evil that has welled up out of the wastes of Asia, that is creeping like a turgid flood, engulfing all before it?

My quarrel is not with the economics of Communism. If a greater measure of equality can be brought about in this world, then I should like to support whatever agency can bring it about by peaceful means. I believe that if British Socialism can be made to work, it will be the greatest social and economic system the world has ever known. I want, as much as anyone, to abolish poverty and misery and privation and unhappiness and unemployment and all the other ills of the world, and if they can be abolished by a greater equality, or even a complete equality of wealth, by State ownership of the resources of production, by economic controls, or by any or all of the remainder of the paraphernalia of Socialism, then I will support them. It is not the economic ideal of Communism that frightens me. I do not oppose Communism because I fear that I may lose whatever wealth or material assets I might possess. With this aspect of the problem I am scarcely concerned.

It is the inhuman brutality of Communism that I despise. I do not know why a particular economic and political creed should attract principally the cut-throats and killers of a community, but it is so. Murder has become a component of Communism. Communists believe that bloody revolution must precede the Utopia without ever suspecting that they themselves become brutalised in the process. They believe that the ends justify the means, and this being so there is nothing to which they will not stoop to bring about their ends. Nowhere in the world has Communism come to power by any means other than the sword. Every advance of Communism has been both preceded and followed by a blood-bath. Is this the creed and are these the people with whom we wish to do business?

And once the revolution has been accomplished, what follows? The imprisonment, the suppression of information, the virulent hate campaigns, the brain-washing, the firing squads, the tragic farce of the Peoples' Court, the concentration camps, the adoration of the Leader, the elimination of undesirable elements, the public confessions, the accusation meetings, the slow poisoning of young minds until they become automatic extensions of the ultimate fount of thought control, the total, abject enslavement of the minds of men. It is of no use to say that if that is the way they like things in Russia, let them enjoy it; that it is no concern of ours as long as they do not interfere with us. Once we were able to speak simply of Russia. Now we have to speak of China and North Korea, of all the ancient states of Eastern Europe and of Indo-China. Soon we shall be able to add to the list and speak, too, of Siam and Burma, Malaya, India and Indonesia. All these countries will become Communist unless the West fights, and is allowed to fight, for their freedom. If this is not so, why, then, is there a Siamese puppet government already operating on the Siamese border? Why have we been fighting this bloody and murderous war in Malaya for so long? What is the war in Burma all about? Why has trouble already begun in that part of Indo-China which is still this side of the Iron Curtain? Why have the Communists tried to stage a *coup d'état* in Indonesia? Why does China shoot down our aeroplanes and imprison our nationals? Why does she assemble invasion forces off Formosa? Why are Hongkong and Macao beds of intrigue and unrest? Why is even Nehru worried about the Communists in India?

I suspect that many people, when faced with such evidence of Communist activity, come to the conclusion that Communism is what the people of these countries want and that it is scarcely their business to try to prevent them from having it. But the fact of the matter is that people of these countries do *not* want Communism; they simply want a better deal, a fair share of the wealth of the world, to which they are entitled by virtue of having been born into it. They will embrace Communism if it means a full belly for once. They are not worried about losing their freedom of speech because they have never had it anyway, or at least they have never understood it as we understand it in the West. But what if these countries go? Then the area of expansionist endeavour changes and advances southwards, and into the Middle East, until we are all gathered within the ravenous maw of the Big Brother of the world. Somewhere a line must be drawn, and that line must be defended—with our lives if necessary.

It is no use simply standing on this line with guns—although the guns must certainly be there. It is no use simply injecting capital into a country and hoping for the best. All the wealth and material in the world did not help in Indo-China. It is no use simply raising the standard of living of the country, because the Communist will burn the rice and fire the houses, kill the people and sabotage the plans—anything to bring about the conditions they require for their revolution. They can often work more quickly than we, for they are prepared to use methods which we shun: while we attempt to create, they destroy; while we try to organise, they disrupt; while we try to help people, they simply kill. The people of the East cannot alone defeat Communism within their frontiers, nor even with the aid of our wealth can they defeat it. They must also accept the aid of our force. Without an efficient army and police force in Siam, for example, Communism will in the end triumph. Since it is unlikely that Siam will ever have either, Communism may triumph there through the sheer absence of an adequate defence.

Malaya, without British power, would become Communist tomorrow. It would gravitate to China as bubbles of tea are attracted to the sides of the cup. Not, I repeat, because the people want Communism, but because they want a fairer share. Therefore in Malaya we must first Socialise, and give every man the better lot he so urgently demands. When a European considers that he cannot live on less than $800 a month, and some Chinese millionaires spend as much as $10,000 a month, how can we believe that we have moved within nodding distance of the problem, when the average monthly wage in Malaya is below $100? Secondly, Malaya must have financial aid so that she can build her houses and roads and hospitals and industries, develop her under-developed land and fish with modern methods in her under-developed seas. Finally, with all this, must come the military aid, the soldiers, who must root out the Communist killers, disarm them and remove them.

If we cannot do this, we may as well all go home tomorrow. The problem is as simple—and as difficult—as that.

Is the problem partly compounded of British confusion? In treading the middle path so assiduously, are we in danger of losing our way? Although we fight Communism in Malaya with guns and men are shot every day of the week, our politicians make a habit of taking their holidays in Communist countries. Although we are at war with Communism, and have been at war with Communism for years, we go repeatedly cap in hand to the ultimate directors of the war, to tell them how nice it would be if they would buy our bicycles. Although we have carried out in Britain the greatest social experiment the world has ever seen, we are yet afraid to transplant it to our overseas possessions, which will surely die without it.

It is, on the whole, better to make a bad decision than not to make one at all. It seems to me and it seems, I know, to a lot of people in Malaya, that Britain must decide whether she is to consort with criminals or avoid them. She must recognise in time the enemy for what he is: an implacable force bent on her destruction. In Malaya the fight must be on a military level, on an economic level and on a social level. Most of the people of Malaya are miserably poor. As long as they remain poor we shall lose the war that began in earnest at Stalingrad.

Perhaps the resources of Britain alone cannot save Malaya. Then the total resources of the West must be brought to bear. Only a gigantic programme of social and economic reform, coupled with military might, can save us. If we do not accept these terms, then such treasure as is being sent to Malaya will be wasted.

February 20th, 1955

The diary is finished, typed and sent to the publisher. Yet there is one more journey to record, a journey we should have undertaken long ago—but one on which we only now embark.

We board the northbound mail train at seven-fifteen from Singapore. Malaya's trains are still for the most part troop trains, and if a person wishes to have the facts of Malaya's war brought home to him he can do nothing better than travel in Malaya by train. At the end of the dining-car there is a bar, and round the bar are a group of young men getting steadily drunker. It is no use to complain. Perhaps if we spent weeks on end bashing through the steaming and insect-ridden jungles of Malaya, with a killer on the end of every trail, we, too, would be more inclined to get drunk when opportunity offered.

In every carriage there are soldiers, and the racks groan with their accoutrements. There is also a mild-looking second-lieutenant with steel-rimmed, army-issue spectacles and an armband pronouncing him to be O.C. troops. It is difficult to escape the conclusion that he will have a great deal of trouble on his hands if he attempts to control the party developing at the far end of the dining-car.

The train draws into the darkness of Johore Bahru station and Malay Customs officers patter through the train, prodding, pushing, feeling, searching for the dutiable bric-à-brac of travellers, unimpressed by the spectacle of their own futility. Then we plod north again, into the night, along the side of the well-worn backbone of the peninsula. The railway is single track and the train travels 250 miles to Kuala Lumpur in not very much under twelve hours—an average speed of about twenty miles an hour. It is not in any kind of a hurry, this railway. But if it were, it would throw its passengers on to Kuala Lumpur railway station at three or four in the morning. Instead, the journey takes all night so they arrive not long after seven in the morning—which is much more sensible.

We eat a steak for dinner and tinned fruit and cream, and coffee quite intolerable. Then we lurch along to our sleeper where the black-faced, moon-faced Tamil with a wide, white grin serves us with whisky-and-soda at the press of the bell. Eventually we fall into our bunks and for the first time wish we had gone by air, for had we done so we would have been there by

now and would not be suffering the hammer, hammer, hammer
of wheels that no longer seem to be round.

February 21st, 1955

The Tamil attendant's grin is no less broad when he brings us
greasy tea in the morning. We lie in our bunks sipping it
as the pale countryside slides past our window, slowly absorbing
the early light that will transform the paleness to the rich greens
and blues of Malaya. A man may forget much of Malaya, but
he can never forget the purity of its mornings or the overwhelming greenness of its colour. Dead on time we steam between the
minarets of Kuala Lumpur's fantastic railway station, built by
a man more in love with temples than modern transport, and
we join the motley crush and push for the barrier. Once outside
we take the lift and check in at the Station Hotel, where we are
given a room so big that its occupant could hold a banquet
within its walls and still sleep soundly. Our predecessors did
themselves well in Malaya—coolness was to be found in space
and, since they had more space than almost anything else, they
did not stint themselves.

In the afternoon we hire a taxi to take us to the Batu Caves.
The caves are situated in one of those gaunt outcrops of limestone which God, or someone equally powerful, at a time immemorial, scattered over Malaya. The Batu Caves have been
adopted by the Hindus, and every year at Thaipusam they flock
there in their thousands, winding in a living scarf of colour up
the innumerable steps that mount the sheer limestone face, some
for the fun of it, some to inscribe their names in great letters on
the softness of the rock, and some from an obscure devotional
impulse. Now, when we approach the Hindu shrine in the chill
and echoing cavern, the temple boy offers us a handful of small,
white flowers which it seems ungracious not to accept, and waves
before us a tray bearing an assortment of dollar notes so that
we feel it would be doubly ungracious to offer him only fifty
cents, which would appear to be more than adequate. We clamber over the crumbling rocks at the end of the cavern where,
hundreds of feet above, the thunderous sky shines as though

down a chimney. Then we return to the high green-streaked cave, a cathedral bigger than any conceived by man, and find, to our disappointment, that the Indian temple boy harbours for the temple attendant an affection of most unnatural proportions, lying across his brown diaphragm as he burbles in clicking Tamil to the uncomprehending stalactites.

On the way back to Kuala Lumpur we stay for a few moments at a tin mine where a gigantic dredge, anchored in its man-made lake of milk-white water, drags up the innocent mud in creaking buckets only to spew it forth again minus its precious content. More tin cans are the product; another desert on the face of Malaya is the result. The dredges, like corrugated monsters from Mars, lumber over the northern plains of Malaya; sinister, rattling contraptions eating the heart out of the land that crumbles like chalk beneath them.

We return to our vast room in the Station Hotel and eat an early dinner before catching the night train south again. Our destination is Kota Bharu in the north, but first we must trundle south until we meet the East Coast line at Gemas. We shall lie for hours in the Gemas siding waiting for the up-train to take us north again. With any luck, we shall sleep through it all.

February 22nd, 1955

Through the jungle of Pahang and on into Kelantan. We follow the rivers and the valleys, but for most of the time the view from the carriage window is obscured by the high jungle on either side. We skirt round the edges of the limestone towers that perch above our tiny train, growing sheer out of flat land, their craggy faces etched deeper by tortured upturned strata. All day we trundle through an undeveloped land towards the north-eastern coast where the Malays live. They say that much of Malaya will grow little but jungle. They say that the soil is no good. I do not believe this. I do not believe it any more than when people say that it is impossible to build more houses here or a main drain there. If it were imperative for Pahang, for example, to grow food on its vast acres instead of jungle, then I think food could be grown all over Pahang. If the soil will

support great and luxurious forests, there must be something
else it will support. And the time will come when the jungles
will have to produce food instead. For if the population of the
East continues to grow as it grows today, if the Singapores of the
East continue to double their populations in twenty years, if,
in China, there continues to be twelve million *more* Chinese each
year, if we are to continue to have one million more Japanese
each year, then more food will have to come from somewhere or,
in spite of the planning, and in spite of the promises, millions
and millions of people will begin to die of starvation.

The jungle is a dead loss. It grows little that is of use. It
is largely impenetrable. It harbours, apart from the aborigines,
little but wild animals and terrorists—and there is small difference between the last two. Nothing will grow in it except the
jungle itself. It is not even pretty to look at. It seems to me that
if we were to set about clearing it and if we were to set about
the problem of growing food in its place, we would be doing
something that is even more important than building schools
and houses, important as the latter are. In the last resort, in
Malaya, a man can live in the open air; our schools are a comparatively recent innovation; but a man cannot live without
food. Unless he stops breeding like the rabbits and unless he
turns his jungles into gardens, he is going to have to try. But
saying so, doesn't win votes. Perhaps, therefore, he will have to
try.

We are met at Kuala Krai and drive by car for the next hour
to Kota Bharu. The jungle has gone from the land and in its
place stand ricefields and rubber plantations. Here is, indeed, a
garden which at one time was as useless as the jungle we have
left behind us.

It is evening when we reach the town of Kota Bharu and
already the prostitutes parade in the town, dressed in their bright
blues and reds—Malay girls for the most part, prostitutes because their environment makes them so. Kota Bharu is the consequence of Malay good nature face to face with alien energies,
both Eastern and Western, that in Malaya are content to express
themselves in a makeshift and rickety impermanence. There is
nothing impermanent about the soft and constant monsoon wind

that sweeps in from the China Sea, bending the tall palms to crooked disfigurement. There is nothing impermanent about the crying, rolling surf, foaming on to white beaches, where brown children play and fishermen look to their boats and tackle. There is nothing impermanent, even, about Malay houses, squatting beneath their shading palms, even though white ants are in the floor-boards and rot eats into the rafters. They belong; and so they do not grow old but only weather and transmute themselves imperceptibly back to the dust from which others will be made to take their place.

Not so the constructional rubbish that forms so great a part of Kota Bharu, whose builders imagined themselves to be superior to those who built Malay houses. Here is the grub in the heart of Malaya: among the beauty squats the horror; among the things that God made stands the decaying rubbish of China and the West. Here, among the silver sand, under a canopy of royal palms, within sight and sound of the blue and white magic of the sea, stand the brick and concrete hovels, the peeling colour-wash and flaking plaster, soullessness supreme.

February 23rd, 1955

Over the hump of Malaya to Penang, an hour's journey by air. Below, the jungle sweeps to the high pinnacles, o'ertops them and plunges again to the plains of the western coast. If you would go by rail, the journey of eight hundred miles will take three days—four hundred miles to the south to where the railway crosses from the east to the west, and then four hundred miles to the north again.

We stay in Penang on the edge of one of the loveliest bays in Malaya. Perfect sands fall steeply to the sea and behind the sands rear the central hills of the island of Penang. We do not swim, for we have had the fear of God put into us with tales of deadly sea-snakes that inhabit this part of the sea. Already two people have died.

On the beach the Tamil fishermen are hauling in their net. They haul on their ropes in two long files stretching from the edge of the sea. Their net, attached at either of its ends to each of these ropes, is almost half a mile out to sea. We can see where the net is, for a boat bobs above it and follows it in.

As the fishermen haul, they chant. I do not know what it is that they chant, but it rises as though from the dust of India. One man leads and calls in a high and rhythmical intonation; promptly the others give the reply. At the same time they haul on the ropes. And slowly the net moves shorewards. As each man reaches the point where the rope piles into huge coils he goes to the front again and attaches himself to the rope with a line that is passed round his waist. Most of the purchase, therefore, comes from his waist.

They are thin and wiry little men, these Tamils, with skins so dark that they are almost black. The cloths that they wear at their waists are drawn up tightly into their loins so that their buttocks are exposed; thin, emaciated, hollow buttocks. It is extraordinary, this steady application of energy. The sweat gleams on their black skins and little balls of muscle stand out on their thin limbs, and for well over an hour they work without pause, straining at the dripping rope. Their splaying toes rip up the sand. The sun pours down and dances viciously off the water so that a man can see only if his eyes are almost closed. And over it all the monotonous, repetitious chant and counter-chant.

The net approaches to within a hundred yards of the beach and suddenly the rhythm of the chant changes—faster, more insistent. The caller cries out in a louder voice and the answer comes more urgently. The black bodies lean more heavily against the rope, and feet in unison hit the sand and fight for a grip in the holes that other feet have made. The sun falls towards the western hills and becomes hotter, and the little black boat bobbing on the silvering sea comes slowly towards us. We can see the rope running along the surface of the sea all the way now to the net and the black boat moving in the sun's reflected fire.

A tall grey-beard, dressed, it seems, in nothing but a western-style shirt and a white turban, goes to the water's edge and turns and faces the men. He stands in the blinding heat like an ancient prophet, raises a hand to heaven and calls with all the power of his lungs, and then throws himself at the rope and hauls so that his body is almost parallel to the ground. At once the timeless answer is given, yet faster, and with a more pronounced and furious rhythm. One, two, three, four; one, two, three, four; and the sand flies as the feet stamp into its softness. I had never seen this operation before and I think now it is one of the most exciting things I have ever seen. I stand there transfixed, among an ecstasy of sound and movement and colour, and I think that if a man lived who combined the genius of a Beethoven, a Pavlova and Leonardo, he could produce nothing so beautiful as this, nor anything so vital and stirring.

The net is only a few yards from the beach now. For the last time the rhythm changes and the call and the answer becomes a one-two rhythm; one, two; one, two; one, two. In their stamping, dancing gait the men run away with the rope and the net lies black and heavy on the wet sand.

Quite suddenly there is quiet and the sound of the sea is heard again, and the men come down to see what the reward for their hours of toil is to be. Under three obscene jellyfish, each eighteen inches across, squirms the thin, grey body of a flat-headed sea-snake. Besides these things there is enough fish to fill a small basket. Another spectator tells me that the catches vary. Certainly a catch worse than this would be no catch at all.

February 24th, 1955

By Malayan Airways to Singapore, our brief interlude over. We land in the evening and drive through the hot and crowded streets. Most of what we see is ugly. There is life here and energy. There are people, but the people have lost their beauty and sold themselves to streets and stinking drains and black cells of houses that stand like serried warts on the face of a mummy. This is also our world and we wonder what we have done that it should have moved so far from beauty.